topics in
cost
accounting
and
decisions

topics in cost accounting and decisions

Harold Bierman, Jr.

Professor of Accounting
Graduate School of Business
and Public Administration
Cornell University

McGraw-Hill Book Company

New York   San Francisco   Toronto   London

X

038129

preface

This book is a collection of discussions of topics in advanced managerial accounting. The general orientation is toward decision-making situations which involve the use of accounting data and which practicing accountants (or other business managers) are frequently called on to resolve or assist in resolving. This book intends to be helpful to the reader who is concerned not so much with record keeping as with the analysis and use of accounting data.

It is assumed that the reader already has a knowledge of accounting entries for both general financial accounting and basic cost accounting, therefore no attempt has been made to include introductory material which describes debit-credit procedures or to include in a complete or extensive manner the material of cost accounting concerned with determining the unit cost of product and the flow of costs through the accounts. A brief discussion of cost-variance factors is included so that the significance of a variance may be considered. Some repetition of introductory topics could not be avoided, however, since readers of this book may have widely different backgrounds. The author has assumed that readers will have had at least one semester of managerial accounting or two semesters of financial accounting with some cost accounting or equivalent training. No attempt has been made to develop systematically the reader's ability to record financial transactions, close accounts, and prepare financial reports.

Calculus is used, but only in one or two appendixes will the reader with no understanding of calculus have difficulty in understanding the significance of the calculations. Some knowledge of statistics and probability is required since these tools are used in several sections of the book.

Although this book is not a text in the usual sense, it may be used for teaching purposes in many ways. The teacher may choose to supplement this book with cases from the Intercollegiate Case Clearing House or with one of the several case books which have been published. Other possibilities are to use this book in conjunction with a standard cost-accounting text or to have the students conduct research on the topics covered in the book and prepare oral (or written) reports.

Some of the material in this book is routine; a portion of the material is original with the author; and a significant part is based on the author's interpretation of journal articles. To some extent these are uncharted waters, and the reader is so warned.

acknowledgments

Many people assisted directly or indirectly in the preparation of this book. The following few names are representative of those to whom the author is indebted.

A great debt is owed to W. A. Paton for many accounting lessons and many points of view. Howard Raiffa, Cornell University, and the Ford Foundation were jointly responsible for an opportunity to learn some mathematics. Betsey, Sandy, and Marie made the request for typing assistance a pleasure; the typing was facilitated by the policies of Deans C. S. Sheppard and D. A. Thomas. Peter Firmin, Richard Brandenberg, and Charles Johnson did a helpful job of reviewing the manuscript; the errors and faults that remain are despite their fine critical advice. Seymour Smidt, Robert Jaedicke, Lawrence Fouraker, and Alan McAdams, my coauthors on other publications, helped develop some of the ideas presented in these pages.

R. Schlaifer and A. Hald graciously gave permission to use tables from their publications.

Appreciation is also expressed to the editors of *The Accounting Review, N.A.A. Bulletin*, and the *Controller*, who gave permission to use extracts of material previously published in their journals.

HAROLD BIERMAN, JR.

contents

cost
control

It is frequently suggested that decision makers should attempt to optimize the profits of the firm and that each decision should take into consideration its effect on the other sections of the firm. There are two difficulties with this global optimization from an operational point of view:

1. Rather than maximize profits the firm may reasonably want to maximize something else (which we shall call utility). The advantage of utility over profits as a goal is that utility takes into consideration psychological reactions to gains and losses. The profit measure ignores them.

2. The decision maker's ability to cope with global optimization may be limited. That is, he may be unable to digest all the information available to him on the ripple effects of a decision, and even the simplest decision may become impossible to make because the decision maker insists on analyzing all implications of the decision. For example, a student may decide to go to a movie because the picture playing is one that he likes and because he has the time to see the picture. Or he can analyze how the expenditure of the admission money will affect his ability to send his unborn children through college or how it will affect his retirement fund. And of course, there is always the possibility the time should be spent studying; thus a complete analysis should take into consideration the effect of going to see the movie on his career.

This book deals with decisions on a suboptimization basis, though frequently decisions are linked together by a rate of interest in order to take into account, in a common manner, time discounting. There is no question that suboptimization has its dangers. For example, an optimum advertising policy may lead to disaster if productive capacity is not taken into consideration. Suboptimization should attempt to include the more relevant effects the decision may have on the over-all well-being of the firm.

Another possible criticism of the approach taken in this book is that the decisions are approached as if they might be solved using a quantitative approach exclusively. There is no question that consid-erations other than money should enter into decisions. For example, a decision to close a plant may be indicated from a quantitative analysis, but the parent firm may still see a responsibility to keep the plant open for a period of time while its employees find employment elsewhere.

Despite the limitations of a quantitative approach to decision making, there is agreement that this approach is frequently of great assistance. Any decision maker should have at his disposal the best quantitative tools which are available, so that he may establish a frame of reference for the decision.

This chapter deals with cost control as if accounting could make a positive contribution toward the effective control of costs. It might be argued that non-accounting methods (such as making all workers part owners of the plant) would be more effective. But even in this situa-tion, some workers would tend to avoid work and others would excel; thus some means of measuring efficiency is still desirable. Therefore we assume that quantitative measures of efficiency are useful, and pro-ceed to seek the best measures that are available.

This chapter briefly reviews different cost classifications and investi-gates the objectives of cost-accounting systems for manufacturing firms and the efficiency of accounting systems in meeting these objectives; it also suggests the use of probability and statistics in solving several cost-control problems.

The Classification of Costs

Costs are defined and classified in many different ways. For example, a cost may be classified by:

How it reacts to changes in activity (fixed or variable)

Responsibility (plant, department, process, or cost center where it was incurred)

The product which the cost helped produce

Natural characteristics (labor, material, supplies, etc.)

Function (manufacturing, administrative, selling)

Reference to a particular decision; and by miscellaneous economic characteristics (joint, common, out-of-pocket, opportunity, unavoid-able, etc.)

The accountant does not set up accounts in the bookkeeping records for every one of the above classifications; in fact, it would not be desirable to do this. A good accounting system will be a ready source for cost information, but generally analysis and rearrangement of the costs will be necessary for specific decisions.

Changes in Activity

The terms "fixed" and "variable" are generally used to describe how a cost will react to changes in activity. A variable cost is a cost which is proportional to the level of activity (total cost increases as

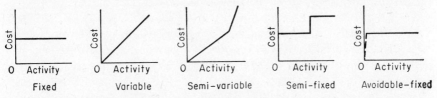

Figure 1.1   Cost characteristics.

activity increases), and a fixed cost is constant in total over the range of activity being considered.

The terms may be made more useful by the addition of three further classifications: "semivariable," "semifixed," and "avoidable-fixed." "Semivariable" could be used to refer to a cost which is basically variable but is not a continuous function of activity; i.e., the slope of the cost curve may change abruptly when a certain point is reached. For example, working hours in excess of the normal 40-hour week will give rise to overtime or shift premiums and will result in direct labor increasing more rapidly as activity increases than if overtime penalties were not incurred at that point.

"Semifixed" refers to a cost which is essentially fixed but which may have to be increased if production is increased.

Figure 1.2   Variable cost with fixed-cost component.

Thus quality control costs may be fixed over wide ranges, but an additional man may have to be hired if production is expanded further. Another example is the addition of another machine.

"Avoidable-fixed" refers to the possibility of avoiding the fixed costs if the plant is temporarily shut down (in the case of a permanent shutdown all costs can be avoided). Thus the accounting department is generally considered to be a fixed cost, but the personnel could be laid off if the plant had to be shut down.

Figure 1.1 shows some cost-characteristic possibilities but does not include all possibilities. For example, a cost may have an avoidable-fixed component at very low levels of activity but may vary directly with increases in activity. This type of cost is sometimes said to be semi-variable (compare Figures 1.1 and 1.2).

Responsibility

Classification of costs by responsibility is important because it is the basis of cost control. The first step in the control of costs is to know where the cost was incurred and who was responsible.

The allocation of service department costs (building, power, heat, cafeteria, accounting, etc.) to operating departments for purposes of computing unit costs or profits by product line often confuses the control of costs. The allocations are thought to be essential to the control of costs, but costs must be controlled where they were incurred, and allocations to operating departments are generally not useful for cost-control purposes. Exceptions to this rule are some repair department costs which are controllable both by the repair department (to ensure that repairs are implemented efficiently) and by the operating department (to ensure that preventive maintenance reduces the number of repairs). However, there may be some repair costs incurred by a department which are not controlled by that department.

Cost-control reports should be prepared so that only costs for which the manager has responsibility are reported as being controllable. The inclusion of costs which he cannot control merely acts as a detraction.

Product Line

The classification of costs by product line is essential in order to determine the profitability of the product line. The rate of profitability of the various products may influence decisions to expand or contract sales.

The main problem in classifying costs by product line is that many costs cannot be directly identified with any one product, since they are associated with several products. We can label a cost of this nature an indirect cost. The term "indirect" is used with a cost which cannot be directly identified with a product line, job, process, department, etc. We must know with what we are trying to identify the cost before we can decide whether or not the cost is indirect.

If there are indirect costs, then reports by product line must be carefully prepared. Instead of showing one income figure it is necessary to show a series of subtotals. The following report highlights those costs directly associated with the product line and subordinates those costs indirectly associated. In addition it distinguishes between variable and fixed costs.

Income Statement
for Product A

Sales	$5,000
Less: Direct variable costs	2,000
	$3,000
Direct fixed costs	800
Excess of revenues over direct costs	$2,200
Less: Indirect variable costs	1,000
	$1,200
Indirect fixed costs	400
Net income—product A	$ 800

Instead of first subtracting the costs directly identified with the product line, we might have subtracted the variable costs first and then the fixed costs, as in the next report.

Income Statement
for Product A

Sales		$5,000
Less: Direct variable costs	$2,000	
Indirect variable costs	1,000	3,000
Excess of sales over variable costs		$2,000
Less: Direct fixed costs	$ 800	
Indirect fixed costs	400	1,200
Net income—product A		$ 800

Natural and Functional Classifications

The term "natural classification" refers to the basic physical aspects of the cost (labor, material, supplies, etc.). "Functional" refers to how the cost was used (manufacturing, administrative, or selling). A need for both natural and functional classifications exists. The prime conflict between the two classifications is in the preparation of income statements. Should the expenses be classified according to natural or functional classifications? The answer must depend on the use of the report; but no matter which classification is used, additional information should be supplied in footnotes. For example, if the functional classification is used, the depreciation expense and labor expense of the period should be shown in a footnote.

Economic Characteristics of Costs

The accountant can classify costs in many ways, but he cannot record a cost as relevant or irrelevant to a decision, since this will depend on the particular decision being made. In like manner the principle of opportunity costs is of great importance to decision making, but the accountant cannot record the opportunity costs since these will generally depend on the alternative uses of the resources at the time of the decision. The term "sunk cost" is frequently used to refer to a cost such as building cost, since the building depreciation will continue even if the plant reduces production. But the accountant cannot record costs as being sunk, since a decision being considered may be whether or not to sell the plant. The same complication is true of avoidable and unavoidable costs.

The accountant does allocate indirect costs to different products, but for most decisions the somewhat arbitrary allocations of the accountant must be placed aside. This is not to say that the accountant is wrong to make the allocations for purposes of income and inventory determination, but it would be incorrect to use these allocations for purposes for which they were not intended and cannot be used.

Thus a cost may have important economic characteristics which do not enter the accounting records. When there is occasion to make decisions, the costs must be extracted from the accounting records and be properly arrayed. It is not possible for the accounting system automatically to record and report costs in all relevant ways, for all possible decisions. However, the availability of high-speed computers has increased the amount of information which can be stored.

The Objectives of Cost-accounting Systems

To justify the millions of dollars spent on accounting for costs, the manufacturing cost-accounting system must be useful to management. Among the most important functions of a cost-accounting system will be to provide necessary information for:

1. Determination of income and financial position
2. Control and reduction of costs
3. Decision making and planning

The above items are not listed in order of importance, and they are not all-inclusive (for example, accounting for defense contracts is excluded).

Determination of Income and Financial Position

While this objective is frequently cited as a prime justification for elaborate cost-accounting systems, it is relatively unimportant compared to the other two objectives. Determination of income and financial position is important, but any determination is going to be inexact and subject to assumptions. For example, are fixed costs period costs, or are they costs which should be attached to product? While a certain amount of cost accounting is necessary to accomplish the objectives of income determination, the system could be much simpler than the cost-accounting systems commonly used in manufacturing companies. Much of the detail could be eliminated with little loss of accuracy. For example, if a department manufactured automobile generators, we might want to know the total costs incurred in the department to determine the cost per unit, but it would not be necessary to know the cost of each step in the manufacture of each part and the exact nature of each cost.

There would still exist the problem of common costs (costs incurred in the production of more than one product), but the importance of common-cost problems would be reduced, since we would be more interested in broad measures needed for financial accounting purposes than in the exact measures needed for cost control and decision making.

It is interesting to note that no matter how elaborate the cost-accounting system, there would still exist problems of income and financial position determination. One problem is whether fixed costs should be considered costs of product (see Chapter 3). If the fixed costs are absorbed to product, there is the problem of the basis for fixed-overhead absorption and the treatment of idle-capacity variance (and other cost variances). Should all the fixed costs be considered a cost of product, or should some of the fixed costs be considered a cost of idleness when less than normal activity is attained? The problems of joint and common costs also prevent exact measures of financial activity, especially where there are inventory changes involving one of the joint products.

These examples are not a complete list of complications arising in the use of cost-accounting information for purposes of determination of income and financial position. If income measurement and determination of financial position were the only objectives of a cost-accounting system, the system could be much simpler. Added accuracy in this area is frequently an illusion. Few managerial decisions can be made using the accounting income which is the product of the conventional cost-accounting system. Mere general impressions are formed, which can lead to decisions only after further information is gathered. The user of the information coming from a cost-accounting system must realize that this is a relatively rough tool. A manager who receives a measure of income which is inexact, and who knows that the measure is inexact, has better information than a manager who receives a somewhat more elaborate measure of income but is misled into thinking that the measure can be used for specific decisions such as expanding or contracting the product line.

Control and Reduction of Costs

Control or reduction of costs requires a detailed cost-accounting system. It is necessary to know when and where the costs were incurred (the accounting period and the department or cost center where they were incurred), and the nature of the costs. And equally important, we must know the actual amount of the cost, and the amount which the cost should have been (the budgeted or standard amount). Unless we have all the above information, the cost-accounting system cannot be effective in the control of costs.

The setting of standards is an important part of the cost-control system. The use of standards enables management to pick out rapidly those areas where there are difficulties (costs significantly in excess of standard) and to take action where action is required. This is an application of managing by exception.

What should be the policy in regard to the difficulty of attaining the standards? Should the standards be very difficult to attain or relatively easy to attain? Actually, there is an entire range of possibilities in setting standards. The problem of setting standards is analogous to the problem of setting par for a golfer.

The theoretical standard is analogous to shooting an 18-hole golf course in 18 strokes. While this is theoretically possible, it is extremely unlikely to occur. Setting standards which are almost certain not to be attained is discouraging to workers and should be avoided.

The practical standard is analogous to shooting an 18-hole golf course in 72 (assuming the 72 is par). This 72 is difficult to attain, but a very good golfer can shoot 72. There is more to be said in favor of this type of standard, difficult to attain but attainable, than for theoretical standards.

The normal standard is analogous to setting a par consistent with the golfer's ability (often by means of a handicap). Par for the course may be 72, but if the golfer is just a "duffer" his par may be 98, where the term par is used in the sense of a goal or standard of performance based on the person's ability. The standard becomes a mean or expected value of the golfer's score. The use of standards which take into consideration the state of experience and skill of the worker are reasonable; ideally, the skill of the worker should increase until the standard finally approaches the high level of performance called par (the 72 of the golf-course analogy). Realistically, we should recognize that not everyone can shoot 72, no matter how hard he practices or how much pressure is applied by the person in authority.

Loose standards are in a sense not standards but reference points.

Thus, if a golfer averages 90, he may set a "standard" for himself of 95 just to make sure that his variance is generally favorable. In like manner the standards of a factory may be set so that the worker's performance is generally favorable, even though he could and should do better.

The use of standards leads to the necessity of interpreting the differences between actual costs and standard costs. (The term "standard" is used here to include budgeted costs adjusted to the actual level of operation.) The analysis of cost variances could be accomplished by comparing the actual costs and standard costs and merely noting the difference. While this would be a big step forward, differences between actual and standard costs have been identified with a greater degree of accuracy by the use of a technique called variance analysis.

Cost Variances

The variances are frequently divided into material, labor, and overhead variances. All the variances except one are the result of paying unit prices which differ from standard prices or of using a different amount of physical resource to accomplish the task. The activity variance is caused by working at an activity level different from that budgeted.

MATERIAL VARIANCES

Material-usage variance is the difference between the standard and actual quantities of material priced at the standard price per unit.

Material-price variance is the actual quantity of material used times the difference between the actual and standard price per unit of material.

DIRECT-LABOR VARIANCES

Efficiency variance is the difference between the standard and actual direct-labor hours, priced at the standard wage rate per hour.

Wage-rate variance is the actual number of hours times the difference between the actual and standard wage rates per hour.

OVERHEAD VARIANCES

Fixed-budget variance is the difference between the fixed overhead budgeted and the amount of fixed costs incurred.

Variable-overhead budget variance is the difference between the variable overhead budgeted (adjusted to the actual level of activity) and the amount incurred.

Fixed-overhead efficiency variance is the fixed-overhead rate times the difference between the actual direct-labor hours and the standard direct-labor hours.

Variable-overhead efficiency variance is the variable-overhead rate times the difference between the actual direct-labor hours and the standard.

Activity variance is the fixed-overhead rate times the difference between the actual hours worked and the budgeted hours for a normal time period.

The significance of the material- and the direct-labor variances will depend on the choice of the policy concerning the type of standard used. If the standard reflects an attainable high level of performance (say, a normal standard), then a variance of significant size should be investigated.

The interpretation of the overhead variances must be exact since the variances do not always indicate what they seem to indicate. The fixed-budget variance shows the difference between the amount budgeted and the amount incurred. The variable-overhead budget variance seems to show the same, but there is one difference. To obtain significant information we must adjust the variable overhead to the actual level of activity attained. Direct-labor hours (or dollars) is frequently used to accomplish this adjustment. This is generally not a bad approximation, but it must be recognized that a cost may vary with other measures of activity. For example, the number of accounts receivable clerks varies with the number of billings. Also, the overhead cost may lead or lag behind the direct-labor cost. Thus a variable-overhead budget variance may be the result of excessive expenditures or merely of the method of computation.

The overhead efficiency variances are somewhat complex. An unfavorable variable-overhead efficiency variance tends to show the amount of variable overhead which was incurred because an excessive amount of direct labor was incurred. An unfavorable fixed-overhead efficiency variance has a different meaning. It shows the amount of fixed overhead not absorbed by product because the amount of actual and standard hours differed. No additional fixed-overhead costs were incurred because of the additional hours worked.

The activity variance shows the amount of fixed overhead which was not absorbed to product because the amount of hours worked differed from the budgeted hours. Instead of direct-labor hours, the number of units of product produced, machine hours, or direct-labor dollars may be used. The amount shown as activity variance will be affected not only by the number of hours worked, but also by the amount of hours originally budgeted. The same type of problem that was encountered in setting standards is encountered in setting the budgeted-level activity which will be used in computing the fixed-overhead rate. At one extreme is the theoretical capacity (assumes the plant can work 365 days a year, 24 hours a day, and not have breakdowns). At the other extreme is the actual activity encountered or the level of activity expected. These extremes are not as desirable as the use of normal capacity.

Practical capacity defies a rigid definition. It is sometimes defined as the most efficient point of operations (where either average variable costs or average total costs are a minimum). Unfortunately, many firms will have relatively flat average variable-cost curves over a wide range of activity, and thus can produce past that point with little loss of efficiency. Practical capacity is also defined as the point at which the firm would operate if there were no shortage of orders, but this would make the practical capacity equivalent to the point of absolute diminishing returns. A common practice is to resort to industry usage. Thus if the industry works six days a week, 20 hours a day, this becomes practical capacity. Another industry may commonly work only eight hours a day, five days a week, and this becomes practical capacity. Obviously, practical capacity is a flexible concept.

Since practical capacity is so difficult to define, normal activity is frequently used. Normal activity has as its objective the absorption of all overhead to product in a normal year; thus it is the mean or expected activity not of one year but of several years.

CALENDAR VARIANCE

The activity variance discussed above may be split into two components, the calendar variance and the idle-capacity variance. This practice helps to extract out from the activity variance that part of the variance which is caused by changes in the number of working days in the month. Supposedly, the variance which is left is controllable by management.

The calendar variance is computed by multiplying the fixed-overhead rate by the difference in the number of hours of direct labor budgeted for a normal month and the number of hours budgeted for this specific month. The idle-capacity variance is the fixed-overhead rate times the difference in the number of hours worked and the hours budgeted for this month.[1]

---

[1] "Idle-capacity variance" is not a good name for this variance when normal activity is used as the basis of burden absorption. The term is used reluctantly.

EXAMPLE

The fixed costs for a year are budgeted at $24,000 for 12,000 direct-labor hours (thus the fixed-overhead rate is $2). The budgeted time for an average month is 1,000 hours. Assume there are 800 hours budgeted for February and the actual hours worked are 700. The three variances being discussed are:

Calendar variance	$2(1,000 − 800) = $400	unfavorable
Idle-capacity variance	$2(800 − 700) = $200	unfavorable
Activity variance	$2(1,000 − 700) = $600	unfavorable

MIX VARIANCE

In certain manufacturing situations factors of production may be substituted for each other. Thus, in an emergency or during slack activity a highly paid worker may be used in a task which ordinarily requires a worker of a lower grade. In like manner one grade of steel may be substituted for another grade. This type of transaction gives rise to mix variances. A mix variance is defined as a cost which is caused by the substitution of one factor of production for another factor of production. We shall determine the variance caused by the difference in wage rates (or prices), but we shall not attempt to determine the change in efficiency which results from the substitution. Generally the information necessary to compute this latter variance is not available.

We shall illustrate the mix variance by the use of a shift in direct labor. The mix variance is computed by multiplying the number of direct-labor hours which are shifted, by the difference between the standard wage rate for the workers who were transferred and the standard wage rate for the task. Several other possible definitions of mix variance would be equally reasonable; thus there is no implication that this is the only correct method of computation. There is too much jointness connected with the incurring of these variances to allow precision in the method of computation.

EXAMPLE

There are two types of workers, "skilled" and "unskilled," working on two processes, grinding and assembly. The standard cost information and the facts for March as as follows:

Standard Costs for One Unit of Product

Process	Type of worker	Standard hours	Standard wage rate	Totals
Assembly	Unskilled	4	$2.00	$ 8.00
Grinding	Skilled	6	3.00	18.00
				$26.00

Actual Costs for Month

Type of worker	Actual hours	Actual wages	Actual wage rate
Unskilled	380	$ 836	$2.20
Skilled	610	2,074	3.40
		$2,910	

Assume skilled workers worked on the assembly line for 10 hours (the total hours worked on assembly operations were 390 and on grinding 600). There were 100 units of product manufactured. The standard costs are $2,600 and actual costs $2,910; thus there were $310 of variance to be identified.

The computation of the variances is as follows:

Efficiency variance: The standard wage rate times the difference between standard and actual hours worked.

Assembly	$2(400 − 390) = $20	favorable
Grinding	$3(600 − 600) = 0	
	$20	favorable

Wage-rate variance: The actual hours times the difference between the standard and actual wage rates (for both types of workers we are using the actual hours worked by that type of worker)

Skilled	610(3.40 − 3.00) = $244	unfavorable
Unskilled	380(2.20 − 2.00) = 76	unfavorable
	$320	unfavorable

Mix variance: The number of hours shifted, multiplied by the difference between the standard wage rate for the task performed and the standard wage rate for the men shifted

$$10(3.00 − 2.00) = $10 \quad \text{unfavorable}$$

Total variance:

The algebraic sum of the three variances

Efficiency	$ 20	favorable
Wage rate	320	unfavorable
Mix	10	unfavorable
	$310	unfavorable

Cost Accounting and Cost Control

The use of cost accounting for cost-control purposes implies that more costs would be incurred if the cost system were not being used. There are basically two reasons why costs may be higher if they are not controlled. For one thing, there would be ignorance of physical waste. Thus a leak in a water pipe may go unnoticed unless the water bill is compared to budgeted amount. Cost savings of this nature probably would rarely justify the installation of a cost-control system, since the water in the basement would probably indicate the leak before the accounting system did.   Nevertheless it is one reason for a cost-accounting system.

The second reason is that workers do not tend to work at highest efficiency unless their performance is being controlled or unless they are very highly motivated.   This statement implies that human beings have certain personality characteristics and that costs may be controlled either by police-type methods or by incentives, or both.   The author is in favor of marrying the control and incentive devices.   Obviously the implementation of the system of rewards and penalties requires great skill and judgment, that is, managerial skill.

Despite the limitations described above, control of costs is the prime justification of a cost-accounting system.   The fact that cost control requires not only a cost-accounting system but also managerial judgment is not surprising.   Jumping to conclusions and taking hasty action on the part of management, or at the opposite extreme ignoring indications of inefficiency, will draw criticism on accounting as a cost-control mechanism.   In such cases the wrong culprit is blamed.   A cost-accounting system can assist management; it is not a substitute for judgment.

Decision Making and Planning

Too often one hears the unfair criticism of cost accounting that the cost figures cannot be used for decision making but must be adjusted. The function of a cost-accounting system is not to supply on a regular basis cost information for decision making and planning but rather to act as a storage space where the information is kept until it is needed. It would be very costly for any one accounting report to be supplied to management to assist in all possible decisions.   First the decision under consideration should be known; then the costs should be extracted out of the records and arranged in a useful manner.   The regular accounting reports produced by the cost-accounting system should give some measure of the profitability of the operation, be useful for purposes of measuring performance, and be useful for cost-control purposes. They cannot also be useful for specific decision-making purposes, since accountants can not know what decisions are to be made.   The following list gives some indication of the variety of decisions which may be made, each requiring different informaton:

Pricing a product line
Expanding productive facilities for a product line
Abandoning a product line
Making or buying a product or part

The first decision (pricing a product line) is a marginal decision; and marginal costs and revenues are relevant to the making of the decisions. The other three decisions are nonmarginal in nature. To expand a product line we must know the expenditures required to purchase the new facilities and the total costs connected with the expansion. To make a decision whether or not to abandon a product line we should know the differential revenues which will be lost and the differential costs which will be saved. The same is true of the decision to make or buy. All these decisions are also functions of factors not entering the accounting records, such as the opportunity costs connected with the building space required and the time of the executives which will be spent on the project or freed if the product is dropped.

A good cost-accounting system will not necessarily report costs in a form which is usable for all decisions. However, a good system will have stored the information required to make these decisions, so that it is readily accessible when needed. A qualification to be noted is that all decisions are based on future costs and revenues; the past is merely an aid in making a judgment of the future. Recorded costs, to be useful, must be projected into the future.

The Investigation Decision[2]

The conventional procedure in evaluating performance using budgeted or standard costs is to look at either the absolute size of the cost variance (the difference between actual and standard costs) or the percentage obtained by dividing the cost variance by the standard cost. Both these measures rely upon the intuition of management in deciding whether further action is desired, i.e., whether the variance should be investigated; the investigation may then lead to either praise or censure for the person responsible for the variance. The following procedure attempts to make the decision to investigate somewhat more exact by adding another measure, the probability of the variance occurring from random noncontrollable causes, and by using that measure to help quantify the costs of investigating or not investigating.

Setting the Standard

The expected value of the cost to be incurred will be used as the standard cost. Assuming the cost is normally distributed, we know

[2] The ideas in this section were developed jointly with Robert Jaedicke and Lawrence Fouraker. See Harold Bierman, Jr., Lawrence Fouraker, and Robert Jaedicke, *Quantitative Analysis for Business Decisions,* Richard D. Irwin, Inc., Homewood, Ill., 1961.

this is the most likely amount of the cost to be incurred. This is a departure from general practice, but it does facilitate the computations and interpretations of the variances. Other budget philosophies may be incorporated, but they would add to the complexity of the analysis and detract from the basic objectives of the chapter.

Having set the standard (or budgeted amount) so that it is the most likely cost to be incurred, we next assume that favorable and unfavorable variances caused by random noncontrollable causes are equally likely to fall on either side of the standard, and we further assume that they are normally distributed about this standard (which is the mean of the distribution).

Establishing the Dispersion

To determine fully a normal distribution we need the mean, which in this case is the standard cost, and the standard deviation (designated by the symbol σ, which is the Greek letter sigma). An approximation of

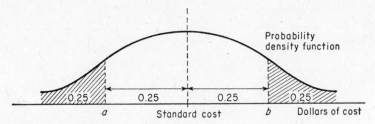

Figure 1.3   A density function for a cost.

the standard deviation may be determined by obtaining the answer to one question which may be worded in several ways. For example:

1. How far from the mean would you place the range of the cost so that the cost would be equally likely to fall either side of the estimated range?
2. In what range would you expect the cost to fall, with equal likelihood of favorable and unfavorable variances, the odds being equal that the cost would fall in that range and out of the range?
3. There is a 50–50 probability that the cost variance (the actual cost minus the mean) will be larger than some amount. What is that amount?
4. Using Figure 1.3, what value would you place on the factors a and b? The hatched area represents one-half of the total area under the curve. The actual cost will land between a and b one-half of the time.

All the above questions refer to variances caused by random noncontrollable causes.

A characteristic of any normal distribution is that approximately 0.5 of the area lies within two-thirds of a standard deviation of the mean. Using any of the four questions listed above, we can determine an approximation of the standard deviation of the distribution.

EXAMPLE

Assume that the budgeted amount for a cost is $10,000 and that the answer to Question 1 is $4,000.   The standard deviation is $6,000.

$$\tfrac{2}{3}\sigma = \$4,000$$
$$\sigma = \$6,000$$

If the answer to Questions 2 and 4 is $6,000 to $14,000, the standard deviation would again be $6,000 by the same computation as shown above. If the answers to all the questions are consistent, the answer to Question 3 will be $4,000.

The standard deviation is a measure of dispersion; thus we have established a measure of the likelihood of the cost varying from the mean.   Assume the actual cost is $22,000, resulting in an unfavorable cost variance of $12,000 (i.e., $22,000 minus $10,000).   We must next compute the number of standard deviations that $22,000 is from the mean, $10,000.

$$x = \frac{\text{actual cost} - \text{standard cost}}{\sigma} = \frac{22,000 - 10,000}{6,000} = 2$$

Referring to a table of normal probabilities we find that the probability of the cost being two, or more than two, standard deviations to the right of the mean is 2.3 per cent.   Thus the probability of an unfavorable cost variance (from random noncontrollable causes) being $12,000 or larger is 2.3 per cent.   The probability of any variance of that size or larger is two times 2.3 per cent or 4.6 per cent (the 4.6 per cent includes the probability of favorable variances as well as unfavorable).   In this example the variance is not likely to have been caused by random noncontrollable factors, and we have more information than we would have without the probability analysis.

Continuing the example, assume the cost of the period was $13,000.   The number of standard deviations from the mean is 0.5.

$$x = \frac{13,000 - 10,000}{6,000} = 0.5$$

The probability of an unfavorable variance being 0.5 or more standard deviations from the mean is 31 per cent.   Thus the probability of the cost variance (from random noncontrollable causes) being unfavorable and $3,000 or larger is 31 per cent. The probability of any variance (favorable or unfavorable) of that size or larger is 62 per cent. The probability of a variance that size or larger, given that an unfavorable variance has occurred, is also 62 per cent.

By this type of analysis we can compute the probability of any cost variance being caused by random noncontrollable causes. This probability can be used to help determine whether or not to investigate the variance.

The Decision to Investigate

We now have three measures of the desirability of investigation:

1. The absolute size of the variance
2. The size of the variance relative to the size of the standard cost
3. The probability of the variance being caused by random noncontrollable causes

Figure 1.4 is a chart showing whether or not to investigate. Measured on the vertical axis is the conditional probability of an unfavorable variance from random noncontrollable causes as large as or larger than the

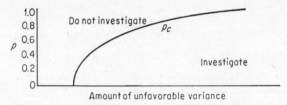

Figure 1.4   Cost-control decision chart—unfavorable variances.

actual variance, given an occurrence of unfavorable variance. The curve p_c gives the critical probability: to investigate or not to investigate. If p is greater than p_c, management should not investigate; otherwise investigation is considered to be desirable. The curve p_c does not go through the origin since there must be some minimum absolute amount of saving before the cost of investigation is worth incurring. This intercept does not depend on the probability of the variance.

As the probability of the unfavorable variance being caused by random causes increases, the absolute size of the variance must also increase if it is to be desirable to investigate the cause of the variance. In like manner, if the absolute variance is small, the probability of the variance being caused by random factors must also be small if investigation is desirable.

One way of setting up the decision chart is to draw it using the intuition of management. A second method incorporates the costs of investigating and not investigating.   Because the second method involves some complexity and considerable estimation of the future, many will prefer to draw a more or less arbitrary curve separating the "Investigate" from the "Do not investigate" region.   In some situations it may be desirable to draw several curves and arrive at three regions, as shown in Figure 1.5. Here the conditional probability of an unfavorable variance from random noncontrollable causes as large as or larger than the actual variance, given that an unfavorable variance has occurred, is measured on the Y axis. This decision chart has an area where the "Investigate" or "Do not investigate" decision is left to the discretion of the analyst.   The advantage of this type of presentation is obvious.   If the analyst has free time, he will be more likely to investigate the variance in the optional area than if he has his time fully scheduled for the coming period.   Over a period of time the analyst may be required to investigate a given percentage of the gray area situations.

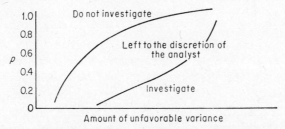

Figure 1.5   Cost-control decision chart—unfavorable variances.

Even if the curves of Figure 1.4 or Figure 1.5 are drawn according to the intuition of management, it is necessary to take into consideration the costs of investigating and not investigating, as well as the probability of the variance being caused by random factors.   Because of the difficulty of intuitively weighting the various factors, a systematic method of computation is desirable.

Derivation of the Decision Chart

The discussion up to this point has analyzed and charted situations where the cost variance is unfavorable.   The same analysis is valid if the cost variance is favorable.   If the cost variance is unfavorable, management will wish to eliminate the cause of the variance and prevent the variance from recurring.   If the variance appears favorable, it may wish to investigate in order to praise the individual responsible or to correct faulty standards or errors in reporting.   Thus the basic analysis is equally applicable to favorable and unfavorable variances.   There follows a procedure which may be used to derive the decision chart using the expected costs of investigating and not investigating.

Instead of drawing the "Investigate" and "Do not investigate" areas using the intuition of management, we can show areas based on explicit computations of the expected cost of investigation versus the expected costs of not investigating.

We have two possible acts:

Act 1. Investigate the variance.
Act 2. Do not investigate the variance.

There are also two possible states:

State 1. The variance was caused by random noncontrollable causes, and no action is required by management.

State 2. The variance was caused by factors over which management does have control, and action by management is desirable.

Designate the cost of investigation by C. The cost of repetition of the inefficiency in the future if investigation is not carried out is designated by L. L is a present value of the estimate of cost inefficiencies in the future which are avoidable. Letting p be the probability of State 1 occurring (the probability of State 2 is one minus the probability of State 1), given an occurrence of unfavorable variance, we can prepare Table 1.1, a conditional-cost table.

Table **1.1**   Conditional-cost Table

States	Acts		Conditional probabilities of states, given an occurrence of unfavorable variance
	Investigate	*Do not investigate*	
1	C	0	p
2	C	L	$1 - p$
Expected cost of acts	$\overline{C}$	$\overline{L(1 - p)}$	

In this table we show that if we investigate, the cost will be C no matter which state is actually the true state. If we do not investigate, the cost is zero if State 1 is the true state (i.e., the variance was from random causes); but the cost is L if the true state is State 2 (i.e., the variance was caused by factors over which management has control).

The expected cost of each act is obtained by multiplying the conditional costs of the acts and summing for all possible states. For example, for Act 1 ("Investigate"):

	Conditional cost	Probability	Cost × probability
State 1	C	p	pC
State 2	C	$1 - p$	$(1 - p)C$
	Expected cost of Act 1		$\underline{C}$

For Act 2 the same type of computations are made.

	Conditional cost	Probability	Cost × probability
State 1	0	p	0
State 2	L	$1 - p$	$L(1 - p)$
	Expected cost of Act 2		$L(1 - p)$

If the expected cost of Act 1 is greater than the expected cost of Act 2, we should not investigate. If the expected cost of Act 1 is less than the expected cost of Act 2, we should investigate.

If $C < L(1 - p)$, then investigate.
If $C > L(1 - p)$, then do not investigate.

If we let p_c be the critical probability, where the expected cost of Act 1 equals the expected cost of Act 2, then we have

$$C = L(1 - p_c)$$

and solving for p_c $$p_c = \frac{L - C}{L}$$

If the actual probability of the variance is greater than p_c, we should not investigate, since C will be greater than $(1-p)L$. If the actual probability is less than p_c, then we should investigate. By plotting p_c for different values of cost variances we can determine the curve shown in Figure 1.4. The factor C will be a constant based on the estimated cost of investigation. The factor L will be a function of the size of the cost variance; the larger the cost variance, the larger is the present value of the costs which will be incurred if the cause of the cost variance is not discovered. For each possible cost variance we can compute the critical probability p_c, making use of the formula, where L will depend on the size of the variance:

$$p_c = \frac{L - C}{L}$$

Instead of using a graph we can compute the critical probability for each situation which arises. For example, returning to the illustration where the actual cost was $13,000, the standard cost $10,000, and the standard deviation $6,000, we found that the probability of a cost variance as large as or larger than $3,000, given an unfavorable variance, was 62 per cent. The probability of an unfavorable variance of that size or larger, caused by random factors, is 31 per cent.

There are several interesting probabilities, and it is important that we distinguish among them.

$P(A)$ = P(unfavorable variance) = .50
$P(B)$ = P(a variance as large as or larger than \$3,000) = .62
$P(AB)$ = P(events A and B both happening)
         = P(unfavorable variance and a variance as large as or larger than \$3,000) = .31. This is the right tail of the distribution.
$P(B|A)$ = P(event B, given that event A has occurred)
         = P(a variance as large as or larger than \$3,000, given that an unfavorable variance has occurred) = .62

The basic formula to obtain this last probability (called a conditional probability) is

$$P(B|A) = \frac{P(AB)}{P(A)}$$

The .62 is computed as follows:

$$P(B|A) = \frac{.31}{.50} = .62$$

The conditional probability, $P(B|A) = .62$, is p of our initial analysis. We must compute the probability of a variance as large as or larger than the actual variance given that an unfavorable variance has occurred. It would be possible to solve the problem using $P(AB)$, the joint probabilities, but the sum of the probabilities of the events would then add up to .5.

We have to determine C and L to compute the critical probability. Assume that the cost of investigation is estimated to be \$40 (i.e., $C = 40$), and that L is equal to three times the cost variance (i.e., the inefficiency is expected to last for about four years, assuming a 10 per cent interest factor). Thus L is equal to three times \$3,000, or \$9,000.

$$p_c = \frac{L - C}{L} = \frac{9,000 - 40}{9,000} = .996, \text{ or } 99.6\%$$

The conditional probability of the unfavorable variance or larger is 62 per cent, which is less than the critical probability of 99.6 per cent; thus the variance should be investigated.

Let us next assume a situation where the standard cost is \$100, the actual cost \$130, and the standard deviation \$60. Here again the joint probability of an unfavorable variance and a variance as large as or larger than the actual variance is 31 per cent. The conditional probability is 62 per cent. Assume that the cost of investigation is \$50 and that L is equal to twice the variance (i.e., L is equal to $60 in the example). The critical probability is

$$p_c = \frac{L - C}{L} = \frac{60 - 50}{50} = \frac{10}{50} = .2, \text{ or } 20\%$$

This critical probability is less than the actual probability $(.20 < .62)$, and investigation is not desirable.

If the cost of investigation is equal to or greater than L, the benefits of investigation, then investigation cannot be desirable, and it is not necessary to compute the critical probability.

Summary

By incorporating the cost of investigation and expected benefits of investigation explicitly into the analysis of cost variances, attention is focused on the important fact that information has a cost, and that there may be cases where it is desirable to forgo investigation. The analysis presented here attempts to go beyond the intuitive decision process, which leaves the cost of investigating and of not investigating out of the analysis completely, or which at best brings them in to it in some unexplained manner.

The fact that the above analysis may be defended on theoretical grounds does not mean that complete and certain information is available with which to make the decision. Both the C and L of the analysis are to some extent matters of judgment, as is the probability of the variance being caused by random causes. We are attempting to bring these factors explicitly into the analysis in a systematic manner.

Probability and Overhead Absorption

The use of probabilities also has an interesting application in the area of overhead-absorption accounting. They assist us in defining terms that are too often used without meaningful definitions.

For cost-accounting purposes there are several methods of accounting for fixed-overhead costs. Among these are:

1. Treat the costs as period expenses and not assign fixed costs to product (see the discussion of variable costing, Chapter 3)
2. Absorb overhead to product, using fixed-overhead rates determined by dividing the fixed costs by one of the following:

   a. Actual activity
   b. Expected activity

    c. Normal activity
    d. Practical capacity

We shall assume here that it is desirable that fixed overhead be assigned to product. The use of actual or expected activity is not desirable, since the activity variance is buried in the cost of product and the per unit cost of product becomes a function of the level of activity.

The prime difficulty with the use of normal activity as the basis of fixed-overhead absorption is that all fixed overhead will be absorbed at a time when the operations are well below capacity; i.e., the activity variance will be zero when the activity is normal. This difficulty does not eliminate normal activity from consideration, but it does lead us to consider another basis, namely, practical capacity.

An important obstacle to the use of practical capacity as a basis of overhead absorption is that practical capacity is difficult to define. However, with the use of probabilities we can arrive at a reasonable definition. For example, if normal activity is 100,000 direct-labor hours per month, and operations has a standard deviation of 30,000 direct-labor hours, we might be able to set practical capacity at 160,000 direct-labor hours, or two standard deviations from the mean. We would then expect that fixed overhead would be overabsorbed less than 2 per cent of the time (assuming the probability distribution of the level of operations is normal). The reasonableness of 160,000 direct-labor hours should be checked. There is nothing mystical about the choice of two standard deviations; we may wish to set the absorption basis at one standard deviation from the mean (130,000 hours) or at some other amount.

Instead of trying to implement the use of practical capacity in the above manner, we could measure the normal activity in terms of the expected level of activity, and in terms of the standard deviation of the expected activity (determined in the same manner that the standard deviations of the probability distribution of costs were determined earlier in the chapter). When the actual activity was determined, the probability of the occurrence could be determined, along with the activity-capacity variance.

EXAMPLE

Normal activity for the month of July is 10,000 direct-labor hours; budgeted fixed-overhead cost is $20,000, and the fixed-overhead rate is $2 (i.e., $20,000/10,000 = $2). In July the actual activity was 8,000 direct-labor hours. Assuming a standard deviation of 3,000 direct-labor hours, what are the activity variance and the probability of an unfavorable variance that large or larger?

The activity variance is

$$\$2 \ (10{,}000 - 8{,}000) = \$4{,}000 \qquad \text{unfavorable}$$

The 8,000 is $\frac{2}{3}\sigma$ from the mean, indicating that the probability of the level of operations being 2,000 direct-labor hours different from the mean or more is 50 per cent. The probability of an unfavorable variance that large or larger is 25 per cent; that is, the probability of the activity being less than 8,000 hours is 25 per cent.

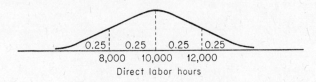

The application of probabilities to the analysis of the activity variance does not solve all problems of absorption of fixed overhead. However, the use of probabilities does enable us to make an intelligible (though flexible) definition of practical capacity. We can define practical capacity in terms of some probability of occurrence. Also, if we use normal activity as the basis of burden absorption, it enables us to place a probability measure on the activity variance. This probability measure assists in the interpretaton of the variance in activity from normal. It does not assist in making specific decisions, since the cost which is being analyzed is a fixed cost and not generally relevant to decisions (unless it is in some sense avoidable).

Appendix 1—Variance Analysis

Material variances

Q_a = actual quantity of material used
Q_s = standard quantity of material
P_a = actual price per unit
P_s = standard price per unit

Material-price variance $= Q_a(P_s - P_a)$
Material-usage variance $= P_s(Q_s - Q_a)$

Labor variances

H_a = actual hours of direct labor
H_s = standard hours of direct labor
W_a = actual usage rate per hour
W_s = standard usage rate per hour

Labor wage-rate variance $= H_a(W_s - W_a)$
Labor efficiency variance $= W_s(H_s - H_a)$

Overhead variances

H_b = budgeted hours for a normal month
H_m = budgeted hours for the specific month
B_f = budgeted fixed-overhead costs
B_v = budgeted variable-overhead costs
A_f = actual fixed costs
A_v = actual variable costs
R_v = variable-overhead rate
R_f = fixed-overhead rate

Fixed-overhead budget variance = $B_f - A_f$
Variable-overhead budget variance $B_v - A_v = H_a R_v - A_v$
Fixed-overhead efficiency variance = $R_f(H_s - H_a)$
Variable-overhead efficiency variance = $R_v(H_s - H_a)$
Activity variance = $R_f(H_b - H_a)$
Idle-capacity variance = $R_f(H_a - H_m)$
Calendar variance = $R_f(H_b - H_m)$

chapter two

cost-
price-
volume
decisions

Decision making involving prices, volume, and costs should be split into two classifications: those decisions made after the capital assets necessary for production have been acquired, and those made in anticipation of the acquisition of the necessary capital assets. It is important to distinguish between the two situations, since considerations which are relevant in the one are not relevant for the other. Applying the same procedures in the two situations will lead to incorrect decisions. This chapter will review the pricing and output decisions in a situation where the capital assets are already owned. The problems of decision making when the capital assets have not yet been acquired are capital-budgeting decisions.

Price-volume Decisions

Assume that the ABC Company owns a new plant which is fully equipped with the latest-model machinery to make lawn mowers. What price does it charge? At what output does it produce? What cost decisions does it have? What profit decisions? We shall review the last two items first.

What profit decisions must be made? The answer is none! The company will decide on a price and an output; it will attempt to produce the goods efficiently; if the planning is correct and is efficiently carried out, then a profit may result. But management does not "plan" profits. In this situation it cannot say that it needs a profit of 20 per cent on the investment of $1,000,000 and therefore must have a profit of $200,000. The profit will be a result of planning and our execution of the plans, but it is a residual of these plans and is not the result of a "profit decision."

The cost decisions of the ABC Company are somewhat less limited. The firm can budget costs for various levels of output, can attempt to control costs and improve efficiency, and can use inventories to stabilize production. However, the basic cost structure has been determined by the characteristics of the machinery and plants which were purchased. Whether overtime will be necessary is a decision to be made in this period, but to some extent the decision was made when the plant was built. If the demand for the product is high enough, it will be necessary to incur overtime; but the decision which determined the size of the plant, which in turn resulted in the necessity to incur overtime, has been made in another period.

We shall explore in more detail the pricing and output decisions. The pricing decision is one of the most important decisions made by management, and one of the most misunderstood. Two pricing methods commonly used which are subject to criticism are the "cost-plus" and the "desired-return-on-investment" methods of pricing.

Cost-plus Pricing

The cost-plus method of pricing is relatively simple. The cost of the product is computed and a reasonable profit is added to obtain the price. With a government cost-plus contract in hand, this is a reasonable procedure; but in a competitive situation (as in bidding for a government contract) this procedure may lead to undesirable results. A primary difficulty is in deciding on the level of activity which should be used to absorb fixed costs to product. The second problem is to decide on the reasonable profit. But most important is the fact that the entire procedure is not a theoretically sound method for determining price.

Assume that the ABC Company can produce 10,000 lawn mowers per month when operating at capacity. The monthly fixed costs are $200,000, and the variable costs are $30 per lawn mower. What is the cost of one lawn mower? One reasonable answer is $50 (the variable costs of $30 plus fixed costs of $20). The absorption of fixed costs is based on capacity. But suppose the company expects to produce and sell only 5,000 lawn mowers during the month. Are the unit costs to be used for pricing then $70 (the variable costs of $30 plus the fixed costs per unit of $40)? Carrying this example to its illogical conclusion, if only one unit is to be produced, we arrive at a cost per unit for pricing of $200,030, or at the opposite extreme, of $30 if the fixed costs are considered period costs.

The desired-return-on-investment pricing method is similar to the above, except that attention is focused on return on investment instead of income. It has no advantage over the cost-plus procedure, and retains all the disadvantages. There is no objection to a company's attempting to recover all costs and to earn as much profit as it can in a competitive environment. But this desire will not necessarily mean that all costs will be recovered, or that the company will earn a profit.

Standard Price

One method of solving the pricing problem is to base overhead absorption on normal activity without regard to the expected or actual level of operations. This procedure is certainly better than adjusting the cost per unit and the price upward as the output decreases. In fact, it sets a sort of "standard" price which must be obtained in order to maintain the productive facilities and earn a fair return on the capital employed. But we must realize that it will not always be desirable to set a standard price. In some situations the firm may be able to charge more than the standard price (for example, if it is introducing a new product which no other competitor has yet), while in other situations it may be desirable to set a price less than the standard price.

Determining Price and Output—Theoretical Solution

The solution to the problem of output and price is an exercise in the application of economic theory. There is a tendency to laugh off the analysis which follows by suggesting that we are determining the point where the angels dance. Rather than pretend to present a procedure enabling us to determine the exact price which will maximize profits, let us reduce our objective to that of developing a theoretically sound guide in determining price and output. The principles will be correct, even though in many situations we shall not be able to apply them with exactness because of incomplete information.

The first assumption which must be made is that we know how many units of product can be sold at different prices. Usually, the lower the price, the more units will be sold. Though this is not always a valid assumption, it will be assumed to be true in the illustration which follows. (The assumption is not necessary for the theory being developed.)

It is possible to plot the number of units which can be sold at all feasible prices. This curve is called the average-revenue or price curve since it shows the price or average revenue necessary in order to sell the different number of units. The average-revenue curve of Figure 2.1 slopes downward to the right since it is assumed that the number of units sold will increase as the price decreases.

Also in Figure 2.1 is a marginal-revenue curve (MR-MR). This shows the amount of revenue added by the sale of one more additional unit. It slopes downward to the right since it is necessary to reduce the price to sell an additional unit. It is below the average-revenue curve since every time the sales price is reduced the price of all previous units also has to be reduced.

No decision can be made with just the revenue curves, but it is interesting to note that when the price is $2, the marginal revenue is zero, and that with a lower price the marginal revenue becomes

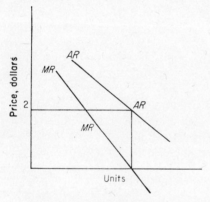

Figure 2.1   Revenue curves.

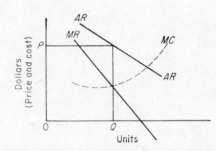

Figure 2.2   Determining output and price.

negative. This means that a further reduction in price results in a reduction in *total* revenue. We would never want to sell for a price lower than $2.

The next step is to add a marginal-cost curve. This curve is presented in Figure 2.2; it shows the amount of cost which is added by the production and sale of one more additional unit of product. If it costs $300 to produce 100 units and $305 to produce 101 units, the marginal cost is $5. The accountant is accustomed to talk of variable, or incremental, costs. In this case the incremental cost of one more unit is $5. The shape of the marginal-cost curve indicates that the firm is at first operating under increasing efficiency (the marginal cost decreases) and then reaches a point where the efficiency decreases (the marginal cost increases). If constant efficiency is assumed, the marginal-cost curve will be a horizontal line.

The point where the marginal-cost curve intersects the marginal-revenue curve (*OQ* units) is very important. This determines the *optimum output*. If the company is producing at less than this level of output, one more unit of production and sale will result in additional revenue greater than the additional cost (the marginal revenue is greater than the marginal cost).

Thus, as long as the value of the marginal-revenue curve is greater than the value of the marginal-cost curve, it will be profitable to increase output. The point where the two curves intersect is the optimum level of output. Let us assume it is decided to increase production by one more unit. Figure 2.2 shows that if production is increased beyond *OQ* units by an additional unit, the additional cost (marginal cost) will be greater than the additional revenue. Thus there will be no profit incentive to increase output beyond *OQ* units.

What price will be charged to maximize profits? To sell *OQ* units it is necessary to charge a price *OP*. This is determined by running a vertical line through the point where marginal cost equals marginal revenue until it intersects the average-revenue line. This determines the price necessary to sell *OQ* units and thus maximize profits. If a lower price is charged, more units than *OQ* will be purchased; but the additional revenue earned by these additional units will be less than the additional costs. If a greater price than *OP* is charged, the number of units sold will be less than *OQ*, and we shall have a situation where marginal revenue is greater than marginal cost. Only an output of *OQ* units sold at a price of *OP* will maximize profits.

Several things should be noted. The output (but not the price) was determined by the intersection of the marginal-cost and marginal-revenue curves. To find the price, it was necessary to know the average revenue. Also, the only costs which entered into the decision were those costs which vary with output. This is a difficult thought to digest; but it is true that costs which are constant in total, and do not vary with output, should not enter into the pricing decision except to set the "standard" price.

The logic of the above analysis is simple and correct. Why is it not more commonly used? There are several reasons, and they are all related to the fact that information is often incomplete. Seldom can the average revenue, the marginal revenue, or the marginal-cost curves be known with certainty. If these curves are not known, then the solution to the problem of output and price cannot be solved with absolute accuracy.

Another objection sometimes offered is that if prices were reduced, competitors would also reduce prices and output would not be increased. Plotters of a firm's average-revenue curve should certainly take into consideration the action of competitors. If this is not done, the curve is meaningless. If it is done, the objection just mentioned is not applicable.

Break-even Analysis

Conventional break-even analysis represents total revenue and total expenses with straight lines. This assumes that output and sales can be increased without changing price (at least, the effect of price changes are not shown) and that the firm operates at the same efficiency at all levels. Thus, to increase profit it is necessary merely to increase the number of units sold. Another assumption which is often made, though it does not bear on our present analysis, is that changes in inventory will not affect income. (A variable or direct-costing technique is implicitly assumed.)

If the firm relaxes the requirements that the price remain unchanged and that efficiency be constant, the plottings of total revenue and total expenses will no longer be straight lines. This type of break-even chart is illustrated in Figure 2.4. It is useful in explaining why the firm should produce at the level where marginal costs equal marginal revenue, since it shows that at this point income is maximized. It also shows that there may be two break-even points. This phenomenon is due to the fact that in order to increase output management must reduce price, but that if it reduces price sufficiently the total revenue will ultimately decrease; thus the total-revenue curve will slope downward and recross the total-expense curve.

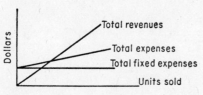

Figure 2.3 Conventional break-even chart.

The X axis of the conventional break-even chart (Figure 2.3) showed the number of units sold. The X axis of the revised break-even chart shows the number of units sold and the price necessary to sell that number of units. Thus, the break-even chart of Figure 2.4 shows the revenues, expenses, and profits for different levels of unit sales and different prices (though for only one level of sales at each price).

Beneath the break-even chart of Figure 2.4 is a chart of marginal costs, marginal revenues, and average revenues. If the two charts are drawn correctly, they will be interrelated in the following ways. The output where marginal cost equals marginal revenue will be the output where the difference between the total-revenue and total-expense curves is the greatest (the income is maximized). The price at which the income is greatest on the break-even chart will be the price determined

by the intersection of the vertical line through the point where marginal cost equals marginal revenue and the average-revenue curve.
The point where total revenue reaches a maximum is where the marginal revenue is equal to zero.

The presentation of a break-even chart with changing prices is not
meant to suggest that the conventional break-even chart with its assumption of constant prices is not useful. In the majority of cases it will
be the more useful of the two presentations. However, if the need

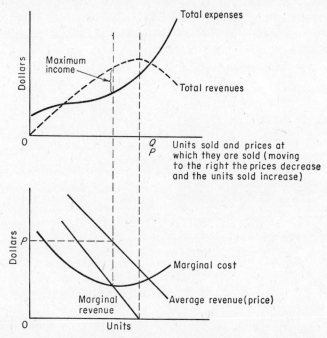

Figure 2.4   Break-even chart with changing selling prices.

is for a chart showing the result of using different possible prices, then
we should use a chart similar to that presented in Figure 2.4.

A common practice of business managers is to draw a break-even
chart assuming the present price and to show that a decrease in price
will require greater sales in order to break even. There is no question
that the lower the price, the higher the break-even point in terms
of units sold and total revenues. The lowest conceivable break-even
point would be a price equal to the sum of the variable costs of one
unit and the total fixed costs. Thus only one unit would have to be
sold to break even. But would that unit be sold? A careful look at
Figure 2.4 shows that the optimum price and output are determined
by reference to the marginal-cost curve and the marginal-revenue curve.

The effect on the break-even point is not considered, nor should it be considered. The conventional break-even analysis is inadequate for determining optimum price and output. For example, Figure 2.5 shows a break-even chart with two possible revenue lines, R_1 and R_2, which are the result of two prices, P_1 and P_2. All other things being equal, the price which leads to the revenue line R_1 appears more desirable since it gives a lower break-even point and higher profits at every point of output. However, it is impossible to determine the better of the two prices until we insert the probable revenues which will be earned following each of the two suggested price policies. Assume that with price P_1, which results in the revenue curve R_1, the firm will operate at the break-even point OB; but with price P_2 the firm will sell an amount equal to capacity OQ. It can now be seen that price P_2,

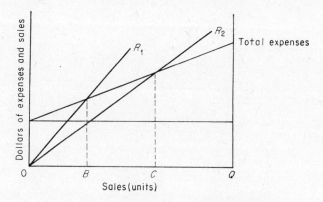

Figure 2.5   Comparing two selling prices.

which results in line R_2, is the more desirable, even though the indicated break-even point is higher. The fact that a larger dollar amount of sales (or of units sold) is needed to break even does not indicate that the break-even point is harder to attain. A price equal to the sum of the variable cost per unit and the fixed costs will give the lowest break-even point, but it may be difficult to sell that one unit necessary to break even.

Break-even Analysis and Changes in Expenses and Sales Price

It is interesting to note that if the firm is selling its product at an optimum price (marginal revenue equals marginal costs) prior to a change leading to increased efficiency (in the form of decreased marginal costs), then the profitable action is for the business manager to decrease his prices and increase his output. Note that this is not done altruistically to share the increased profits but to increase the profits of the firm. Inspection of Figure 2.4 shows that any lowering of the marginal-cost curve will result in the optimum output being increased, and the optimum price will be lower in order to sell these extra units. The profits of the firm will be increased by the amount of the increase in the area between the marginal revenue and marginal-cost curves.

If the break-even chart consists of total expenses and revenues on the Y axis plotted against *total revenues* on the X axis, then a change in the price per unit of the product will require *not* a change in the revenue line (the revenue line does not have to change, since it is measuring dollars of sales, no matter what the price) but a change in the expense line. The change in the expense line is required because the costs per dollar of sale are changed by the fact that each unit sold will now bring in a different amount of revenue while incurring the same amount of expense.

If a change is made in selling expenditures, it can be expected that the break-even chart will change. For example, increased advertising expenditures may enable the firm to increase its prices.

Break-even Analysis and Cost Control

Break-even charts have considerable use as cost-control mechanisms since they show at a glance when favorable or unfavorable expense

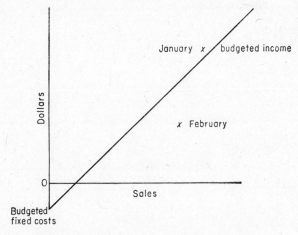

Figure 2.6   Budgeted and actual income.

variances exist. Frequently it is easier to get executives to look at charts than at tabular presentations.

One popular type of break-even chart used for profit control is shown in Figure 2.6. Instead of revenues and budgeted expenses, just the difference between the two (budgeted income) is plotted for different levels of sales. The actual income for the month is marked on the graph; the location of the actual income in relation to the budgeted income determines whether the budgeted income for the actual level of activity was attained. In Figure 2.6 the income for January is more than budgeted and the income for February is less than budgeted. One explanation could be that expenses were not reduced rapidly enough as sales declined.

An alternative presentation would show only the budgeted expenses for the different levels of sales and the actual expenses for the different time periods. This is shown in Figure 2.7.

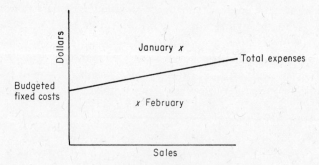

Figure 2.7   Budgeted and actual costs.

In addition to showing the budgeted and actual total expenses, it is desirable to break down the totals by types of expense, by departments, and by product lines. Charts may be prepared for any of these breakdowns, so that the budgeted and actual results may be compared for any level of operations. For many expenses, measures of activity other than sales will be more appropriate. Thus the direct-labor costs incurred should be plotted against number of units of product actually produced, and the wage costs of accounts payable clerks against invoices processed. For each cost classification an appropriate measure of activity should be determined.

Break-even Analysis and Uncertainty

Assume two different break-even charts as shown in Figure 2.8.

Situation B may be interpreted to be the same as situation A, except that the income line results from a higher price. Is the higher price of B more desirable than the price of A? The break-even point is lower, but this is an inevitable result of price increase and tells us nothing about the likelihood of occurrence of the different possible profits following either pricing policy. We cannot use the change in break-even point as the criterion in making the decision.

For a more reasonable decision-making process, we should establish the probability density function, showing the likelihood of selling different amounts of product.[1] See Figure 2.9.

For purposes of this discussion we consider a probability density function to show the relative likelihood of each event occurring. The

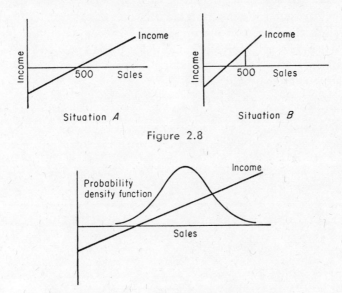

Figure 2.8

Figure 2.9 A probability density function.

area under the curve is equal to one. Figure 2.9 has two scales on the Y axis, one to measure dollars of income and the other to measure the height of the density function. The area under the function enables us to determine the probability of sales being less than or greater

[1] In this chapter we have assumed that the probability distribution of the number of units sold is the same as the number of units demanded. We could allow the possibility of the firm's being unable to fill an order because demand is in excess of the number of units on hand, with the result that the customer buys elsewhere. The solution to this problem then becomes more complex, because it combines pricing, production, and inventory decisions. The separation of pricing, production, and inventory decisions is unrealistic, but it is helpful in that it allows us to understand one segment of the decision. Also, while optimizing segments of the firm may not be the ideal solution, it is frequently an important feasible solution.

than any given amount. (The area under the curve and to the right of some given amount, say $1,000, is the probability of the sales being greater than $1,000.)

To simplify the computations of expected profit,[2] we shall assume a normal-density function.

$$\text{Expected profit} = \sigma C D_b$$

where σ = standard deviation of probability distribution of sales
   C = slope of income line (price minus incremental cost per unit)
   D_b = number of standard deviations break-even point is distant from mean sales

The above equation may be simplified. As long as the income function is linear, we can also determine the expected profit by computing the income for the mean sales. For example, if sales are expressed in units of product,

Expected profit = (mean sales — break-even sales) $\times$ income per unit

EXAMPLE

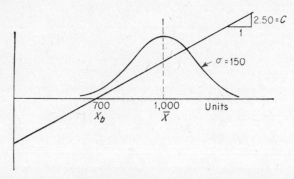

With a price of $4 per unit, the distribution of sales has a mean of 1,000 units and a standard deviation of 150. The incremental costs per unit are $1.50 per unit. The break-even point is 700 units.

$$\sigma = 150$$
$$C = 4.00 - 1.50 = 2.50$$
$$D_b = \frac{\bar{X} - X_b}{\sigma} = \frac{1000 - 700}{150} = 2$$

Expected profit = $\sigma C D_b$ = 150 $\times$ 2.50 $\times$ 2 = $750

We can also compute the expected profit by computing the income for the mean sales of 1,000 units.

Expected profit = (1,000 — 700)2.50 = $750

[2] See the Appendix to this chapter for the derivation of the expected profit. The derivation is more important than the formula, since the formula may be replaced by a simplified computation.

In addition to the expected profit we can compute several measures which give an indication of the risk of the decision. For example, the probability of operating at less than break-even is

$$F(-2) = 0.023$$

where $F(-2)$ is read as "the probability of being more than 2σ to the left of the mean." It is the left tail of the probability distribution.

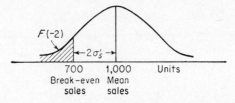

700   1,000   Units
Break-even   Mean
sales   sales

Another useful indication of the risk of the decision is the expected loss. This is equal to the sum of the product of each loss and the probability density of the loss; the resulting equation is

$$\text{Expected loss} = \sigma C N(D_b)$$

where σ and C are as defined previously, $N(D)$ is called the loss function, and $N(D_b)$ is the value of the loss function for $D = D_b$. Values for $N(D)$ are given in a table in the Appendix to the book.[3] D_b is the number of standard deviations that the break-even point is distant from the mean. The value of D_b is positive if the mean sales is to the right of the break-even level of sales.

In the above example

$$\sigma = 150$$
$$C = 2.50$$
$$D_b = 2$$
$$N(D_b) = N(2) = 0.008491$$

$$\text{Expected loss} = 150 \times 2.50 \times 0.008491 = \$3$$

[3] The loss function is computed

$$N(D) = f^*(D) - DG(D)$$

This function is used in computing the expected profit in the Appendix to this chapter.

Definition of terms:

$f^*(D)$ is the value of the standard normal-density function at D standard deviations from the mean.

$G(D)$ is the probability of being more than D standard deviations to the right of the mean. It is the right tail of the normal probability distribution.

We shall define as expected gross profit the expected profit, taking into consideration all possible nonloss levels of operations.   We then have:[4]

$$
\begin{aligned}
\text{Expected gross profit} &= \sigma C[f^*(D_b) + D_b F(D_b)] \\
&= 150 \times 2.50[f^*(2) + 2\,F(2)] \\
&= 150 \times 2.50[0.054 + 2(0.977)] \\
&= 375(0.054 + 1.954) = \$753
\end{aligned}
$$

The expected profit of the decision is equal to the difference between the expected gross profit and the expected loss.

$$
\text{Expected profit} = 753 - 3 = \$750
$$

This is the same amount of expected income that was computed previously.

The ratio of expected loss to expected gross profit gives an indication of the risk of the investment:

$$
\frac{3}{753} = 0.004
$$

The decision being considered has little risk since the expected sales is two standard deviations to the right of the mean and the probability of a loss is small.

Nonlinear Income Functions

In the previous example we assumed income was a linear function of sales; i.e., the income plotted against sales is a straight line.   Because of this we could just as well use the income resulting from the mean sales since that amount is equal to the expected income.   Whenever the income plotted against sales is a straight line, we could use mean sales in computing expected income, or, equivalently, we could use the incomes of the different possible sales weighted by the probability of the occurrence.

The following example assumes that income is not a linear function of sales.

EXAMPLE

Assume the break-even level of sales is 700 units.   The probability distribution of sales is:

[4] See the Appendix to this chapter for the derivation of the expected gross profit. *Definition of terms:*

σ is the standard deviation of the probability distribution of sales.

C is the slope of the income line (price minus incremental cost per unit).

$f^*(D_b)$ is the value of the standard normal-density function D_b standard deviations from the mean.

D_b is the number of standard deviations that the break-even point is distant from the mean sales.

$F(D_b)$ is the probability of being less than D_b standard deviations to the right of the mean.   It is the left tail of the probability distribution.

Sales (in units)	P (sales)	Expected sales (in units)
1,200	0.30	360
700	0.50	350
0	0.20	0
		710

The expected income is:

Sales (in units)	Income*	P (sales)	Expected income
1,200	20,000	0.30	$6,000
700	0	0.50	0
0	(35,000)	0.20	(7,000)
			($1,000)

* The expected incomes for different levels of sales are assumed to be the result of economic analysis and are not linear functions of sales.

The expected income results in a loss of $1,000; thus the decision being considered is not desirable.   If the mean sales of 710 units were used, the decision would be to accept, since 710 is larger than the break-even level of sales of 700 units.   Remember, the income is not a linear function of sales in this example.

Break-even Analysis and Changes in Product Mix

Break-even analysis is at its best when there is a set price and only one product being sold. The problems of price changes have been discussed and a reasonable solution has been offered. The problem of product mix is more complex. Not only may the total output vary, but also the amount of each product sold may change from period to period. The different products may have different profit margins; thus the profit per dollar of sales will vary.

One possibility is to draw break-even charts by product lines. The costs which can be directly identified with the product line are plotted to obtain a break-even point of direct costs (direct in terms of the product line). On top of these costs may be plotted the costs which are assigned to the product as the result of indirect cost allocations, to obtain another break-even point. This second break-even point cannot be used for decision making.

If one break-even chart is desired for the company which produces several different products, we can make the assumption of a normal product mix and make clear the assumption on which the chart is based. In any event, it is clear that the usefulness of a break-even chart for the company as a whole decreases as the number of products made by the firm increases.

Break-even Analysis and Changes in Inventory

A break-even chart implicitly assumes that the fixed costs incurred by the firm will be charged against the revenues of the period. This is consistent with the variable-costing procedure which charges only variable costs to product but is not consistent with normal cost-accounting procedures (except when there are no changes in inventory and cost variances are charged off against the income of the period).

Let us assume that a firm is using a cost-accounting system with overhead absorption based on normal activity. If there is an increase in inventory during the period, then some of the fixed costs incurred during the period will be applied to the goods in inventory and will not be deducted from the revenues of the period. If this income is compared to the budgeted income (the amount the firm expects to earn according to the break-even chart) we shall find that the reported income will be greater, all other things assumed to be equal. There are two solutions to this problem. One would be to use variable-costing procedures in computing the income of the period. The second would be to adjust either the budgeted income of the break-even chart or the income which is a result of the cost-accounting system.

The PV Ratio

Should a company produce aluminum if it is currently in the chemical industry? Should it expand the productive capacity for aluminum if it is currently in the aluminum industry but finds its productive capacity too small? These are examples of investment decisions which must be faced. Before expanding the productive facilities for a present product, or adding a new product, management must decide as to the relative desirability of the different profit possibilities of the different product lines. This is a normal capital-budgeting decision, and the discounted cash flow capital-budgeting procedures will usually result in a correct decision (assuming reliable information) for this type of problem.

Some companies use a different technique in deciding which product is worthy of additional sales effort and productive capacity. The procedure makes use of the ratio of the variable margin to sales (the excess of revenues over variable costs, divided by sales). This ratio is called by various names, but the exact title is unimportant. We shall call it the PV ratio (PV standing for Profit Value).

The PV ratio fails as a guide to the problem being considered, for two reasons. First, it relies on the excess of variable costs over revenues for the present manufacturing process. The manufacturing process being considered for the additional productive capacity may make use of a different degree of automation and thus may have a different PV ratio. The PV ratio, by eliminating from consideration fixed costs, fails to take into consideration the capital outlays required by the additional productive capacity and the additional fixed costs which will be added (for example, the additional accountants, quality control personnel, and foremen who will be required for the operation and who will become fixed costs). Secondly, the PV ratio fails to consider the number of units sold, or which can be sold.

Inspection of the PV ratios of products can certainly *eliminate* from consideration unprofitable lines (those with a low PV and a low volume), and can indicate the lines which appear to be relatively more desirable (those with a high PV). But until we broaden the analysis to take into consideration *all costs directly associated with the product line*, especially those incremental costs which will be incurred because of the expansion, a decision cannot be made whether or not to expand the line.

The PV ratio is a questionable device, but it does give an indication of the relative profitability of the different profit lines, if all other things are equal. For example, an automobile manufacturer may make ten different models of his low-priced car. Should a car be pushed by salesmen because of the high PV ratio? In this case the fixed costs connected with building additional cars will be approximately equal; thus the car with the highest PV ratio seems to be the most desirable car to sell. But even here the conclusion may not be correct, for the PV ratio is generally a ratio of average revenues and average variable costs. The decision is one which should be made using marginal analysis.

The use of PV ratios defined in terms of marginal profits per marginal dollar of costs will lead to reasonable decisions. But even this ratio cannot be used in decisions which are of a nonmarginal nature (such as one involving plant expansion). The PV ratio as generally computed is useful for forming impressions, not making decisions.

Summary

It is possible to arrive at a "standard" price of a product by computing the cost of product and adding a reasonable profit. The cost of product should include fixed overhead absorbed, using normal activity to compute the overhead rate. The use of the standard price is frequently reasonable in setting a target price. In the long run the price of the product must be close to the standard price in order to attract additional investment into the industry. With incomplete knowledge as to the characteristics of the demand curve (because of uncertainty as to the reaction of competitors and customers to price changes), it may be sensible for a firm to charge a standard price for its product. A "fair" profit resulting from the use of a standard price may be more desirable than the dangers accompanying a price reduction justified on the basis that the firm is attempting to find the sales volume which equates marginal cost and marginal revenue. Failure to predict correctly the firm's demand curve (average-revenue curve) can result in a situation where sales and output are expanded beyond the point of optimum sales, and the additional costs are greater than the additional revenues. Why was the price reduced? Because it was thought that the increase in the number of units sold would be greater than actually resulted (the elasticity of demand was overestimated). Thus, setting a standard price and keeping that price may not be an uneconomic decision if we take into consideration the element of uncertainty which accompanies any price change. But it should be remembered that the standard price will not always be the most desirable price. The theoretical solution to the problem of determining the optimum price requires a knowledge of the number of units likely to be sold at different prices and the marginal costs for different levels of output. To as great an extent as possible, this theoretical solution should be applied to the actual situation requiring a pricing-output decision. The theoretical solution does not prevent the selling price from being greater than the marginal costs, but it does mean that the fixed costs do not enter into the decision.

Frequently prices will be set with reference to other factors than those mentioned in this chapter. Long-run considerations may enter into the decision; for example, the effect a price will have on customer goodwill, or the possibility of competitors entering the market if the price is high enough. These factors may lead to setting a price lower than a price which would maximize short-run profits.

One final comment. The output and pricing decision may be made to maximize profits, but a firm does not know if it is going to make a profit. It may very well be that it will be minimizing a loss. To determine whether a profit will be made, it is necessary to compare average total costs and average revenue, or total costs and total revenue. But the pricing and output decisions may be still made without knowing whether or not a profit will be earned.

Appendix

We shall derive the value of expected profit of a given price policy, assuming linear revenue and expense relationships, and a normal-probability distribution of sales.

$$E(\text{profit}) = \sigma C D_b \tag{2.1}$$

where σ = standard deviation of sales

C = slope of income line

D_b = number of standard deviations break-even point is distant from mean sales

For values of X larger than the break-even point X_b, the conditional income is $C(X - X_b)$.

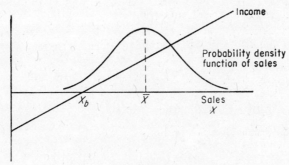

Figure A2.1

To find the expected profit for Xs greater than X_b, it is necessary to multiply the conditional income by the probability density function $f(X)$, and to integrate for all values of X from X_b to ∞. Let $\underset{X_b}{\overset{\infty}{E}}$ (profit) be the partial expectation of profit described above; then:

$$\underset{X_b}{\overset{\infty}{E}} \text{ (profit)} = \int_{X_b}^{\infty} (X - X_b)Cf(X)\ dX \qquad (2.2)$$

We define D as being equal to the number of standard deviations X is distant from $\bar{X}$. It is defined to be positive if X is to the right of the mean and negative otherwise.

If X is larger than $\bar{X}$, then

$$D = \frac{X - \bar{X}}{\sigma} \quad \text{or} \quad X = \sigma D + \bar{X} \quad \text{and} \quad dX = \sigma\ dD$$

If X is less than $\bar{X}$, say X_b, then

$$-D_b = \frac{X_b - \bar{X}}{\sigma} \quad \text{or} \quad X_b = \bar{X} - D_b\sigma$$

If $f^*(D)$ is the standardized normal-density function (mean 0, variance 1), then

$$f^*(D) = \sigma f(X)$$
$$f(X) = \frac{f^*(D)}{\sigma}$$

Returning to Equation (2.2), we accomplish a change of variable, substituting D for X, and obtain Equation (2.3).

Determining new limits of integration:

lower: substitute $-D_b$ for X_b (D_b is negative since X_b is to the left of $\bar{X}$.)
upper: when $X = \infty$

$$D = \frac{\infty - \bar{X}}{\sigma} = \infty$$

$$\underset{-D_b}{\overset{\infty}{E}} \text{ (profit)} = \int_{-D_b}^{\infty} [(\sigma D + \bar{X}) - (\bar{X} - D_b\sigma)]C\frac{f^*(D)}{\sigma}\sigma\ dD \qquad (2.3)$$

Rearranging terms and simplifying:

$$\underset{-D_b}{\overset{\infty}{E}} \text{ (profit)} = \sigma C \int_{-D_b}^{\infty} (D + D_b)f^*(D)\ dD \qquad (2.4)$$

The above integral can be divided into two parts:

1. $\displaystyle\int_{-D_b}^{\infty} D f^*(D)\, dD = \frac{1}{\sqrt{2\pi}}\left(-e^{-\frac{D^2}{2}}\right)\Big|_{-D_b}^{\infty}$

$$= \frac{1}{\sqrt{2\pi}}\, e^{-\frac{D_b^2}{2}} = f^*(D_b)$$

2. $\displaystyle D_b\int_{-D_b}^{\infty} f^*(D)\, dD = D_b G(-D_b) = D_b F(D_b)$

Substituting in Equation (2.4),

$$\mathop{E}_{-D_b}^{\infty}\ (\text{profit}) = \sigma C[f^*(D_b) + D_b F(D_b)] \tag{2.5}$$

Equation (2.5) may be called the expected gross profit. It is also necessary to compute the expected loss:

$$\mathop{E}_{-\infty}^{-D_b}\ (\text{loss}) = \int_{-\infty}^{-D_b} (X_b - X) C f(X)\, dX \tag{2.6}$$

Following a procedure similar to the derivation of Equation (2.5), we obtain

$$\mathop{E}_{-\infty}^{-D_b}\ (\text{loss}) = \sigma C[f^*(D_b) - D_b G(D_b)]$$

$$= \sigma C[f^*(D_b) - D_b + D_b F(D_b)] \tag{2.7}$$

The expected profit is the difference between Equations (2.5) and (2.7):

$$E\ (\text{profit}) = \sigma C[f^*(D_b) + D_b F(D_b) - f^*(D_b) + D_b - D_b F(D_b)]$$
$$= \sigma C D_b \tag{2.8}$$

which is what we wanted to show.

chapter three

variable
costing[1]

The term "variable costing" is frequently used in two different ways. First, it can refer to a method of accounting which considers fixed costs as costs of the time period and treats only variable costs as inventoriable costs. Second, variable costing may refer to a system of internal reporting and analysis for decisions which differentiates between fixed and variable costs. We shall use the former, more restrictive definition since the question whether or not fixed cost should be included in computing the costs of product is controversial. The distinction between fixed and variable costs is clearly useful for decision making, but this necessity to determine the nature of costs for purposes of decision making is not dependent on the method of accounting for fixed costs for financial reporting.

The Need for Variable Costing

The need for variable costing arises because certain costs are constant over wide ranges of production. Under generally accepted methods of accounting, which absorb all or a portion of fixed costs as costs of product, the income of a period is affected not only by sales and efficiency but also by the amount of production and by the change in inventory. Thus the income of a period may be increased not only by more sales or better efficiency but merely by producing more and by putting the excess production into inventory.

[1] The terms "direct costing" or "marginal costing" are frequently used instead of variable costing. They all refer to a procedure which considers fixed costs an expense of the time period and only variable costs as a cost of product.

EXAMPLE

Assume that a company in the months of March and April has $20,000 of sales (5,000 units sold).   The production cost information for the two months is as follows:

Fixed costs $100,000 (per month)
Variable costs $1 (per unit)

The production for March was 10,000 units and for April 100,000 units.   The normal activity for both months is 50,000 units.

A variety of income statements are possible for the two months, depending on the policy regarding the accounting for the absorption of the fixed costs.

	"Actual" costs		Normal activity costing (overhead variance allocated to product)	
	March	April	March	April
Sales	$20,000	$20,000	$20,000	$20,000
Less: Variable costs	5,000	5,000	5,000	5,000
Fixed costs	50,000*	5,000†	50,000‡	5,000§
	$55,000	$10,000	$55,000	$10,000
Income (loss)	($35,000)	$10,000	($35,000)	$10,000

* The fixed cost per unit produced was $100,000/10,000, or $10 per unit. There were 5,000 units sold; thus the fixed costs charged to expense were $50,000.

† The fixed cost per unit produced was $100,000/100,000, or $1 per unit. There were 5,000 units sold; thus the fixed costs charged to expense were $5,000.   This assumes a lifo flow of costs.

‡ On the basis of normal activity the fixed cost per unit was $100,000/50,000, or $2 per unit.   There were 10,000 units produced in March; thus the fixed cost absorbed by product was $20,000 and the unabsorbed fixed cost was $80,000.   Half of the unabsorbed overhead, $40,000, is charged to inventory and half to expense since 5,000 units were sold and 5,000 units remain in inventory.   Thus the total fixed cost charged to expense was $40,000 of allocated, unabsorbed overhead and $10,000 of normal overhead.

§ During April the production was 100,000 units; thus there was $200,000 of fixed overhead absorbed to product.   There was a favorable activity variance of $100,000.   The fixed cost charged to expense was the number of units sold times the normal overhead rate of $2 (this assumes a lifo flow of costs), minus 5,000/100,000 of the $100,000 variance:

$$5,000 \times \$2 \qquad \$10,000$$
$$\text{Less } \tfrac{5}{100} \times \$100,000 \qquad \underline{5,000}$$
$$\text{Charged to expense} \qquad \underline{\$\ 5,000}$$

It is important to note that the "actual" cost procedure and the normal costing procedure give the same income, if the unabsorbed overhead is allocated back to the product sold and to the ending inventory.   Both procedures result in the income of the period being distorted by the level of production in relation to sales.

Frequently the activity variance is handled as an expense of the period in which it is incurred, instead of being considered a cost of product to be allocated to the cost of goods sold and to the ending inventory. In the one procedure it is included with other expenses of the period and allowed to affect the income. In the other procedure it is subtracted from the operating income so that the operating income is not affected by the level of activity.

	Normal activity costing (activity variance included as an expense)		Normal activity costing (activity variance subtracted from the operating income)	
	March	April	March	April
Sales	$20,000	$ 20,000	$20,000	$ 20,000
Less: Cost of goods sold*	15,000	15,000	15,000	15,000
Activity variance	80,000	(100,000)		
	$95,000	($ 85,000)		
Operating income (loss)	($75,000)	$105,000	$ 5,000	$ 5,000
Less: Activity variance			80,000	(100,000)
Income (loss)			($75,000)	$105,000

* The $15,000 is equal to $5,000 variable costs and $10,000 fixed overhead.

It is interesting that the normal costing procedure will give equal incomes for the two months if we focus attention on a subtotal before the deduction of the activity variances. However, this might result in the reporting of profits for each of 12 months, but then a loss for the year when the activity variance was taken into consideration.

The last procedure illustrated will be variable costing. When this process is followed, all fixed costs are accounted for as expenses of the period in which they are incurred, and only variable costs are considered to be inventoriable.

	Variable costing	
	March	April
Sales	$ 20,000	$ 20,000
Less: Variable costs	5,000	5,000
Excess of revenues over variable costs	$ 15,000	$ 15,000
Less: Fixed costs	100,000	100,000
Income (loss)	($ 85,000)	($ 85,000)

Under variable costing the incomes of the two periods are the same. This is consistent with the fact that the sales and efficiencies of the two periods were exactly the same, and that the only difference in the two periods was the level of production. While the other methods all arrived at a profit for one period and a loss for the other, the variable costing procedure shows a loss for both periods.

The primary advantage of variable costing is that income is not directly affected by changes in inventory and changes in production. Thus, to increase income we must increase the total sales or change the cost-revenue relationship in some meaningful way. The profits which result from increases in inventory are not real profits, and any procedure which eliminates them from the records is accomplishing a worthwhile objective. An increase in inventory, rather than indicating efficiency, may be indicating inefficiency since excessive inventory may result in additional real costs, which may be undesirable from the point of view of the firm.

Variable Costing and Financial Reporting

In recent years variable costing has increased in popularity for purposes of internal reporting and decision making. The increased use by management of this technique has brought into focus a companion question. Should variable costing be used for financial reporting purposes, especially statements issued to stockholders?[2] Does the generally accepted accounting practice of absorbing fixed overhead to product result in situations where the reader of a widely distributed annual report may be misled?

Criteria for Judging Financial Reporting Procedures

What is good financial reporting? The decision whether or not to use variable costing for financial reporting must be decided by whether it is good reporting. Generally speaking, there are three criteria which are used in deciding what shall constitute suitable reporting. These are:

1. Is it in accordance with generally accepted accounting practice and conventions as set forth by professional organizations and governmental bodies?
2. Is it in accordance with basic accounting theory as described in accounting literature?
3. Is it useful for decision making?

[2] For points of view which are different from those of the author see S. R. Hepworth, "Direct Costing: The Case Against," *Accounting Review*, pp. 94–99, January, 1954; R. Lee Brummet, "Direct Costing: Should It Be a Controversial Issue?" *Accounting Review*, pp. 439–443, July, 1955. These two articles state in excellent fashion the arguments against using variable costing for financial reporting.

All too frequently the first two criteria are cited as the determining factors in choosing the proper method. The third criterion is neglected or assumed to be automatically covered by accounting practice or basic accounting theory. This assumption is unwarranted.

If accounting practice is to be the determining criterion, then change is impossible since by definition what is being done is correct. The accounting practice in effect today is of interest, but a statement of convention should not be used to prove that a procedure is correct or incorrect. The fact that Accounting Research Bulletin 43 approves absorption costing tells us what is currently approved by the American Institute of Certified Public Accountants.[3] It does not help us decide whether variable costing would be a more reasonable procedure than current practice.

The criterion of accounting theory should not be discarded lightly. The authors of the past fifty years have contributed tremendously to raising the level of accounting practice. The fact that thought-provoking writings have been produced by such men as Cole, Hatfield, and Paton makes us reluctant to modify time-honored concepts. But it must be recognized that these men changed accounting practice, advocated further changes not accepted, and certainly did not intend to freeze accounting thought. Thus, to quote accounting authorities as justification for an accounting procedure is meaningful only to the extent that the logic of the authority is applicable to the present situation, and does not actually prove that one or another position is sound. And even where it is logically presented that one position is sound, it does not follow that another position is not sound.

Fixed Costs as Product Costs—Pros and Cons

The adherents of variable costing for financial reporting purposes argue that only variable costs may be said to be costs of product. Fixed costs would be incurred in any event, and thus are said to be costs of the period, not costs of product. This argument has some validity but falls short of proving the case for variable costing. A fixed cost may not be as inevitable or as nonrelevant as the variable-costing adherents suggest.

Let us analyze the wages of a plant manager and the depreciation of the plant. These are fixed costs, but it is possible that if there were no intention of producing the product the plant could be sold or diverted to producing another product. The plant manager could be switched

[3] Committee on Accounting Procedure, *Restatement and Revision of Accounting Research Bulletins,* Bulletin 43, American Institute of Certified Public Accountants, New York, 1953, p. 28.

to another job.   The fixed costs are relevant costs of product when there are opportunity costs connected with factors of production which in turn give rise to the fixed costs.   Thus the value of the plant manager's services, if he were performing other tasks, represents the opportunity cost of the plant manager working on the present product.   In like manner the funds which would result from the sale of a plant or the net revenues which would result from other uses of the plant are the opportunity costs of using the plant to make the present product.   It may not be unreasonable to substitute the wages of the plant manager and the depreciation of the plant for the opportunity costs of these factors of production, and to consider these costs as a cost of product.

Another strong argument in favor of including fixed costs as a cost of product is the concept of matching expenses with the revenues which they help earn.   If the fixed costs are a valid cost of product (as is indicated above), they should not be recognized as an expense until the product is sold.   The accounting treatment of the variable- and fixed-cost factors identified as costs of product should not be different.   This is the position of the Committee on Accounting Concepts and Standards of the American Accounting Association.[4]

In many cases the factors of production which give rise to the fixed costs do not have alternative uses; thus their opportunity costs are zero. The fixed costs are time period costs, not costs of product, since they would be incurred even if no product were produced.   The variable (or incremental) costs incurred in producing the units of product are the costs of product, not the total costs incurred during the period.   If this argument is accepted, then the fixed costs are considered expenses of the period in which the cost expiraton occurred.

The Usefulness Criterion

There would seem to be reasonable arguments for both inclusion and exclusion of fixed costs.   On the basis of the arguments presented above, the balance is in favor of including the fixed costs in the cost of product, thus including them in inventory.   This is the point of view of accounting practice and the majority of academic authors.

However, the third criterion remains to be considered.   What is the usefulness of the procedure?   Certainly the criterion of usefulness is relevant in making the decision as to whether fixed costs should be included in inventory.   The reasons for including fixed costs based on identification of the cost with product seem more logical than the reasons

[4] Committee on Accounting Concepts and Standards, *Accounting and Reporting Standards for Corporate Financial Statements and Preceding Statements and Supplements*, American Accounting Association, Columbus, Ohio, 1957, p. 4. See the dissent of Mr. Hill and Mr. Vatter from the majority position, p. 10.

for excluding fixed costs.   But this is not to say that the opposition does not have a reasonable position.   For practical purposes, many fixed costs are unavoidable and thus may logically be considered costs of the time period rather than of the product.   If we recognize that there is *some* justification for excluding fixed costs, then we are receptive at least to looking at the relative usefulness of the several possible procedures.

THE CHOICES AVAILABLE

It will be assumed that there are three choices available to the accountant maintaining the records of a manufacturing firm.   He can compute the cost of product by:

1. Dividing the total costs incurred during the period by the number of units produced.
2. Using a standard overhead rate based on a predetermined level of activity (for example, normal activity or practical capacity) and considering any idle-capacity variance as a cost of the period.   To distribute the variance to product would make this procedure the equivalent of the first procedure.   To have the variance bypass the income statement would solve several difficulties with this procedure, but the cure would be worse than the ills.
3. Including only variable costs as a cost of product, fixed costs being considered as expenses of the time period.

All three procedures give the same results if in every period the plant sold all of the product it produced.   The classification of the items carried to the income statement would differ, but the net income resulting would be the same.   However, these are obviously unrealistic assumptions, for some of the product produced will not be sold, and the problem is made even more complex by the fact that production as well as the amount produced but unsold will change from period to period.

The first procedure suggested above will result in the incomes of successive periods being affected by the changes in production and the changes in inventory.   With the second procedure, income will be affected by changes in production.   Using a predetermined overhead rate based on normal activity, the company can show an income with zero or near zero sales.   (If the overhead is overabsorbed to product, the activity variance is favorable, and this reduces the expense and increases the income of the period.)

Unlike the first two procedures, variable costing results in income being reported which is undistorted by changes in production or changes in inventory.   This occurs because fixed costs are considered expenses of the period.

Absorption Costing and Income Theory

Accounting theoreticians do not intend income to be generally a function of production or of the level of inventory which is carried (especially where the higher the inventory the higher the resulting income). Revenue is not recognized at the production stage except in special cases where the sale is certain and the production period is long.[5] Generally a completed legal sale is necessary to justify the recognition of revenue. It is paradoxical that the accountant, who is so careful about when to recognize revenue (and rightly so), allows the income to be distorted by the inclusion of fixed manufacturing overhead in the cost of product. If fixed costs are included in inventory, under conventional accounting procedure, then the income will be affected by changes in inventory and changes in production, as well as by the level of sales and efficiency.

If this is acceptable accounting theory, let accountants acknowledge the fact that such a situation exists and state the explanation. It is unlikely that the opponents of variable costing are arguing in favor of recognizing revenue at the time of production. Then, is revenue to be unaffected but income to be affected by changes in production? This is not a logical and acceptable addition to the theory of income.

Variable Costing and Financial Reporting

What would be the effect of using variable costing for financial reporting? Income would not be distorted by changes in production and inventory. Management currently obtains financial data of this nature. Other readers and users of financial reports need undistorted information no less than internal managements.

The inventory presented in the position statement would include only variable costs. The advantage of this procedure is that, in the absence of price changes, the inventory reported in the position statement would reflect changes in the physical units on hand. This is to be preferred over fluctuation in the cost per unit caused by variations in the level of production, which fluctuation would happen if the cost per unit was determined with actual costs divided by actual production, or with activity variance distributed back to inventory and cost of product sold. The disadvantage of variable costing for financial reporting is that inventories are recorded at less than they would be with the use of full cost.

How meaningful is the fact that inventories are recorded at a lesser amount than would be found under any absorption costing system?

[5] In certain industries (for example shipbuilding and gold mining) it is not unreasonable for income to be a function of production.

What decisions would be made differently because of the exclusion of fixed costs from the inventory position? Even in the computation of financial position, variable costing gives information which is generally as useful for decision making as absorption costing; and if absorption costing is used incorrectly, then variable costing is even more desirable.

But the argument that fixed costs are a valid cost of product still remains. One possibility would be to indicate the standard cost of the product, undistorted by the actual level of production, in a footnote. The disadvantage of this procedure is simply that the inventory on the position statement is not presented in a manner to reflect all costs related to its production.

A Possible Solution

We have discussed the paradoxical situation where the logical correct method of inventory presentation results in distorted income measurement. Efforts to eliminate the distortions to income arising from variable costing result in an understatement of inventory. The following solution attempts to correct both these major problems, substituting a relatively minor difficulty.

It is suggested that income be measured by an accounting procedure which considers all fixed costs as expenses of the time period. Thus the fluctuations in income caused by changes in production and inventory are eliminated.

To avoid the understatement of inventory, the unwanted by-product of a variable-costing procedure, the inventory will be presented at full cost, the presentation using one of the relatively sound methods of absorbing overhead to product. The fixed overhead in the inventory of the present period will be compared to the amount of fixed overhead in the inventory of the previous period, and the change will be recorded to the retained earnings account. The change in fixed costs in inventory at the end of the period will appear in the reconciliation of retained earnings, but will not affect the reported income of the period.

A compromise is needed here since both absorption and variable costing assume that income is being measured in terms of the difference between revenues and expenses of the period. If income were to be redefined in terms of the change in the stockholders' equity at the beginning and end of the accounting period, excluding new capital and capital distributions, the need for the special adjustment to retained earnings would be eliminated. If production actually increased the well-being of the stockholders, this fact would be noted in the income statement. As long as accountants consider realization of income to be accomplished by a completed sale, and cost to be the basis of asset accounting, then the basic inconsistency between absorption and variable costing will continue to exist, and with it a need for reconciliation of the two conventions.

Possible objections to the suggested procedure are that it makes use of the retained earnings reconciliation to adjust the amount of fixed costs remaining in inventory and considers the fixed costs an asset after they have been expensed. Against these objections must be balanced the improved measures of income compared with those of generally accepted accounting procedures, and the improved valuation of inventories and presentation of financial position compared with those under variable costing. The following illustration is designed to show the operation of the suggested procedure. It also compares the results from the suggested procedure with conventional accounting, and with variable costing.

ILLUSTRATION

The ABC Company produces one product. The budgeted and actual fixed manufacturing costs of each year are $10,000. The standard and actual variable manufacturing costs are $2 per unit. The company has a normal capacity of 10,000 units and uses normal capacity to absorb fixed overhead to product (the fixed overhead rate is $1 per unit). Assume zero work-in-process inventories.

At the beginning of 1965 the company had the following position statement:

Position Statement
as of January 1, 1965

Other assets	$40,000	Capital stock	$20,000
Finished goods	....	Retained earnings	20,000
	$40,000		$40,000

During 1965 the company finished 10,000 units of product and sold 4,000 units for $3.10 per unit. During 1966 the company finished 2,000 units and sold 4,000 units. Assume the only expenses are costs of manufacturing.

Under the suggested procedure the following reports could be prepared:

Income Statement

		1965		1966
Sales revenues (4,000 × $3.10)	......	$12,400		$12,400
Manufacturing costs				
Variable costs (4,000 × $2)	$ 8,000		$ 8,000	
Fixed costs	10,000	18,000	10,000	18,000
Operating loss		($ 5,600)		($ 5,600)

Retained Earnings Reconciliation

	Dec. 31 1965	Dec. 31 1966
Retained earnings, January 1	$20,000	$20,400
Less: Operating loss for year	5,600	5,600
	$14,400	$14,800
Plus: Adjustment for changes in amount of fixed costs in inventory*	6,000	(2,000) †
Retained earnings, December 31	$20,400	$12,800

* The fixed costs are charged to expense in the period in which they are incurred, to avoid distortions in the measurement of income caused by changes in inventory. However, generally accepted accounting principles properly consider the cost of manufactured goods to include a pro rata share of the fixed manufacturing costs incurred. Thus the inventory and retained earnings are adjusted for the amount of fixed costs considered to be associated with the goods in inventory.

† An accounting entry would be required, decreasing the inventory by $2,000 and decreasing the retained earnings—adjustment account.

Retained earnings—Adjustment for amount of fixed costs in inventory	2,000	
Finished goods—fixed costs		2,000

The above entry adjusts the amount of fixed costs presented in inventory to be consistent with the number of units in inventory as of December 31, 1966. It will not affect the income of this period or future periods.

Position Statement

	Dec. 31 1965	Dec. 31 1966		Dec. 31 1965	Dec. 31 1966
Other assets	$22,400	$20,800	Capital stock	$20,000	$20,000
Finished goods	18,000	12,000	Retained earnings	20,400	12,800
	$40,400	$32,800		$40,400	$32,800

This procedure accomplishes several goals. The inventory is stated at full cost, thus satisfying those concerned with the omission of fixed costs from inventory that results when using variable costing. On the other hand, the incomes of the two periods are equal, as they should be for two accounting periods where the revenues were equal, where the total number of units sold were the same, and where there were no changes in efficiency. Under the conventional variable-costing procedure the income statements would be exactly the same as above, but the inventories would be so presented as to include only variable costs. The income statements in generally accepted absorption accounting would be as follows:

Income Statements
Using Absorption Accounting

	1965	1966
Revenues	$12,400	$12,400
Manufacturing costs		
Standard cost of product	12,000	12,000
Activity variance—Loss		8,000
Total expenses	$12,000	$20,000
Net income (loss)	$ 400	($ 7,600)

Generally accepted accounting procedures lead to the interesting (though misleading) conclusion that there is an income of $400 in one year, and a loss of $7,600 in the other, when the only difference between the two years is the level of production.

Conclusions

Some accountants have reacted disapprovingly to the suggestion that variable costing be allowed for financial reporting as if the very basis of double-entry bookkeeping was being challenged. Present-day accounting is not based on full cost-absorption accounting. Absorption of fixed costs to product is logical, but it inevitably results in a joint-cost situation. One problem is to separate the cost of product and the cost of idleness as the use of the production facilities fluctuates. But even if the joint costs could be separated, there would still exist the fact that the income is affected by the level of production activity. A possible solution has been offered in this chapter which removes the distortion from the measurement of income (essentially a variable-costing procedure) but retains a full-cost basis of inventory presentation.

chapter four

joint
cost
and joint
products

Joint cost relates to a situation where the factor of production by its basic nature results in two or more products. This differs from indirect costs, which represent the cost of using factors of production where the number of products produced is a decision of management. For example, indirect costs will occur if a plant produces beer cans and soda pop cans, since some of the same equipment may be used to produce both products yet both need not be produced. An example of a joint cost is the cost of a pig purchased by a meat company. There will be several products resulting from the processing of the pig, and these products will have a common cost, the purchase price of the pig. No one product could be economically produced from the pig without producing many other products.

Thus there are two types of costs which we cannot directly identify with the end products when there are two or more types of products being made. It might be said that these costs are common to both products; in fact, the term "common costs" is sometimes used to describe this classification of cost.

Indirect costs result from the production of more than one product, but the decision to use these factors of production to produce several products is a decision of management. Any indirect cost could be directed to the production of one product.

Joint costs result from the production of more than one product, and the multi-products are the result of the method of production or the nature of the raw material, not of a decision of management (though management may find the production of one of the resulting products uneconomical and drop the "finishing" process). By the nature of the raw material (or the productive process) several products result; thus the costs are "joint" to these products. An example of a raw material which results in a joint cost is oil. From the raw material, crude oil, come such products as gasoline, fuel oil, tar, and chemicals. An example of a productive process which leads to joint costs is railroading, with the cost of rails being a joint cost to both freight and passenger travel.

The products resulting from joint costs are called joint products if they are approximately equal in importance. Thus, ham, pork chops, and bacon would be joint products of the purchase cost of the pig. In some situations products of little value may be obtained, and these are called by-products. This meaning of the term "by-product" is different from common usage, in which the product so referred to may be of considerable value even though it is subsidiary to the main product. An example of a by-product in a cost-accounting sense is the metal scrap resulting from the production of an airplane. This scrap has considerable value in absolute amount, but compared to the value of the primary product, airplanes, it is of small value and is considered a by-product. As we shall see, the by-product classification has accounting implications. Any product producing salable scrap has at least one by-product.

Accounting for Joint Costs

The first thing to note concerning the accounting for joint costs is the fact that the joint costs cannot be split up and identified *with certainty* to several joint products. There is no way to split the cost of a pig into components and say that the cost of ham *is* X dollars and the cost of bacon *is* Y dollars and prove that we are absolutely correct. We know the cost of the entire pig, but we cannot determine with certainty the costs of the several products processed from the animal.

Having recognized the impossibility of the job, the accountant is still faced with the necessity of preparing reports of financial position and income. To determine the financial position and income, estimates must be made of the value of the inventory, and the same is true of measuring income. Thus, procedures must be established for determining reasonable values for the joint products.

A possible method is to take the expected sales value of each component product and compute the costs so that they are proportionate to the sales value. One objection to this procedure is the fact that different products may require different finishing costs to prepare them for the market. If the finishing costs are subtracted from the sales value, then it would be reasonable to charge each product with an amount of the common cost in proportion to those amounts. The assigned cost would then be in proportion to the value of the products to the firm.

Assume that a certain raw material costs $200 per unit and that three joint products are made from each unit. The characteristics of the three products are:

Product	Pounds	Sales revenue	Finishing costs	Net sales value	Per cent of total value
A	70	$130	$30	$100	25%
B	20	210	50	160	40%
C	10	150	10	140	35%
				$400	

Using the net sales value to prorate the $200 of costs, we would charge product A with 25 per cent, or $50; product B with 40 per cent, or $80; and product C with 35 per cent, or $70. A different allocation of the common costs would have resulted from the use of the sales revenue of each product. Assuming that it is reasonable to charge each product in proportion with its value, we shall do better to use net sales value.

If the units are sold for the predicted prices, it is interesting to look at the resulting income statements.

	Product A	Product B	Product C
Sales	$130	$210	$150
Finishing costs	30	50	10
Cost of raw material	50	80	70
Total expenses	$ 80	$130	$ 80
Gross profit	$ 50	$ 80	$ 70
Gross profit as per cent of sales	38.5%	38.1%	46.7%

The percentages of gross profit to sales for all three products differ. Let us now assume that there were no unequal finishing costs, but that the net sales value was actually the sales price and that all finishing costs were of a joint nature and were included in the $200 figure. The income statements now become:

	Product A	Product B	Product C
Sales	$100	$160	$140
Less: Raw material and finishing costs	50	80	70
Gross profit	$ 50	$ 80	$ 70
Gross profit as per cent of sales	50%	50%	50%

Note that the ratio of gross profit to sales is now the same for all three products, a result of the method of computing the allocation of the common costs. The percentages will be different only where there are finishing costs which can be directly identified with the end product, and where those finishing costs are not in proportion to the net sales value of the product. The tendency of the joint-cost allocations to result in an equal ratio of gross profit to net sales values warns against placing excessive faith in profit figures for product lines resulting from arbitrary joint-cost allocations.

The preceding method of cost allocation is probably the most reasonable method, but there are many other methods used in practice. One common method is to allocate the costs on a physical measure. For example, the pounds of product in the above illustration could be used. This would result in product A receiving 70 per cent of the $200 common costs despite the fact that its net sale value is only $100. This does not seem to be reasonable procedure, since the allocations are made on a basis unrelated to the value of the product.

By-products

Assume that in addition to the products A, B, and C there is another product, Z, which is relatively small in value (similar to the scrap metal accumulated and sold to scrap dealers). Assume that 50 pounds of Z are generated from each unit of raw material, that Z sells for $0.40 a pound, and that it costs $0.10 a pound to prepare it for sale.

Each unit of raw material results in $50 \times \$0.40$, or $20 of sales value of Z. But preparing Z costs $0.10 a pound, or $5. The net value of the scrap is $20 less $5, or $15. A reasonable accounting procedure for by-products is to remove from manufacturing costs the net value of the by-product and set it up in a by-product inventory account. The following T accounts illustrate the above situation:

Raw material		Material in process	
200	(1) 200	(1) 200	(4) 15

By-product processing costs		By-product inventory	
(2) 5	(3) 5	(3) 5	
		(4) 15	

Miscellaneous credits (such as wages payable)	
	(2) 5

Explanation of entries

1. The placing of one unit of raw material in production
2. The incurring of costs related to processing the by-product
3. The transfer of by-product processing costs to inventory
4. The transfer of by-product material costs to by-product inventory

The transfer from material in process is priced at the net sales value of the by-product.

Note that the by-product inventory is priced at its sale price. This procedure results in the by-product's showing neither a profit nor a loss unless there is change in the price of the by-product after it has been transferred to inventory.

If the by-product becomes significant in size, then the procedure described above can distort the relative performance of the by-product compared to the primary products since it tends to show no profit for the by-product. It should thus be treated as a joint product.

Note that the preceding T accounts show that $200 less $15 will be allocated to the three joint products. An increase in the value of the by-product will result in a decrease in the amount to be allocated to the three joint products since the transfer to the by-product account will be increased.

By-products are also accounted for by recognition of the revenues produced by the sale, but without assignment of any material costs to the by-products. If the amounts are small, this procedure can be excused since the errors are not material. However, the procedure is not theoretically sound.

Joint Costs and Decision Making

The preceding section indicated that any allocation of joint costs to joint products was arbitrary at best, though there were some methods which were more reasonable than others. The function of the allocation is to obtain some notion of the cost of the inventory and the income of the period. If we shift attention to making decisions, then we must shift from making arbitrary allocations, since the allocations will not be the basis of decisions. In the preceding example the $20 cost of the by-product did not determine the price of the by-product, but rather the cost of the product was determined by the price. In like manner the cost of product C may be found to be $70, but this does not mean that the firm should not sell the units of C on hand if the price drops to $60.

Let us assume a situation where two joint products A and B are made from a raw material which costs $2 per pound and which weighs 10 pounds.

	A	B
Weight of product resulting from		
10 lb raw material	4 lb	6 lb
Direct finishing costs	$1.25 per lb	$0.50 per lb
Indirect finishing costs $7 (applies jointly to A and B)		

Both the direct and indirect finishing costs indicated above are of an incremental nature. (Any purely fixed costs have been omitted since they do not affect the decisions.)

Neither cost, of A or of B, can be determined with certainty since they have common costs of $20 for material and $7 of processing costs. However, we can determine the cost of making both A and B. To manufacture four pounds of A and six pounds of B costs $35.

Raw material	$20
Joint processing costs	7
Direct costs—A(1.25 × 4)	5
Direct costs—B(.50 × 6)	3
	$35

We also know that if the company made just A and did not finish B, the costs would be $32 (made up of $20 plus $7 plus $5). If it made just B and did not finish A, the costs would be $30 (made up of $20 plus $7 plus $3).

From the above information we can make several conclusions that do not depend on an allocation of joint costs and which are theoretically sound:

1. If the revenues from the sale of A plus B are in excess of $35, the firm should produce. (It does not follow that if the revenues are less than $35 it should not produce.)
2. If the revenues from the sale of A are greater than $32, the firm should produce A. It should not finish B unless the revenues arising from the sale of B are in excess of the $3 of costs of finishing B.
3. If the revenues from the sale of B are greater than $30, the firm should produce B. It should not finish A unless the revenues arising from the sale of A are in excess of the $5 of costs required to finish A.
4. If the revenues from the sale of A and B are less than $30, then the firm should not produce A or B.

Though the products A and B are joint products, the manufacturer may choose not to produce one or the other or both products. Thus, a chemical company may find that it is commercially sound to produce one joint product, but that the use for another of the joint products has decreased, with a resulting decrease in price, so that production is no longer economically sound.

Determining the Price of Joint Products

It is frequently assumed that the pricing policy for joint products requires a cost allocation of an arbitrary nature. That is not true. It is possible to establish a theoretically sound framework for determining price and output decisions for joint products.

Let us continue the example of the preceding section dealing with products A and B, which are produced in fixed proportions. These products will be assumed to have independent demand curves (average-revenue or price curves). (See Figure 4.1.) The demands for the two products may be independent or mutually dependent, but for simplicity we shall assume that the prices and total sales at different prices of the two products are independent of each other. The only assumptions made are that the demand curves slope downward to the right (the number of units sold increases as the price is decreased), and that the output of product B will depend on how many units of A are produced.

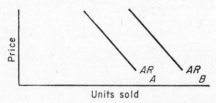

Figure 4.1   Demand curves for two joint products.

Instead of separate demand curves for the two products, we may consider the 10 pounds of raw material as making one product, namely, four pounds of A and six pounds of B. We can then draw average-revenue and marginal-revenue curves for this new product. The average-revenue curve for one unit would consist of the price necessary to clear four pounds of A plus the price necessary to sell six pounds of B. Both these amounts may be obtained from Figure 4.1.

Several complications should be noted. Where the marginal revenue of B falls below \$3 per unit of B (that is, \$3 for six pounds of B), then B should not be finished, and the marginal-cost curve for the product A plus B should take this into consideration by elimination of the \$3 of finishing costs. In like manner, when the marginal revenue of A falls below \$5 per unit of A (that is, four pounds of A), then A should not be finished, and the marginal-cost curve should take this into consideration. For simplicity in drawing the curves, we shall assume that the relevant parts of the graphs occur before either of these possibilities takes place.

The only cost curve shown in Figure 4.2 is the marginal-cost curve.

The curve is assumed to be a horizontal line; thus, it will also serve as an average variable-cost curve.

Figure 4.2 shows that the optimum solution to the problem of deciding the output is OQ units, where the units are expressed in terms of four pounds of A and six pounds of B. At that output, prices will be charged so as to result in average revenues of OR. OR is not the price, since OQ units will not be sold, but rather units of products A and B will be sold. To find the prices at which the units will be sold,

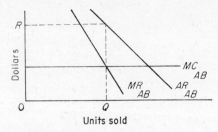

Figure 4.2   Marginal analysis for two joint products.

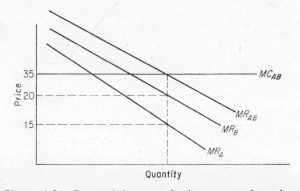

Figure 4.3   Determining marginal revenue of product.

it is necessary to return to Figure 4.1 and find the prices for A and B that will clear the market of the number of units which we have decided to produce. The price of A times the number of units of A, plus the price of B times the number of units of B, will be equal to OR times OQ (the number of units) from Figure 4.2.

The reader may object to a pretense of accuracy in the solution offered since not all the information necessary for this solution is often known in practice. The objection has merit, but the importance of the presentation is not in terms of its being applied exactly as illustrated but rather in terms of a method of reasoning. This reasoning shows clearly that the allocation of joint costs is not essential to a clear and definite solution to the problems of output and pricing of joint products.

However, we may wish to determine the cost of the two products A and B for purposes of presenting an inventory figure and measuring income. Figure 4.3 shows the marginal-revenue curves of product A and product B as well as the sum of the marginal-revenue curves. The marginal cost curve includes finishing costs. The total marginal cost of the two products at the point of optimum output is equal to $35. It is reasonable to divide the marginal cost into two parts based on the marginal revenue of each product. At the optimum level of output the marginal revenue of A is $15 and the marginal revenue of B is $20; the marginal revenue and the marginal cost of the joint product is $35. Dividing the $35 of cost between A and B results in $15 being allocated to A and $20 to B. This procedure is somewhat different from the method of allocation presented earlier in this chapter, which based the allocation on the price (average revenue) less any finishing costs. The two procedures would be equivalent if the average-revenue curve were horizontal since the average-revenue and marginal-revenue curves would coincide.

It is important to distinguish between two situations:

1. The raw material has been purchased, and we have sold all of product A; some product B is still on hand (A and B are joint products). If the firm could not economically store any more B or sell B, then the cost of product A is the entire cost of the raw material. The cost (and value) of B is zero.
2. The firm is considering purchasing more raw material, and our analysis is similar to that presented in Figure 4.3; then it is reasonable to split the cost of the raw material between A and B, using the expected marginal revenues of the products. These costs would be relevant for decision making (though the price would be set by reference to the average-revenue curves).

Mr. A. A. Walters has described a joint-cost model where demand is in the form of a joint-probability distribution for a given price. (Up to this point we have assumed that the amount demanded for different prices was known.)[1] The specific model presented by Walters is limited by his assumptions that price is fixed at the beginning of the marketing period and is held throughout the period and that product is impossibly expensive to store; but he does show that under certain conditions the allocation of fixed cost based on expected sales is reasonable.

[1] See A. A. Walters, "The Allocation of Joint Costs," *American Economic Review*, June, 1960.

chapter five

analysis
of distribution
costs

Traditionally cost accountants have concerned themselves with manufacturing costs. In recent years an increasing amount of attention has been directed to the control and analysis of distribution costs. This has occurred primarily because of the increased relative importance of distribution costs is a per cent of total costs.

What Are Distribution Costs?

The function of distribution begins after the manufacture of the product and continues until the cash is collected. Under this broad definition distribution costs would include:

1. The costs of handling and storing the completed product and of shipping it to the customer
2. The costs of promoting customer goodwill and making sales
3. The costs of recording and collecting the amount owed to the company by its customers

What Is Distribution Cost Analysis?

Distribution cost analysis includes an analysis of distribution costs and revenues by product line, by sales outlets and methods of selling, by types of customers, and by geographical locations. For example, the following are samples of how the revenues and distribution costs may be analyzed.

Sales outlets (customer type)	Methods of selling
Wholesalers	Mail order
Retailers, independent	Company salesmen, outside
Discount houses	Company salesmen, inside
Chain stores	

Geographical location

Product line

Cities over 1,000,000

Product *A*   Cities over   100,000

B   Cities over   10,000

C   Cities under   10,000

or

Sales districts, counties, states, countries

Uses of Distribution Cost Analysis

The uses of distribution cost analysis are very similar to the uses of manufacturing cost analysis. The broad categories of use are decision making, cost control, and financial reporting. As in cost accounting for manufacturing costs, we can expect to accomplish several of our goals more accurately than we can others. Some of the distribution costs are common to several functions and are going to have to be allocated on relatively arbitrary bases. We should attempt to allocate these costs on the basis of benefit received, but we shall still be allocating common costs. Some cost allocations will be useful for making specific decisions, some will not.

Decision Making

Many decisions in the area of marketing are made intuitively, and it is unlikely that distribution cost analysis will improve significantly the quality of these decisions. For example, it will probably never be possible for the accounting department to tell the marketing staff that they are spending too much or too little on advertising and prove the statement. On the other hand, the accounting department can tell the top management that the revenues of a product are not recovering the manufacturing and distribution costs directly associated with the product, including advertising. This may lead indirectly to a decision concerning advertising.

In the type of cost analysis being considered it is useful to think of three layers of costs:

1. Direct costs are costs which can be directly identified with the product, division, geographical unit, etc.
2. Allocated costs with traceable benefits are costs which cannot be directly identified, but which have a close correlation with the activity of a unit. For example, costs of writing bills may be allocated on the basis of the number of lines on an invoice.

3. Allocated costs with indirect benefits are costs which cannot be directly identified and which have little correlation with the activity of a unit. For example, the benefits derived from the sales manager's salary may not be closely identified with any one product line and thus must be arbitrarily allocated to the several product lines.

In addition to the above three distinctions we want to know if the cost was fixed or variable. The classifications take on a different meaning in the analysis of distribution costs from that of manufacturing costs. In manufacturing cost analysis we were interested in how the cost reacted to changes in manufacturing activity. With distribution costs we are interested in how costs react to changes in sales. An example of a variable distribution cost is a salesman's commission. An example of a fixed cost is the salary of the sales manager. The problem is complicated, however, by the fact that costs may be fixed in one sense, but not in another. Thus advertising costs may be fixed by a managerial decision, but in order to increase sales it may be necessary to increase the amount spent on advertising. On the other hand, a given amount of advertising may result in increased sales if the sales price is lowered. Thus advertising may be considered fixed when the firm is considering a change in sales price.

The decisions made with the help of distribution cost analysis are varied. Among the most important are:

Setting prices of the product

Expanding, contracting, or abandoning product lines or sales effort

Expanding, contracting, or abandoning specific customer outlets or geographical locations

Establishing warehouses and supply points

Determining the relative merits of different sales efforts (including performance of salesmen)

The above decisions will require cost and revenue information classified in several different ways. For example, where possible, each cost must be identified as to product line and geographical location. Also of interest is the relation of the cost to any particular type of sales outlet, its functional classification (delivery, warehousing, billing, collecting, sales, etc.), and its natural classification (labor, supplies, utilities, etc.). Costs which cannot be directly identified with product lines, geographical locations, etc., present a problem. Should they be allocated? All costs may be allocated, but we should carefully distinguish among the direct costs, the allocated costs with traceable benefits, and the allocated costs which have no close correlation with the unit to which the cost is being allocated.

Let us assume a situation where the Tall Bottle Company makes four different types of bottles. Management is reviewing the profitability of the milk bottle line. The income statement for the most recent period is:

Milk Bottles
Income Statement
For year ending December 31, 1960

Sales		$30,000
Less: Manufacturing costs of goods sold		
(includes fixed costs of $3,000)	25,000	
Gross margin		$5,000
Less: Distribution costs		
Directly identified with product		
(includes fixed costs of $2,000)	$6,500	
Allocated costs	2,500	
		9,000
Net loss		($4,000)

Assume that all the fixed costs are unavoidable and would be incurred even if the product were abandoned, and that the $2,500 of allocated costs includes $1,000 of costs which are variable and closely related to the sale of milk bottles (these include delivery expense, which is allocated by weight, bulk, and mean distance of the deliveries).

What action, if any, should management take? If we rearrange the income statement as below, we find that the sale of milk bottles is contributing $2,500 to the recovery of common costs and fixed costs, and should not be abandoned. Note that $1,000 of the allocated costs is considered relevant to this decision.

Income Statement

Sales		$30,000
Variable costs		
Manufacturing	$22,000	
Distribution ($1,000 + $4,500)	5,500	$27,500
Contribution to recovery of fixed costs		$ 2,500
Fixed costs		
Manufacturing	$ 3,000	
Distribution	3,500	$ 6,500
Net loss		($ 4,000)

The fact that the product is recovering more than the variable costs does not mean that no action is required. A company may recover variable costs every day right up until it has to file bankruptcy papers. The analysis indicates that, assuming the fixed costs are unavoidable, the company is better off with the milk bottle business than it would be without it. It is possible that more or less selling effort is required or that the price should be raised or lowered. The income statement presented shows that management should not be complacent. It does not indicate the nature or the direction of managerial action.

Note that in recommending the decision not to drop the product we did not consider the unavoidable fixed costs or the allocated costs not closely related to the product. If some of the fixed costs could be avoided by the dropping of the product, these costs should be considered.

If the problem were changed so that there were the option to sell the milk bottle portion of the business, then most of the fixed costs could be avoided. The price that could be obtained for the business becomes a type of opportunity cost. We can solve the problem by implementing the theory of capital budgeting (see Chapter 8). The procedure would be to compare the present value of the cash flows resulting from retaining the business to the present value of the cash flows which would result from the sale of the business.

There are a variety of decisions which will require different arrays of cost information. The main point to be noted is that all costs are not relevant for all decisions. Costs to be especially watched are costs which are fixed but avoidable and costs which are common to many products or other units. The inclusion or exclusion of costs of these types will depend on the exact nature of the decision. The inclusion of allocated costs should never be automatic, nor should the exclusion of fixed costs.

Cost Control

The control of distribution costs is especially difficult since, in contrast with many manufacturing type operations, there is no easily measurable output and standards of performance are much more difficult to set. Nevertheless it is sometimes possible to set standards which are effective enough to assist in the control of distribution costs.

Where the action is repetitive and of a fairly uniform nature, the setting of the standards is relatively simple. Thus the billing department may be judged on how much it costs to turn out invoices, with due consideration of the characteristics of the invoices. The shipping and receiving departments may be judged on the number of items handled and the weight of the items. The credit and collection departments may be judged on the record of collections versus the uncollectible accounts and receivables outstanding. Thus some distribution costs may be fairly effectively controlled in a manner similar to that used in the control of manufacturing costs.

The problems of controlling the costs of selling are more complex since the effectiveness of the costs in gaining sales is affected by variables beyond the control of the sales department, such as general business conditions, the actions of competitors, the design of the product, the price of the product, and changing habits of consumers. In the control of selling costs, the quantitative measures must sometimes be tempered by qualitative judgments as to whether the sales department or a particular salesman is doing a "good" job.

Companies frequently use measures such as selling cost per order, or selling cost per call, or calls per day as control devices. But there is some danger in comparing different salesmen where the geographical and economic characteristics of the different sales areas differ considerably. Used with discretion, these measures can be useful in forming an impression of how effectively a salesman is performing.

Financial Accounting

Distribution cost analysis does not have a large impact on the overall financial accounting of a firm. The greatest portion of the distribution costs are considered expenses of the time period in which they are incurred, and little attempt is made to assign the costs exactly to the periods which benefit from the incurrence of the costs. Thus advertising costs are generally considered an expense in the period in which the advertising medium appears, rather than a cost allocated over the periods which benefit from the advertising. In like manner, the selling costs connected with obtaining unfilled orders are only infrequently carried over to the period in which the order is filled.

For internal purposes we desire income statements prepared by product line, by type of customer, and by geographical location. Here the distribution cost analysis system is important since there will be common costs which will be allocated. Where there are common costs, the degree of association of the costs and the benefit derived from the costs must be clearly defined.

The Robinson-Patman Act

The Robinson-Patman amendment to the Clayton Act makes it unlawful to offer price concessions to any customers unless the concessions are justified by differences in the cost of manufacture, sale, or delivery.[1]

The existence of the Robinson-Patman Act means that a company

[1] For a more complete description of the Robinson-Patman Act see Herbert F. Taggart, "Cost Justification: Rules of the Game," *Journal of Acountancy*, December, 1958, pp. 52–60; or *Cost Justification*, Michigan Business Studies, vol. xiv, no. 3, University of Michigan, Ann Arbor, 1959.

should charge all customers the same price and not offer special discounts to any class of customer, or any quantity discounts, unless the company is prepared to defend with cost studies the price differentials.

How does a firm prove that a price differential is based on cost saving? One approach that is unacceptable is the use of differential costs. If the additional business would only result in additional variable costs, and no additional fixed costs, it would not be acceptable to use only the variable costs to show that this additional business has a lower average cost than other business currently being serviced.

EXAMPLE

Ten thousand units of a product are being produced and sold at a price of $10. The product costs $5 per unit (variable costs are $3, and fixed costs are $2 per unit and $20,000 in total). An order for 10,000 more units can be obtained if they are sold at a price of $8 per unit.

Should the order be taken, from the point of view of economic considerations (assuming the order will not reduce the present sales)? Since the price per unit of $8 exceeds the variable cost per unit, the additional business is desirable from an economic point of view.

Should the order be taken, from the point of view of legality under the Robinson-Patman Act? Can the $2 difference in price be explained by a "saving" of $2 in fixed costs? The answer is no. This defense would be rejected by the government. If the company wants to accept the business, it will have to change its basic price to all customers to $8 per unit, change the price for the order to $10 per unit, or find another defense. One possible defense would be to show that the fixed costs of $20,000 should reasonably be allocated to the other sales. For example, assume the $20,000 is related to packaging equipment which will not be used with the new order since there is going to be bulk shipment. In this case a price difference could be justified by real cost savings.

Another method of cost allocation which is not accepted by the government is the allocation of general overhead costs among customers or sales classes on the basis of sales dollars. This has been given the colorful title of the "bootstrap" method. On the other hand, the use of sales dollars is acceptable to the government in allocating costs to product lines or geographical locations, which are a direct function of sales dollars (for example, sales commissions).

In many situations, to justify a cost allocation it is necessary to produce time studies showing how the personnel spent their time. Fortunately, this may be done on a sample basis, and in some cases reasonable relationships are acceptable. For example, a sales manager's pay may be allocated in the same proportion as that of the salesmen for whom he is responsible.

The exact defenses acceptable under the Robinson-Patman Act may be expected to change through the years. However, if the government questions a price differential offered to customers, a reasonable type of defense based on cost analysis would probably be acceptable, and should certainly be the basis of the pricing policy used.

Conclusions

If X dollars are expended for direct labor, it is not difficult for the accountant to suggest that Y units of product should be forthcoming. The benefits of the expenditures are concrete and relatively easy to measure. If significantly less than Y units of product result, there is cause for suspecting some type of inefficiency.

With distribution costs the cause-and-effect relationship is not as easily measured. Two salesmen may be doing equally good work, but one has a better territory and so is making more sales. Or, the automobile traffic in one city may be heavier than another, resulting in fewer calls per day for one salesman than another. In one year the advertising campaign may be considered a big success, but in the second year sales go downward and it is a complete bust. Are sales declining because of changes in the quality of advertising, changes in styling of the product, changes in prices, changes in actions of competitors, or because of a general business recession? Is a salesman efficient if he reduces his selling expense, or is he just making fewer telephone calls and traveling less?

There are too many variables connected with distribution costs for the accountant to offer definitive advice in this area. He can report magnitudes of expenses and sales, and break these down in various ways, but it will generally be rash to draw conclusions and recommend decisions about performance on this information. It would be better for the accountant to obtain the assistance of a statistician and by the use of experimental and statistical techniques attempt to determine the impact of the several types of distribution costs on sales and profits. For example, by varying the advertising expenditures in one market area while not changing the expenditures in other areas, management may obtain some insight into the effectiveness of the advertising. It would seem better for the accountant to supplement his skills in this field rather than to offer advice based on incompletely analyzed information.

chapter six

measuring performance; transfer pricing

One of the most important and at the same time most difficult tasks of an administrator is to measure the performance of subordinates. Too frequently the measure being used cannot do the job satisfactorily. Sometimes a measure is useful for one purpose but not for another. The fact that a golf drive went 250 yards is useful in judging the force with which the ball was hit, but knowledge of the total distance covered is not useful in judging whether the drive was good or bad. We need information relating to the location and distance of the hole before we can make that type of decision.

How do we measure the performance of a member of management? The first step is to establish objectives. The second step is to see how well these objectives are met. We shall assume a prime objective of the firm is to maximize profits and that from the accountant's point of view this is the most important consideration. Other objectives such as maintaining continuity of existence will not be considered.

The extent of success in attaining objectives may be assessed quantitatively or qualitatively. The qualitative criterion will include such things as relations with superiors and subordinates, training of subordinates, professional attainments, civic activities, and ability to get things done. The qualitative factors are certainly relevant in judging performance, but are more the province of the industrial psychologist than of the accountant. This discussion will be limited to the use of following quantitative factors as measures of performance:

1. Costs and cost variances
2. Physical production (quantity and quality)
3. Sales
4. Income
5. Return on investment
6. Investment turnover
7. Income per dollar of sales (operating rate)
8. Share of market
9. Rate of growth
10. Changes from period to period of any of the above

The One-measure Approach

There is danger in seeking out the one best measure of performance and using it to the exclusion of all other measures. Most of the quantitative measures just listed are not above unintended distortion or manipulation. The manipulations may be a product of figure juggling or the result of managerial actions designed to obtain the result looked for by superiors, even though the end result may not be consistent with the end objectives of the corporation. It is important to ensure, to the extent possible, that the measure of performance being used does not hinder performance and that the measure of performance is consistent with the basic objectives of the firm. To obtain a valid measure of performance we may have to use several measures and then apply judgment by weighing the importance of each measure. If this is not done, we shall not be measuring performance but rather the ability of a clever manager to obtain a favorable report on his performance.

The measures of performance used should be influenced materially by the functions of the manager (or organization) whose performance is being measured. Where possible, items which are not controllable by the manager should be excluded from the measure. The measure must also indicate how well the man or organization is meeting the predetermined objectives. We shall find that to accomplish these goals of measurement not only must we use more than one measure of performance, but different measures will be suitable for different organizations.

We shall first briefly describe the limitations of several of the measures, and then describe suitable measures for different levels of organizations.

Investment Turnover

Investment turnover may be defined as the sales of a period divided by the average investment.

$$\text{Investment turnover} = \frac{\text{sales}}{\text{average investment}}$$

The investment turnover gives an indication of how intensively the investment is being used. If more sales are generated, the turnover increases. Taken by itself the investment turnover is not a good measure of performance since total sales and the turnover can be increased by increasing selling effort. However, when used in conjunction with the other measures it may be helpful in pointing out a cause of decreased profits, namely, less intensive use of the resources committed to the operation.

Operating Rate

The operating rate is the operating profit per dollar of sales.

$$\text{Operating rate} = \frac{\text{operating income}}{\text{sales}}$$

The operating rate gives an indication of the efficiency of operations, but only an indication since in addition to efficiency the profit per dollar of sales is affected by:

1. Changes in the level of sales
2. Changes in the product mix sold
3. Changes in price of product sold
4. Changes in the costs of materials and services used to produce the product sold

If each of the above influences is isolated and the effect of each computed, then the operating rate is useful. The inclusion or exclusion of income taxes is not important so long as the same procedure is followed for the different operating localities being compared. If attention is focused on the operating rate, without proper analysis, incorrect conclusions may be drawn as to the causes of the changes in the rate. For example, assume the following situation:

	Period 1	Period 2
Sales	$1,000,000	$1,500,000
Income	50,000	300,000
Operating rate	5%	20%

Here the operating rate increased from 5 per cent to 20 per cent. Does this reflect increased efficiency?[1] To answer this question we need to know what the income should be for sales of $1,500,000. It may be that the income should be $400,000 for sales of that level, and instead of being "good" the operating rate of 20 per cent for sales of $1,500,000 reflects inefficiency. Or, the increase in operating rate may have occurred merely because of the increase in sales, for which the sales manager should receive credit.

In another situation, sales may not have changed at all, but the operating rate may change because different products are sold. For example:

	Period 1	Period 2
Sales	$1,000,000	$1,000,000
Income	100,000	200,000
Operating rate	10%	20%

Does this situation reflect increased efficiency? Maybe not; it may reflect merely a change in the composition of sales from low-margin items to high-margin items. Our lack of information can be rectified by preparing operating rates for each product line.

We could enlarge on the complications arising with the use of the operating rate. But all the problems cited, or problems which could be cited, can be solved. They are, however, real problems which must be given thought and which enter into any analysis of the operating rate.

Return on Investment

The return on investment may be computed dividing income by average investment or by multiplying the investment turnover (sales divided by average investment) by the operating rate (income divided by sales).

$$\frac{\text{Return on}}{\text{investment}} = \frac{\text{sales}}{\text{average investment}} \times \frac{\text{income}}{\text{sales}} = \frac{\text{income}}{\text{average investment}}$$

Just how important these three percentages (investment turnover, operating rate, and return on investment) are considered by management is difficult to guess. There are some indications that they are thought to be important devices for measuring efficiency of utilization of resources.

The return on investment as a measure of performance will obviously be only as good as the numbers used to compute it. It will come as no

[1] The term "efficiency" is used here to describe a situation where the assets of the firm are being employed most effectively for the given level of output.

surprise to anyone familiar with accounting literature that the problems of measuring sales, income, and average investment are numerous.

Measuring sales is often spoken of as the problem of revenue recognition. Is revenue to be recognized as the order is received, the product made, the product shipped, or the cash received? Since most companies are on the accrual basis of recognizing realized revenue, the revenue is recognized when the goods are shipped or the services performed. Only in relatively rare cases will this method of accounting cause difficulties in computing the investment turnover. For example, a shipbuilding firm which uses the accrual method and recognizes revenue only on a completed sale might have a low investment turnover in a period of great activity if no ships were delivered during this period. This specific difficulty might be readily solved by shifting to a production basis (percentage of completion basis) of revenue recognition, but the general problem of revenue recognition does exist.

The problems of measuring the income of a corporate entity are many, and they increase when attention is focused on the component parts of an organization. The main problems are the pricing of transfers and the splitting of common costs. The problems become more relevant when the component parts of the company are compared to each other. Accounting procedures which are generally accepted from a financial reporting point of view may result in a report of income completely worthless from the point of view of comparing different operating units. The report of income can be qualified by footnotes, but these qualifications tend to be lost when attention is focused on the return on investment.

Problems of income measurement which are particularly relevant for the purpose of measuring return on investment are:

1. Revenue recognition and the matching of expenses with revenues.
2. Treatment of repairs and maintenance costs.
3. Inventory procedure. During periods of fluctuating prices income will be affected by the choice of inventory valuation basis, fifo, lifo, average cost, etc.
4. Treatment of nonproductive supplies. Should they be expensed when purchased or inventoried?
5. Choice of depreciation procedure. Are all plants using the same procedure (straight-line, declining balance, sum of the year's digits, activity basis, etc.)?
6. Adjustment of depreciation for changes in price level.
7. Allocation of common cost, especially central office expenses.
8. The effect of changes in the level of production on income (caused by absorption costing combined with changes in production).

Fortunately, theories and techniques have been developed to handle all the above problems. Unfortunately, the theories and techniques are frequently not applied uniformly to all plants and all divisions of a company. Thus, one plant may use lifo and another fifo. One plant may expense supplies when purchased, another may inventory them. One plant may use straight-line depreciation, another may use some method of accelerated depreciation. For any of the eight items listed above examples can be presented showing two plants (assumed to have the same physical characteristics) which will have different return on investment, such difference caused by the accounting methods, not by variations in efficiency.

Measuring Average Investment

Many of the problems of measuring average investment are directly related to the problems of income measurement. The list will be shortened here in order to focus attention on the three primary problems:

1. Valuing long-lived assets
2. Valuing inventories
3. Allocation of assets administered directly from the central office

The problem of valuing long-lived assets is actually a triple-headed problem. First, what items should be capitalized and what items charged to expense? This is particularly troublesome with repairs, maintenance charges, and any large expenditures for developing new procedures or products. For example, in the oil industry would the costs of digging dry wells and producing wells be treated as assets or as expenses?

The second problem is to decide what to do about depreciation. Should the accrued depreciation be subtracted in computing the average investment? This is a troublesome question, to which there is no one simple answer. There are, however, several observations which may be made. With constant revenues and maintenance charges an asset will have an increasing return on investment through the periods of use if:

1. Straight-line depreciation is used (and the accumulated depreciation is subtracted)
2. Any of the decreasing-charge methods of computing depreciation is used (and the accumulated depreciation is subtracted)

With the above assumptions, the depreciable asset will have an equal return on investment through the periods of use only if a compound-interest method (an increasing-charge method) of computing depreciation is used. But this method will complicate the analysis of income (revenues of the later periods will be charged with larger and larger depreciation charges), and is not generally used by industrial firms.

The third problem of valuing long-lived assets for purposes of determining the average investment is possibly the most important. What should be done about the fact that the unit used to measure the investment in long-lived assets is the dollar when the dollar has different meaning in different years? The purchasing power of the dollar has changed significantly in the last thirty years. Ignoring this fact means that an implicit assumption is being made that inflation and technological progress both have the same rate of increase. If the return-on-investment measure is to have any significance, the effect of the change in the price level has to be solved.

The problem of measuring the value of inventories is related to the fact that lifo is generally accepted for accounting purposes. The first or oldest goods purchased are the last goods to be charged as an expense. This means that if lifo is used, the inventory will often represent goods dating back to the moment of introducing lifo. In any event the inventory resulting from the use of lifo will only rarely give an indication of the actual cost of the inventory, nor will it give an indication of the present value of the inventory.

Other problems of measuring inventory include the writing down of obsolete or spoiled items, the taking of a meaningful physical inventory, and the deciding of what costs are inventoriable in the case of a manufacturing firm.

When assets are administered directly from the central office, should these assets be allocated for purposes of computing the return on investment of a division or plant? This is the cousin of the familiar problem of common costs and may well be termed the problem of common assets.

If there are some reasonable grounds for allocating the asset, then it should certainly be allocated. For example, if the payroll is paid out of a centrally administered payroll fund, then the cash held in this fund should be considered an asset assignable to the individual plants. In this simple example the take-home pay of the workers of each plant would seem to be a reasonable basis for allocation.

Some companies do not allocate cash administered by the central office. This is not harmful if all the operating units being compared have like characteristics, but if they are unlike (one plant having a large amount of long-lived assets, another a large number of workers), then the failure to allocate common assets may give misleading results.

Return on Investment and Decision Making

The usefulness of return on investment (income divided by investment) for decision making is limited. Among the more questionable uses of the return on investment are:

1. Capital-budgeting decisions. (Included in this classification are equipment replacement, capacity expansion, research, buying versus leasing, making versus buying, introducing new product line or other new activities.)
2. Pricing decisions.

The objection to return on investment as a guide for capital-budgeting decisions results from the fact that the procedure ignores the time shape of earnings and the discounting of future earnings back to the present. The present-value approach to capital budgeting is certainly not perfect, but it is to be preferred over the return-on-investment method (see Chapter 8).

It is sometimes suggested that pricing decisions should be made with one eye on the return on investment, and that an "optimum" return on investment should be the goal. It is well to keep a few economic principles in mind. A company may set a price, but the buyers will determine how much is purchased; that is to say, each product has a demand curve. The mere fact that a set return on investment is desired does not mean that it will be attained by changing the price. The successfulness of a change in price will depend on the demand curve, which will in turn depend on the degree of competition to be found in the industry and among industries. Theoretically, a price should be established which will equate marginal revenue and marginal cost. If profits can be increased by raising or lowering prices, this decision can be reached without looking at the return on investment.

Measuring Performance on Different Levels of Organization

The Department

The term "department" is used here interchangeably with cost center or burden center. Assume that we are attempting to measure the performance of a manager such as a foreman or a department head.

The foreman's task is to accomplish his set objective with a minimum of cost. Recognizing that he could accomplish his task with more dispatch with the incurrence of more cost, he compromises between cost and dispatch. Thus a controller might prepare his reports two days sooner by hiring ten more accountants but still not hire the additional accountants because the costs would be greater than the value of the expected benefits. To say that costs are too high must mean either that there is gross inefficiency and waste of resources or that the benefits of the costs do not equal the cost of the benefits even if the costs are administered effectively.

In a research and development department the quantitative measurement of costs incurred is exact, but the measurement of the benefits is very inexact. Hence it is very difficult to control or measure the performance of this type of department with quantitative measures. On the other hand, both the costs and the benefits of a production department may be determined with relative accuracy. The benefits in this case will be the units produced. Generally the costs are measured in terms of the labor, material, and overhead costs which are used by a department. The benefits may be measured by converting the physical product into the amount of labor, material, and indirect costs which should have been used (the standard costs of the product) and then computing variances; low or favorable variances indicate good management, and unfavorable variances indicate poor management. It is also desirable to focus attention on the trend of the variances, the direction of the cost changes being as important as the total amount of the variance.

In addition to the variance analysis it is necessary to control the scrap or spoilage which results from the manufacturing process. A large production with low costs per unit may be desirable, but not if it results in large amounts of unusable product. This undesirable outcome may be prevented by excluding bad product in computing the production of the period (if the bad product was caused within the department) and by carefully controlling the amount of spoilage.

The main pitfall in measuring the performance of a foreman is one which applies to all levels of management, namely, the inclusion of items not controllable by the person whose performance is being measured. The foreman should be held accountable for costs which can be directly identified with his department where he can exert control over the total amount of costs incurred. Thus the measure of performance of the foreman of an operating department should not include the allocation of accounting department costs which is made for cost-accounting purposes, since this cost cannot be directly identified with the operating department. Also, the measure should not include the depreciation of machinery which the department uses but which is purchased without the approval of the department head. While this cost may be directly identified with the department, it is not a cost item which is controllable by the department head.

The Plant

We shall assume that the plant manager has no control over the sale of the product but that he is concerned with all phases of production.[2]

---

[2] Even though the production manager does not control sales, he can indirectly influence the level of sales. Availability of product of good quality will lead to satisfied customers, which in turn will influence the demand schedule. While the production and inventory control policies of the plant manager can influence sales, it is not desirable to measure his efficiency on the basis of sales, or a figure which is influenced to a great extent by the level of sales.

Frequently attempts are made to compute a profit and a return on investment for the plant. It is the opinion of the author that this computation is often a waste of time and misleading. The profit of the plant will be a function of the level of sales, the sale price, and the cost of product. The plant manager has control over only the last item; thus his performance should be measured only by the cost of product, or better yet by the costs incurred in relation to the level of production.

Computing a profit for a plant is generally thought to supply both a measure of performance and an incentive. It may seem to accomplish this goal during prosperous periods, but in periods of slack activity it supplies an excuse for the plant manager. He can blame the poor showing on low unit sales or a low sale price. While these two items will probably be the more dramatic of the causes of low profits, there may also be inefficiencies which should be corrected.

A suitable measure of the performance of the plant manager is similar to the measure of performance of the foreman. His task is to complete good product at as low a cost as possible. Thus we may reasonably compute the cost per unit of product, or under a standard cost-accounting system the variances from standard cost. If the cost per unit is used, it should be computed with references to overhead rates based on practical or normal capacity so that the cost per unit is not affected by the level of activity. A desirable situation is one in which the costs of production of one plant may be compared to the costs of similar plants.

In addition to the quantitative measures centering around the costs of production, the over-all evaluation of performance should include the quality of the work performed and the timeliness of production (i.e., ability to meet production schedules). While sometimes difficult to quantify, these factors can be extremely important in relation to the maintenance of the firm's profits.

Since the authority of the plant manager is broader than that of the department head, more costs incurred in the plant are controllable by him. In fact any out-of-pocket expenditures originating in the plant will usually be subject to his control, and thus should be used in measuring his performance. Should expenses such as depreciation of plant and equipment be included in the computation of the cost of product? While the plant manager may not have had a voice in the original purchase of these assets, he does control their use, and the opportunity cost of these assets may well be included as a cost. The measure of the opportunity cost would be the incremental revenues resulting from the best alternative use.

The Division

The measurement of the performance of the division manager who does not control sales is exactly analogous to that of the plant manager.

The use of costs of production is a better measure of performance than a fictitious profit figure. Where the division manager is also in charge of the sales force, the problem of measuring performance is broadened. The division then becomes an entity very similar to a small corporation, and many of the measures of performance relevant for corporate organizations can be used. These may include total sales, income, return on investment, investment turnover, income per dollar of sales, share of market, and changes in any of the above items.

Two problems which are encountered with a division but not with a separate corporation are the problem of common costs (costs of central office incurred in servicing several divisions) and the problem of pricing transfers to and from other divisions.

In measuring the performance of a division the allocations of central office costs should be excluded. The division manager has no control over these costs, and while the division may benefit from the incurrence of the expenses, it may do more harm than good to include these costs in divisional income statements and computations of return on investment. On the other hand, it may be desirable to inform the division that it is billed a certain amount for central office services and that in order for the corporation to be profitable these costs must be recovered.

A very difficult and interesting problem of measuring performance is caused by the use of return on investment (income divided by average investment). If this is used to measure the performance of a division, then a high return on investment would be considered desirable. Let us assume that division A has a return on investment of 35 per cent and division B a return on investment of 20 per cent. Division B may actually be the better managed division. If division A is rejecting all investment proposals of less than 35 per cent, this will lead to a high return on investment but a less than optimum amount invested in the division from the point of view of the firm as a whole, assuming the firm has a cost of capital of less than 35 per cent. In one company a division employed a very high cutoff rate for investments while the home office had a great quantity of idle cash which it wanted invested.

The conflict of interests created by the use of a measure of performance is not unique to return on investment. For example, a grocery chain employed profit per dollar of sales as a measure of a store manager's efficiency. Since certain items in the store had profit margins below the "standard required" margin, some store managers would allow these items to run out on busy days so that the profit per dollar of sales figure would not be decreased. It was recognized that this would decrease the profit of the store, but since the major emphasis was on profit per dollar of sales, this decrease in profit was not considered important compared to the objective of meeting the required profit per dollar of sales.

Rate of Growth

One method of counteracting the above distortions is to include the rate of growth among the measures of performance. Since growth for growth's sake is not desirable, the most significant measure we want to have grow is income. If income is growing at the same time that return on investment is maintained at a desirable level (or is increased), then according to quantitative measures the manager is doing a reasonable job. Including the rate of growth in our measures points the spotlight on the manager who is willing to be satisfied with the status quo. Balancing growth against return on investment ensures that the manager will not be obsessed with growth at the expense of profits.

EXAMPLE

Assume the income and investments of successive years are as follows:

Year	Income	Average investment
1965	$10,000	$100,000
1966	11,000	110,000
1967	14,300	125,000

The growth rates are as follows:

1965–1966
$$\frac{1,000}{10,000} = 10\%$$

1966–1967
$$\frac{3,300}{11,000} = 30\%$$

1965–1967
$$14,300(1 + r)^{-2} = 10,000$$
$$(1 + r)^{-2} = \frac{10,000}{14,300} = 0.6993$$
$$r = 19.5\% \text{ (approximately)}$$

The returns on investment are:

1965
$$\frac{10,000}{100,000} = 10\%$$

1966
$$\frac{11,000}{110,000} = 10\%$$

1967
$$\frac{14,300}{125,000} = 11.4\%$$

The manager is accomplishing growth and an increase in the return on investment simultaneously, and thus seems to be doing a good job.

The Company

The measures of performance used in the case of the division which controls its sales force can also be used for the company. Several problems are eliminated, such as transfer pricing and allocation of overhead costs, but the many problems of financial accounting remain. For example, should variable costing be used so that effects of changes in inventory are eliminated? In computing the return on investment, should the investment be net of depreciation? What method of inventory flow and depreciation should be used? Obviously, there are no shortages of accounting problems.

There are other problems also. If the decreased sales are a result of general business conditions, does this absolve the company president from the blame of having a bad year? The president is responsible for how well the company does, but he cannot control the business cycle. Thus the quantitative measures of performance may assist in measuring performance, but they are not the complete answer. If enough measures are used, always in reference to trends and changes, and with such factors as general business conditions eliminated, then we shall be able to obtain a reasonable indication of the performance of the management team. For example, the use of share of market can be a measure of performance when business conditions change, but this has to be supported by analysis of changes in prices or selling expenditures to make sure the market gain did not result in decreased profits rather than increased profits.

Transfer Pricing

Since the end of World War II there have occurred two interesting business phenomena which in many respects are contradictory. One has been the large number of business combinations (mergers and acquisitions) which have resulted in an increase in the complexity of business organizations. The other has been the increased use of decentralization or divisionalization as a means of controlling large corporations. Many of these corporations are the result of business combinations. Thus firms seek the advantages of large size and smallness simultaneously.

The Need for Transfer Prices

If an automobile company buys its glass from an independent glass company, the price is set by market forces. The automobile executives can determine the cost of glass by looking at purchase invoices. If the automobile company creates a glass division to manufacture all its glass, a transfer-pricing problem is created. The assembly division will "buy" from the glass division. The units sold must be priced, and by necessity the price set will not be the true market price since the sale is not an arm's-length transaction.

However, this price will determine to a large extent the glass division's profits (by affecting revenues) and the profits of the assembly division (by affecting costs). The price will not directly affect the profits of the company as a whole, though there may be indirect effects via the decisions made from the accounting information which incorporates the transfer prices.

Conflict of Interests

Decentralization does not change the basic goal of profit maximization for the corporation as a whole. Decentralization attempts to gain that goal by having division managers act in the interest of their own divisions. To the extent possible, the intracompany pricing method should be consistent with the goals of maximizing the profits of the company and the division.

Will it always follow that a division manager acting to maximize the profits of his division will be acting to maximize the profits of the corporation? Hirshleifer and Cook have both supplied illustrations where the rational action of the division manager (consistent with maximizing the profits of the division) is not consistent with maximizing the profits of the company.[3]

Do the gains arising from simulated competition and decentralized authority exceed the losses arising from decisions aimed at maximizing division profits rather than corporate profits? We shall avoid answering this question by assuming there is agreement that the intracompany pricing scheme should be designed to facilitate the maximization of corporate profits rather than divisional profits.

Many executives would object to the weakening of decentralization by the procedure which overrules decisions made at the division level, because the decisions were not consistent with the maximization of the profits of the company. The objections have some validity, but are not possible of being proved or disproved.

Transfer Prices Available

The intracompany prices may be established in several ways. These include:

1. Market price. (This may be determined by printed price lists, invoices, or other evidence.)
2. Marginal cost.
3. Variable costs. (Variable costs may be used as a substitute for marginal costs because of the difficulty of determining the marginal-cost curve.)

[3] J. Hirshleifer, "On the Economics of Transfer Pricing," *Journal of Business*, vol. 29, no. 3, pp. 172–184, July, 1956; Paul W. Cook, Jr., "New Technique for Intracompany Pricing," *Harvard Business Review*, vol. 35, no. 4, pp. 74–80, July–August, 1957.

4. Full cost.   (This may be actual or standard cost, and may or may not include an amount of "reasonable" profit.)

5. Negotiated price.

The pricing problem has frequently been approached from the point of view that only one procedure is correct.   This chapter will attempt to show that all the above alternatives are reasonable and that the choice of method can be made only after the purpose for which the information is to be used is determined.   At its best, accounting information is raw material, which to be useful to management must be processed.   Without analysis any intracompany pricing scheme may lead to faulty information and decisions.

Uses of Divisionalized Data

What are the uses of the accounting data of the decentralized operating units?   The intracompany prices are the basis of the revenues of one division and the costs of the other; thus the pricing method directly affects the basic reports of the operating units.   These reports may be used as follows:

1. Measuring performance of division management
2. Decision making

   a. Make-or-buy decisions
   b. Pricing policy for the end product
   c. Output decisions of components and end product
   d. Capital-budgeting decisions and decisions to drop products

3. General financial information

   a. Determination of income of the corporation
   b. Determination of financial position of the corporation

We shall attempt to analyze which one or more of the intracompany pricing methods best fill the needs of management in accomplishing the uses listed.

Measuring Performance

The best method of intracompany pricing for purposes of evaluating divisional management of the selling division is market price.   In the absence of an easily determined market price it may be necessary to use negotiated prices or a combination of market and negotiated prices.   The use of market price simulates the market conditions which the divisions would face if the divisions were separate corporate entities rather than subdivisions of one business organization.

While market price may be the most desirable method, it will not lead to 100 per cent correct answers.   For one thing, there is the problem of determining the market price. Anyone who has purchased an automobile knows that market price is not always equal to list price. Industrial prices are also confused by special terms of payment, freight absorption, quality concessions, etc.

Even if we assume the market price can be determined, the question still remains as to whether it is a fair price. For example, the manufacturing division may have a more or less captive market, and so have less selling expense than the firms setting the market price. Should the manufacturing division get the entire benefit of these savings?

A more troublesome problem exists when there is no market price. For example, if one division conducts research which is applicable to another division, at what price should the research be sold? Obviously the sale price must be negotiated, possibly arbitrated. In a research type of operation there is frequently no market price, and costs incurred are not relevant in setting the value of the research.

In the absence of a market price, any reports or measures resulting from the intracompany price are even more arbitrary than the normal accounting report. Do such reports and measures of efficiency do more harm than good? A management faced with recurring situations where intracompany transfers cannot be priced objectively should reconsider the pros and cons of decentralized accounting reports aimed at measuring income and return on investment. In situations of this nature other measures of performance than the above should be established.

There are several reasons for not basing the transfer price of the selling division on cost. The use of variable costs (or marginal costs) would almost automatically lead to a deficit for the supplying division. The use of full cost, with or without a reasonable profit, would be better than variable costing. The prime difficulty is the determination of the cost of the product. Should actual or standard costs be used? Are inefficiencies to be passed on to the purchasing division? The use of cost as the basis of the transfer price places a large burden on the cost-accounting department. A by-product of a transfer-price system based on cost is a welter of arguments and hassels on what is cost.

While it is suggested that the selling division use a market price to compute its revenues, the marginal costs of the selling division should be used to determine the cost to the purchasing division. The use of marginal costs to determine the transfer price to the buying division is not a sufficient constraint to lead to optimum output, but it is a necessary one.

Decision Making

Four general types of decisions were listed under decision making. These were (a) make-or-buy, (b) pricing of end product, (c) level of output, (d) capital-budgeting decisions and decisions to drop products.

All the above decisions must be made on the basis of either marginal-
or incremental-cost techniques from the point of view of the corporation as a whole. Hirshleifer has shown systematically that the pricing-
and-output decisions must be solved with the use of marginal costs
of the several divisions, but the individual division's best interests may
not be the same as those of the corporation. Neither full costs nor
market prices can be used as transfer prices in making these decisions.

The make-or-buy decision requires knowledge of those costs which
can be avoided by purchasing the product. This requires a cost break-
down which is not supplied by the market price. The same type of
information is required for the decision as to whether or not to drop a
product. These are nonmarginal decisions and must be made on the
basis of differential-revenue and cost techniques.

The effect of transfer pricing on capital-budgeting decisions has been
somewhat confused by the literature on the subject. Actually, a capital-
budgeting decision made by a division buying components from another
division should be based on the incremental cash inflows and outflows
which will result from the investment. These flows are tied to variable
and semivariable cost, not to the market price of intermediate products
purchased from other divisions of the company.

Thus for some decision-making purposes (make-or-buy, capital-budgeting or abandoning a product), the differential costs of the goods transferred from division to division should be known. For decisions such
as pricing or output the marginal costs of the product must be known
in order to determine optimum solutions.

General Financial Accounting

The general financial accounting reports require that inventories be
recorded at cost to conform to generally accepted accounting principles.
This cost must be full cost, including manufacturing overhead but not
including any element of unrealized profit (i.e., profit not realized by
sale to a party outside the corporate organization). This requires that
the accounting group in the central office be supplied with unit cost of
product by the selling division. The element of divisional profit (or
loss) must then be eliminated from the inventory of the purchasing
division and the income of the selling division in preparing consolidated
financial statements.

Limitations

This section attempts to show that no one method of transfer pricing
can fill the needs of a decentralized corporation. The uses of the in-

formation and the methods best accomplishing the objectives of significant reporting have been identified as follows:

Use	Method of pricing
Measuring performance	Market price (negotiated price if market price is unavailable)
Decision making	Marginal costs, variable costs (as substitute for marginal costs), and differential costs
Generally accepted financial accounting	Full cost of product (excluding intracompany profits)

No pretense of absolute correctness has been made for any of the pricing methods. The admitted inaccuracies must be weighed against the unmeasurable gains resulting from having decentralized operations and decision making. The greater the significance of the intradivisional transfers, the more unreliable are the measures of income of the divisions.

The Economics of Transfer Pricing

The solution to the transfer-pricing problem has sometimes been expressed in naïve terms, as if the use of marginal costs of the selling division (or a competitive price, or a negotiated price) would enable managers to make correct decisions and measure performance. There is no simple solution to the problem of pricing products sold within the company; the solution is complex and requires rigorous analysis. The most meaningful analysis which has been presented in business literature has been made by J. Hirshleifer, and the analysis which follows is based on his articles in the *Journal of Business*.[4] There are, however, several places where Hirshleifer differs in detail and method from the present author; thus the reader should refer to the Hirshleifer articles.

To simply the first explanations as much as possible we shall make the following assumptions:

1. A manufacturing division makes a product which has no intermediate market; that is, it must be sold to the distribution division.
2. The price of the product sold by the distribution division is set by purely competitive forces, and the company cannot influence the price. The average-revenue or price line is horizontal, and the same line also measures the marginal revenues.

The two assumptions are not essential to the basic analysis and will be changed later.

[4] Hirshleifer, *op. cit.* Also see a later article by Hirshleifer, "Economics of the Divisionalized Firm," *Journal of Business*, vol. 30, no. 2, pp. 96–108, April, 1957.

Optimum Output for the Firm under Perfect Competition

The first objective will be to determine the optimum output for the firm. (Remember that the firm does not have a pricing problem since it faces a price set by purely competitive forces.) Figure 6.1 shows the solution of this problem. A marginal-cost curve is drawn for the marginal costs of the distribution division (curve MC_d) and the marginal costs of the manufacturing division (curve MC_m). A curve may be drawn representing the total marginal of the firm ($MC_d + MC_m$). The intersection of this total marginal-cost curve with the price line, PP, determines the optimum output of the product. At that point the marginal costs of the product are equal to the marginal revenue of the product since the marginal revenue is equal to the price. The optimum

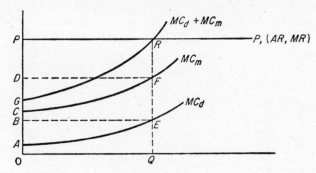

Figure 6.1   Perfect competition for end product.   No intermediate market. Determining optimum output.

output is PR or OQ. The firm will maximize its profits if OQ units are produced since a production of fewer units would mean that not enough would be produced to make marginal revenues equal to the marginal costs. To produce more than OQ units would mean that for each unit produced the costs would be greater than the additional revenues.

The next problem is to determine a reasonable transfer price which will result in the divisions' arriving at the optimum-output decision. The manufacturing division should transfer to the distribution division at its marginal cost QF. If the manufacturing division transferred at a higher price, the autonomous distribution division would decrease end sales since the marginal costs of some of the sales would be greater than the division's marginal costs. A transfer price of QF will result in an optimum output for the firm. It will be shown that marginal-cost pricing by itself is not sufficient to insure the firm's arriving at the optimum output OQ. Other constraints are necessary.

If the goods are transferred at the marginal cost QF, the profits of the distribution division will be ABE and the profits of the manufacturing division will be CFD, which in sum will equal the total profits of the firm, PGR. The curve of average revenues for the manufacturing division will coincide with the marginal-cost curve (since the transfer price will be equal to the marginal cost). The curve of the net average revenue of the distribution division would pass through point E and be equal to the difference between the average-revenue curve for the end

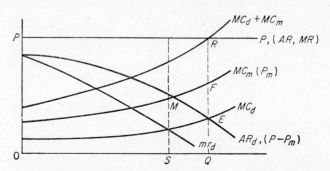

Figure 6.2   Perfect competition for end product.   No intermediate market.
Distribution division as monopolistic buyer.

product and the price paid to the manufacturing division, MC_m (see Figure 6.2).

The Distribution Division as Monopolistic Buyer

Can the distribution division, by limiting output and acting as a monopolistic buyer, maximize its own profit at the expense of maximum profit for the firm?

Figure 6.2 shows the distribution division acting as a monopolistic buyer. Assume that a curve AR_d is drawn, which shows the net average revenue of the distribution division (the difference between the price of the end product and the price P_m which must be paid to the manufacturing division). The curve MC_m and the curve P_m follow exactly the same path since the marginal cost represents the minimum price necessary to draw forth an additional unit of product and P_m is that price.

The curve AR_d passes through point E at an output of OQ units (the optimum output for the firm) since the firm is operating under perfect competition and its average revenue is equal to its marginal revenue. Thus AR_d is equal to $P - P_m$, $AR - P_m$, and $MR - P_m$; and at an output of OQ it is equal to the marginal cost of the distribution division.

In addition to the net average-revenue curve AR_d, we may draw a marginal-revenue curve mr_d for the distribution division. If the distribution division restricts sales to OS and pays the manufacturing division a price equal to the marginal cost SM of the manufacturing division, then the distribution division will be maximizing its own profits. The profits of the firm will decrease since the output OS is less than the optimum output OQ. The profits of the distribution division are increased at the expense of the manufacturing division and the over-all well-being of the firm. Note that the transfer price SM is the marginal cost of the product, but that in this case the use of marginal cost does not lead to the optimum output for the firm.

The Manufacturing Division as Monopolist

It has been shown in Figure 6.2 that the profits of the distribution division may be increased by the division's acting as a monopolistic

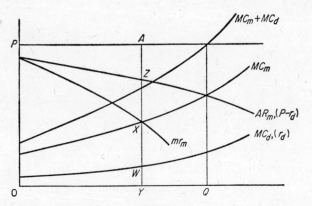

Figure 6.3   The manufacturing division as monopolistic seller.

buyer. The manufacturing division can increase its profits by acting as a monopolistic seller. This is also adverse to the interests of the firm since its over-all profits will be decreased.

Figure 6.3 shows the results of the manufacturing division's acting as a monopolist. Let us suppose that the manufacturing division correctly assumes that the distribution division will require a net revenue equal to its marginal cost if the divison is going to increase its sale of the product. Thus the curve MC_d may be labeled r_d, indicating that this is the minimum net revenue or net price required by the distribution division.

A net average-revenue curve $P - r_d$ or AR_m may be drawn for the manufacturing division, showing the net average revenue to that division. (This is the difference between the price curve of the firm, P, and the average-revenue curve for the distribution division). A curve may then be drawn representing the marginal revenue to the manufacturing division, mr_m. The manufacturing division will produce OY units since at that quantity of output the marginal cost XY of manufacturing equals the marginal revenue. The manufacturing division will, however, charge a transfer price equal to YZ, which is greater than YX, the marginal cost of manufacturing. The output OY which results from this price is less than the optimum output OQ, and the over-all profits of the firm will be less because of the actions of the manufacturing division aimed at increasing its own profits.

Thus the distribution and manufacturing divisions could enter into a form of competition which might not be desirable in terms of maximizing the profits of the firm as a whole. This analysis argues against allowing the divisions to "battle it out" or negotiate prices. The division with the better poker player may win out to the detriment of the firm as a whole. But even if the manufacturing division charges a price equal to its marginal costs and does not act as a monopolist, this will not ensure an optimum output since the distribution division may be acting as a monopolistic buyer. Both the selling and buying divisions (the manufacturing and distribution divisions) must be coerced to take the interests of the firm into consideration if the profits of the firm are to be maximized.

Relaxing the Assumptions of Perfect Competition

Let us next relax the assumption of perfect competition. The firm may now regulate the price at which its product is sold. Reacting to some imperfection in the market, in order to increase production and sales the firm may decrease its sale price. Thus, instead of a horizontal line, the average-revenue curve of the firm will slope downward to the right, and the firm will have a marginal-revenue curve which is below the average-revenue curve. The optimum output for the firm may be obtained from a graph similar to Figure 6.1, except that the price line (average-revenue curve) will not be horizontal; and a marginal curve can be drawn for the end product. The intersection of the total marginal-cost curve and the marginal-revenue curve will determine the optimum output.

If it is desired to find the optimum output for each division with the aim of maximizing its income instead of the income of the firm, then a diagram similar to Figure 6.2 may be used. The average revenue of the distribution division would again be obtained by subtracting the price curve of the manufacturing division (P_m) from the average-revenue curve of the end product. A marginal-revenue curve would be obtained similar to the mr_d curve of Figure 6.2. The distribution division acting as a monopolistic buyer could restrict output to the intersection of this marginal-revenue curve and its marginal-cost curve.

The best transfer price for decision making is the marginal cost to the manufacturing division; but again this does not ensure that the purchasing division will not act as a monopolistic buyer. Centralized action is required to ensure that an optimum output is attained.

Competitive Intermediate Markets

Up to this point it was assumed that the product could be sold only to the distribution division. Let us now assume that the product can be bought or sold by the manufacturing division in a purely competitive market at a price p, and that the end product is sold in a purely competitive market at a price P. Figure 6.4 shows that the manufacturing division will produce Oq_m units of manufacturing product and that the distribution division will sell Oq_d units. The output of the manufacturing division does not have to equal the units sold by the distribution division.

The manufacturing division would produce Oq_m units since, if it produced more, its marginal cost would then exceed the market price. The distribution division would not pay in excess of the market price p to the manufacturing division since it could purchase the product in the market for that price. Thus the marginal-cost curve of the firm would be the sum of the marginal costs of the distribution division, MC_d, plus p, the effective cost of the product to be sold. The transfer price should be p, the competitive price, which is also the marginal cost of the manufacturing division.

If the additional requirement were made that the distribution division could sell only the product of the manufacturing division, then the competitive price p of the intermediate product would not be relevant to the decision. The relevant costs would become the marginal costs to the manufacturing division and the marginal costs of the distribution division. The solution would be similar to the solution illustrated in Figure 6.1. Referring to Figure 6.4, we see that the output would be Oj.

Explanation of curves

P, AR, MR are the price curves of the end product.
p is the market price of the intermediate product.
MC_m is the marginal-cost curve of the manufacturing division.
MC_d is the marginal-cost curve of the distribution division.
DRT, or $MC_m + MC_d$ is the sum of the marginal-cost curves of the manufacturing and distribution divisions. The marginal-cost curve DRT is based on the assumption that the product of the manufacturing division must be sold to the distribution division and the distribution division must buy from the manufacturing division.

CRT is the sum of MC_d plus p, the intermediate price of the product, up to q_m, after which it is MC_d plus MC_m. This curve is based on the assumption that all product produced at a marginal cost of less than the competitive price p has a marginal cost to the distribution division equal to the opportunity cost p.

CRS is the sum of MC_d plus p.

Restricting the distribution division to selling only the product of the manufacturing division reduces the number of units sold by the distribution division from Oq_d to Oj. The number of units sold by the manufacturing division will increase from Oq_m to Oj. The increase in profit of the manufacturing division will be less than the loss in profit suffered by the distribution division. The total loss of profit to the firm will be the area *RST*. The transfer price should be the marginal cost to the manufacturing division, but the distribution division

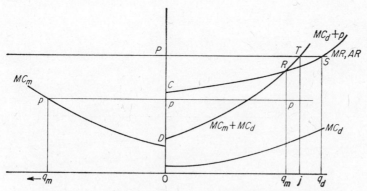

Figure 6.4   Competitive intermediate and final markets.

is being penalized (as is the firm) by management's restricting the distribution division to the selling of product made by the manufacturing division.

Transfer Price and Decision Making

The limitations of transfer pricing for decision making should be carefully noted. We have already discussed the fact that using marginal costs as the basis for the transfer price may not lead to the optimum output decisions at the division level. We can generalize and say that there is no one method of transfer pricing which can be used for all varieties of decision making.

Let us examine the problem of whether or not to drop a division. Assume that the transfer-pricing system uses marginal costs, that a computation of the income of the division manufacturing widgets indicates that the income computed in accordance with accounting procedures is negative, and that a computation of the contribution of the division to the recovery of fixed costs not directly identified with the division indicates that the division is not making any contribution. Should the division be abandoned? Not necessarily. The production of widgets may have the effect of increasing the profits of the division which manufactures a component part of widgets. Thus, to determine whether the widget division should be dropped we must look beyond the information obtained from using transfer pricing to the effect of the abandonment on the income of the entire firm.

The same type of analysis must be used in make-or-buy decisions. The use of marginal costs as the basis of transfer pricing would not be useful for making a decision unless *each unit* was priced on the basis of its marginal cost. This would be difficult at best, but for a theoretically sound decision it should be attempted by the decision maker, or a differential-cost analysis procedure should be followed.

Transfer Price and Measurement of Performance—A Paradox

Difficulties of applying the transfer prices to decision making have been noted. We shall now call attention to a paradox which may

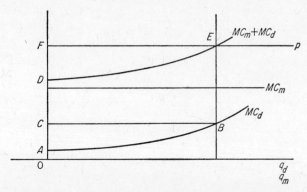

Figure 6.5   Transfer pricing and constant efficiency.

result from the use of marginal cost for transfer pricing. If the marginal costs of the division are purely variable (the marginal-cost curve is a horizontal line) with no increase as production increases, the manufacturing division will show no profit if we use the marginal cost as the transfer price. (See Figure 6.5 and assume that there is no intermediate market for the product.) The profit of the distribution division is ABC, which is equal to the area DEF, which is the profit of the firm. The manufacturing division makes no profit since it charges a price which is equal to its marginal costs and it has a horizontal marginal-cost curve.

A division can determine which type of marginal-cost curve will maximize profits under a transfer system based on marginal costs. While this may not be consistent with the firm's objective of maximizing profits, in certain cases inefficiencies increasing the marginal costs may actually be desirable from the point of view of the selling division.

Summary

Attempting to administer separate components of one industrial firm as if they were separate competing entities frequently results in the necessity for the use of transfer prices for accounting purposes and for decision making. The economic analysis of transfer pricing indicates that the solutions can become extremely complex if the demand and the production of the products are dependent on each other (technological dependence may also be introduced). However, several conclusions may be noted:

1. Marginal cost and competitive prices of the product being transferred may be equal. But it should be noted that there is an entire schedule of marginal costs, so that this equality, or the appropriateness of the marginal cost, should not be assumed.
2. The use of marginal costs for transfer pricing will not ensure that the company is operating at its optimum output. Divisions may act to maximize their own profits to the detriment of the profits of the company. This is possible even if either competitive prices or marginal-cost pricing is used.
3. The use of marginal-cost transfer pricing may result in weird actions, such as attempting to decrease efficiency or aiming to have an increasing marginal-cost curve in order to increase divisional profits (by increasing marginal costs and thus increasing the price of the product).
4. The transfer-pricing procedure will not generally give good results for nonmarginal decisions such as abandoning a plant and make-or-buy decisions. These decisions require a differential-cost and revenue analysis.

The choice of the transfer-pricing method will depend on the information available; for certain decisions transfer prices are not useful at all. The extent to which transfer prices are an artificial compromise should be recognized by the user, so that he may be alert to those cases where they cannot be used for decision-making purposes.[5]

It is likely that in many cases profit centers have been created which

[5] Several complications have been omitted from the discussion. Among these are situations of demand dependence for the intermediate and end products, and cost or technological dependence. See Hirshleifer, *op. cit.*, for discussions of these items.

require the use of transfer prices, when cost centers would have been a more effective means of controlling costs and measuring performance. The use of a profit center requires that revenues be computed, and this in turn requires the use of prices where there may not have been an arms-length transaction; in fact, the profit center may not be able to control the number of units sold. Consider a parts division of an automobile company making components of the new model, for which components there is no replacement market. The parts division cannot control the number of units sold and the transfer price cannot help but be somewhat arbitrary. In a situation of this type it would be more desirable to measure performance of the parts division by cost of product rather than by a fictitious profit figure at least two steps removed from the correctly measured variables (i.e., those which are controllable by the parts division).

The first question raised by management must be whether the use of transfer prices is appropriate at all. Only if the answer to this question is yes, should the question of the method of computing and controlling the transfer price be raised.

chapter seven

cash
and
decisions[1]

The focus of attention in accounting literature has been on internal control measures to prevent fraud and theft and on cash budgeting as a general planning device, but little has been written about the optimum amount of cash on hand and the decision whether to invest in readily marketable government securities. If a person is caught after having stolen $100,000 over a period of ten years, the system of internal control is brought under scrutiny, and the higher levels of management want to know why this was allowed to happen. If $1,000,000 of interest is not earned because of faulty decision rules concerning cash administration, there is less likely to be uniform agreement that the past decisions were bad, and certainly the general reporting methods will fail to indicate an inefficiency.

Decisions in the area of corporate administration of cash and short-term securities are not subject to simple rules. Part of the difficulty arises because a decision depends to a great extent on the subjective feelings about risk of the treasurer and other officers of the firm. In a sense the corporation is buying peace of mind for its treasurer when it has a $20,000,000 credit agreement costing $50,000 a year which it has not used in five years. This may seem to be a high cost to pay,

[1] For a survey of corporate practices, see Harold Bierman, Jr., and Alan K. McAdams, *Management Decisions for Cash and Marketable Securities*, Graduate School of Business and Public Administration, Cornell University, Ithaca, N.Y., 1962. Much of the material in this chapter is adapted from that publication and was developed in cooperation with Professor McAdams.

but the elimination of one type of financial risk may be worth $50,000 a year because it enables management to take risks in other areas.

This chapter will describe decisions which should be explicitly made in the management of cash and near-cash resources, and possible methods of analysis for making these decisions. It is an attempt to point up some of the relevant considerations and the methods of incorporating these considerations into the decision process, and to develop specific decision-making procedures.

Types of Decisions

The basic types of decisions involving cash or near-cash faced by corporations are:

1. Cash decisions

    a. Amount to be held in banks to satisfy banks
    b. Amount to be held in banks for transactions
    c. Amount to be held for contingencies

2. Credit agreement decisions, i.e., need for and amount of credit agreement
3. Security purchase decisions

    a. Amount to be invested
    b. Timing of purchase
    c. Composition of portfolio
    d. Maturity dates of securities

Each of these decisions interacts with the other decisions. For purposes of study we shall look at them primarily as independent decisions and then briefly discuss their interaction.

Cash Decisions

There is essentially one cash decision, namely, determining the amount of cash to be retained in the bank account. There are three basic reasons that corporations hold cash, though there are subdivisions of each basic reason:

1. Compensating balances, i.e., the amount to be held in the bank to satisfy the bank for:

    a. account activity
    b. services
    c. goodwill
    d. float (collections being made by the bank)
    e. lines of credit or credit agreements
    f. bank loans

2. The amount to be held for:

    a. normal operations
    b. capital expenditures

3. The amount to be held for contingencies

The amount to be held to satisfy banks is to a great extent dependent on the amount desired by the banks; there is a wide range of possibilities. Where the bank has not clearly defined the amounts to be held for one or more of the six purposes listed under 1, then the amount held is a matter of managerial judgment. The decision will depend to some extent on the bank's reaction to the balances held by the corporation in the past and to some extent on the corporation's judgment on how much it should hold as a demand deposit.

The decision as to the amount of cash needed for transactions frequently becomes obscured by the need to hold cash to keep the bank contented. One dollar of bank balance may sometimes satisfy several balance requirements of the bank (for example, the requirement for balances for account activity and the line of credit). But a further complication arises when the corporation has a credit agreement since its need for an additional balance to cover routine transactions is reduced.

Some corporations hold cash in anticipation of contingencies. To be reasonable, contingencies must be interpreted to mean relatively minor unforeseen transactions, not a major catastrophe such as a depression. The desire to avoid arranging a loan for each unanticipated need for cash is reasonable. The holding of cash in anticipation of a catastrophe is not reasonable, since at a minimum it would be more desirable to invest such funds in securities, and besides the basic assumption that a corporation can or should hold liquid assets of the magnitude necessary to shield against the effects of a major catastrophe is questionable.

Credit Agreement Decisions

There is no question that the ability to borrow bank funds at the prime rate of interest is of value to a corporation. However, banks review the financial affairs of corporations frequently, and if the financial health of the corporation changes, the terms of the credit agreement also change. The presence of a credit agreement in period X does not insure an ability to borrow in period X *plus 1*.

During the period for which the credit agreement is applicable the corporation has access to bank funds. How much is this access worth? It must be remembered that the existence of a credit agreement is not a guarantee of funds during a period of prolonged hardships. The bank will periodically review the credit relationship, and the terms of the credit agreement will reflect the health of the corporation. A credit agreement is useful in obtaining funds quickly when the funds are needed for operations and for unforeseen circumstances likely to arise in the normal course of business; it is not useful for cash needs of a long-run nature.

There are two primary questions which a corporation must answer:

1. How large a credit agreement is needed?
2. How much is it willing to pay for a credit agreement?

The answers to these two questions are tied together. One can imagine a corporation having a demand curve for a credit agreement (see Figure 7.1).

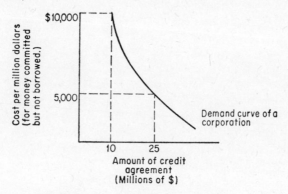

Figure 7.1   Demand for credit.

Figure 7.1 shows that if the cost of the credit agreement is 1 per cent, or $10,000 per million dollars, the corporation is willing to have a $10,000,000 credit agreement. If the cost is $\frac{1}{2}$ per cent, or $5,000 per million dollars, the corporation is willing to have a $25,000,000 credit agreement.

It is important that the cost of different lines of credit be computed and that this cost be explicitly recognized. Instead of the cost being expressed in terms of dollars it is likely that the bank will require a compensating balance. In this case the compensating balance should be converted into dollar cost and an analysis similar to the above carried out.

From the bank's point of view, an outstanding credit agreement is desirable for several reasons:

1. There is a return from the line (perhaps in the form of a compensating balance).
2. It tends to tie the corporation to the bank.

3. It gives some indication of the loans to be expected in the coming period.

From the point of view of the corporation the credit agreement is desirable since it makes borrowing from a bank a relatively routine procedure, thus simplifying the job of the treasurer. It is necessary for the corporate management to decide on the total amount to be paid for this service. The cost of the service is fairly readily measured; the benefits are much more difficult to measure. Nevertheless an attempt must be made to measure them if the decision is to be consistent with the desires of the management of the corporation.

Security Decisions
We shall discuss four marketable decisions:

1. Amount of cash to be invested in securities
2. Timing of security purchases
3. Composition of portfolio
4. Maturity dates of securities

The amount of securities held is a residual decision, i.e., it is the result of other decisions such as the amount of cash to be held, the dividend policy, and the internal investment policy (investment in real assets). Since it is a residual decision, there does not seem to be a clearcut policy as to the maximum amount of securities to be held.

There are two important reasons for a corporation to hold marketable securities:

1. In anticipation of monthly or seasonal transaction needs. (For example a firm may make collections on the tenth of the month but not have payments until the end of the month. The funds must be invested for 20 days. Another example is an income tax payment, since the payment rarely coincides with the cash flow into the firm.)
2. In anticipation of capital investments

There are two other reasons that a corporation may hold securities, which are less clearcut than the above:

3. To insure the ability to pay future dividends equal to past dividends (a stable-dividend policy)
4. To soften the consequences of possible adverse business conditions (contingencies)

The first two reasons are natural results of the normal uneven flows of cash into and out of the corporation. Reasons 3 and 4 are based on assumptions about stockholder preferences. It has not been proved that individuals prefer the corporation to hold securities in order to accomplish a stabilization of dividends, or to avoid embarrassment if business conditions are not good. It may be that individuals prefer the corporation either to invest the funds internally or, if suitable internal investments are not available, to return the funds to the stockholders.

If we agree that securities may rightly be purchased in anticipation of future transaction needs, then the problem reverts to determining the optimum amount of cash to be held, an excess being invested in securities (the maximum amount being equal to the anticipated needs) and a shortage being made up through short-term borrowing.

Corporations should, generally, purchase securities when they possess cash in excess of the amount needed, without attempting to forecast interest rate changes. This is a reasonable policy if the investor has a symmetrical probability distribution relative to the direction of interest rate changes in the future, i.e., if the rate is as likely to go up as down, or if the cost of obtaining better information is higher than the expected benefits.

In any investment situation the composition of the security portfolio is a complex problem since the addition of certain types of securities may increase or decrease the risk connected with the portfolio. For example, short-term government securities are less risky than long-term, since they may be converted to cash at a relatively close maturity date and at a known price. Long-term securities will change in price as interest rates change through time. Thus the price of the security when the cash is expected to be needed is an unknown.

In addition to different maturities, there are also different types of securities in which a corporation may invest and from which higher returns may be expected than from Federal government securities. (They also have higher degrees of risk.) The composition of the portfolio of a particular corporation would depend on the other characteristics of the corporation (such as capital structure) and on the risk preferences of the individual officers. In many corporations the board of directors specifies the type of securities which are eligible for investment, and in most corporations a senior officer has to approve the actual investment.

It is reasonable for a corporation to invest in long-term or non-Federal government securities and to bear the accompanying risk if the management thinks the differential in interest, as compared with short-term Federal government securities, is such that the risk is outweighed by the expected return. Management should have enough flexibility to be able to take advantage of this type of situation.

Some managements have a policy of buying securities which mature on a date close to the date on which the funds are expected to be needed. This policy should not be rigidly followed since there may be occasions when a security which matures after the date when the funds are needed could be more desirable. This security could be sold on the exact date the funds are needed. There is the added consideration that a security could be purchased at a discount and sold before maturity in order to have the gain taxed at the capital gains rate. Rigid rules about the type of security purchased may be undesirable. General rules about the composition of the portfolio are desirable since they will give the manager of corporate cash and securities useful guide-lines.

Decision Rules for Managing Corporate Cash Balances

The specific decisions we shall discuss in this section are the determination of:

1. The optimum amount of cash to be held if the future is known with certainty
2. The optimum amount of cash to be held on deposit under uncertainty about future needs
3. The size of the credit agreement to be negotiated

The term "cash" is used here to refer to the total demand deposits held by one corporation; it includes the amount which represents compensatory balances.

Assuming Certainty

Let us first assume that the future is known with certainty and that we possess a large quantity of marketable securities for the future cash needs of our company. In this situation there is no need for a larger demand deposit balance than the sum of the minimum balance required by the bank plus the current day's transaction needs. If the demand deposits exceed the expected value of today's needs, the excess may be invested; if there is a shortage, marketable securities may be liquidated to obtain the required funds.

Let us next assume that we do not own any marketable securities. There are three possible situations:

1. We have a demand deposit balance which is less than the minimum required balance plus the current day's needs. In this case we might let our balance go below the minimum balance required (or desired) by the bank, or we could borrow to make up the difference. The alternative chosen would depend to some extent on the state of our relations with the bank. Some banks focus attention on average balances, making a short-term dip below the minimum balance an acceptable situation.

2. We have demand deposits equal to minimum balance plus current needs. No action is required.
3. We have demand deposits in excess of minimum balance plus current needs. In this situation the excess should be invested, unless the corporation wishes to build up bank goodwill. In the latter case the funds would be left on deposit.

In summary, under an assumption of certainty it is necessary only to determine the minimum balance required by the bank plus the current day's needs. Theoretically, any amount in excess of this sum should be invested; deficits should be made up by borrowing or by allowing the demand deposits balance to go temporarily below the target balance.

Assuming Uncertainty

Since the future is rarely certain in the real world, it is necessary to investigate cash decisions made under assumptions of uncertainty. It is interesting that despite the elimination of the certainty assumption there is no change in the decision rules developed above. As long as there is a competitive money market which the firm can enter and leave with a minimum lapse of time, there is no reason to maintain cash in excess of a minimum balance. Uncertainty does affect the maximum amount of marketable securities we should hold, since we may choose to hold marketable securities as a buffer against contingencies. But we do not need to hold cash for these contingencies. Since the marketable securities may be liquidated almost instantaneously, it is necessary only to hold the sum of the minimum cash balance plus the expected needs of the current day.

Determining the Size of the Credit Agreement

Most banks indicate that the borrower without a credit agreement is charged the same rate of interest as a comparable firm with a credit agreement. The function of a credit agreement is to make funds more readily accessible to a firm.

What is a credit agreement worth to a corporation? What size credit agreement should it purchase? We shall illustrate one possible method of analysis. It is not assumed that the numbers which follow will have meaning to any specific corporation but that the general procedure may have application to all corporations:

EXAMPLE

Assume that the cost of a credit agreement is $\frac{1}{2}$ per cent of the unused credit, i.e., $5,000 per year per million dollars of credit which is not used.

This is the cost of the credit agreement, not the cost of an actual loan or loans. The service to be paid for is the bank's readiness to grant loans on short notice without any groundwork, equal in total to the amount of the credit agreement. We shall assume that there is an implicit psychological cost of $6,000 per million dollars of funds needed in excess of the credit agreement. To simplify the computations we shall assume that if the money is borrowed at all, it is borrowed immediately for an entire year. We shall assume further that there are five possible events (or, as they are sometimes called, "states of nature"). The amount needed during the year may be 0, 1, 2, 3, or 4 million dollars. There are five possible (and reasonable) acts; have a line of credit of 0, 1, 2, 3, or 4 million dollars.[2] The conditional costs associated with each of the acts and each event are shown in Table 7.1.

Table 7.1   Conditional Costs

Act: Credit agreement of:	Events: Demand for cash (In millions of dollars)				
	0	1	2	3	4
0	0	6,000	12,000	18,000	24,000
1	5,000	0	6,000	12,000	18,000
2	10,000	5,000	0	6,000	12,000
3	15,000	10,000	5,000	0	6,000
4	20,000	15,000	10,000	5,000	0

To find the optimum act it is necessary for us to indicate the probability of each event's occurring.[3]

Let us assume that the probabilities of the various events' occurring are:

Event: Demand for cash in millions of dollars	Probability of event
0	.10
1	.20
2	.30
3	.30
4	.10
	1.00

[2] Since the maximum demand is $4 million, it would not be reasonable to have a line of credit of $5 million (the probability of cash demand's being $5 million is equal to zero).

[3] Other methods of solution are possible. For example, we may choose to minimize the maximum cost (minimax decision rule) and to select a line of credit of $2 million, since the maximum possible cost which would occur if the demand were $4 million is $12,000, or the minimum maximum cost of any act.

By multiplying the costs of each event for each act by the probability of the event, we can compute the expected cost of the act. For example, the act "obtaining a credit agreement of $2 million" has an expected cost of $5,000.

Event	Conditional cost	Probability	Expected cost
0	$10,000	.10	$1,000
1	5,000	.20	1,000
2	0	.30	0
3	6,000	.30	1,800
4	12,000	.10	1,200
		1.00	$5,000

Repeating this computation for each act gives the expected cost of each act.

Act: (Credit agreement in millions of dollars)	Expected cost
0	$12,000
1	7,700
2	5,000
3	5,600
4	9,500

On the basis of expected cost, the credit agreement should be $2,000,000 since this act has the lowest expected cost.

If management has a strong aversion to borrowing money without a credit agreement, it can place a higher cost on these situations where the demand for cash is higher than the credit agreement. This will tend to change the decision toward a higher credit agreement. In like manner, if management thinks it could go to the market and do just about as well as it could do with a credit agreement, then there will be a low cost associated with those situations where the demand exceeds the credit agreement; this will lead toward a decision for a smaller credit agreement. Thus the basic procedure is applicable to any management. It will lead to decisions which are consistent with the subjective preferences of the management since these preferences are incorporated into the decision process.

The probabilities assigned to the several states of nature (the possible demands for cash) may be based on past experience, or they can be a combination of past experience and the feelings of management about what is going to happen in the future.

Decision Rules for Obtaining Cash-like Assets

In the previous section an attempt was made to set forth a procedure to determine the optimum amount of cash and the optimum size of a credit agreement. We shall now discuss decisions involving both cash and marketable securities.

The decisions we want to make are:

1. The optimum amount of cash and marketable securities under assumption of certainty
2. The optimum amount of cash and marketable securities under assumption of uncertainty

There is a problem of terminology we have to solve. We shall be speaking of the total of cash and marketable securities and need a term to express that sum. "Liquid assets" is one possibility, but this conflicts with the common definition of liquid assets which includes accounts receivable. "Funds" is another possibility, but this conflicts with a commonly used definition of funds that equates funds to working capital. Out of desperation we shall use the awkward term "cash-like" assets for the sum of cash and marketable securities.

Like many other decisions the decisions involving cash-like assets are solved indirectly. Instead of determining the optimum amount of cash-like assets to be held, we shall determine the optimum amount of cash-like assets to be obtained when we go to the market for new funds, and also the moment when we should obtain new funds.

The discussion which follows makes the assumption that the marketable securities considered are very close to being cash and for purposes of decision making may be considered in the same category as cash.

Optimum Amount of Cash-like Assets (Assumption of Certainty)

The administration of cash-like assets is very similar to the administration of inventory. Some of the same tools and techniques can be applied. In inventory control, to determine the optimum order size, assuming demand is known with certainty, we use the following equation:

$$Q = \sqrt{\frac{2KD}{k_c}} \qquad (7.1)$$

where Q = optimum order size
K = fixed cost per order (or set-up cost)
D = usage per time period (say, a year)
k_c = carrying cost per time period (same time period as D)

In administering cash-like assets we modify the definition of the symbols as follows:

Q = the optimum amount of cash-like assets to be obtained from outside sources.

K = the fixed or lump-sum cost of obtaining money on a loan basis (e.g., bond issue costs).

D = the amount of cash to be used in the next time period (say, a year). This is the excess of disbursements over receipts and is assumed to be known.

k_c = the interest cost (expressed as an interest rate) of having the cash-like assets on hand. To compute k_c subtract the interest earned on short-term marketable securities from the interest cost of obtaining the capital.

EXAMPLE

K = $40,000, fixed cost of financial transaction involving issue of new securities
D = $1,000,000, net outlay of cash expected in next year (exclusive of new financing)
k_c = .02 per year (assume cost of obtaining funds is .05 and marketable short-term securities earn .03)

$$Q = \sqrt{\frac{2KD}{k_c}} = \sqrt{\frac{2 \times 40,000 \times 1,000,000}{.02}}$$

$$Q = \sqrt{2,000,000^2} = \$2,000,000$$

The optimum amount of new funds to be obtained is $2,000,000. The procedure would be to borrow $2,000,000 and recompute the optimum amount for the next period on the basis of additional information available later in the year. It should be noted that the optimum size of borrowing is affected by the square root of demand (the amount of cash needed). If the expected usage increased fourfold, the optimum size of borrowing would double.

In the above example we would go to the money market for two years' supply of cash-like assets. The model indicates that it is better to obtain the funds and invest at an inferior rate than to go to the market more frequently.

If the corporation can obtain the cash which is needed from its bank, then K, the fixed cost of obtaining money, is very low. Some corporations indicate it takes only a phone call to obtain the funds. But firms would not want to call their banks every day (as they would be doing if K were zero or very small). Thus firms must decide on the implicit cost of calling their bank and insert that amount into the formula for the optimum borrowing size.

Optimum Timing (Assumption of Uncertainty)

The next model is grounded on the assumption that we do not know the demand for cash in the coming period with certainty, but that we have some notion of the probability distribution of demand. (By demand for cash we mean the amount by which outlays exceed inflows during the period being considered.)

To simplify the computations we shall assume it is reasonable to use the certainty model (the square root formula) to determine the optimum order size and shall concentrate on determining when to go to the market for additional funds (i.e., we shall determine the order point).

One possible decision rule is to hold enough cash-like assets so that the probability of running out of cash and having to arrange a sudden loan is zero. This is not an optimum decision since it would mean holding large idle balances. A more desirable procedure would be to balance k_c, the costs of carrying the funds, and C the cost of running out of cash, taking into consideration the probability that demands for cash will vary during the replenishment period. Assume k_c is the cost per dollar of carrying cash-like assets for a given period of time, and C is a fixed penalty, in dollars, associated with being short of cash. R is the amount of cash which signals our going to the market. Q is the optimum size of borrowing. By equating the marginal expected cost of running out of funds and the marginal expected cost of having excess funds, and solving for the cumulative probability $F(R)$ we obtain:[4]

$$F(R) = \frac{Cf(R)}{k_c \left(\dfrac{Q}{D}\right)} \qquad (7.2)$$

$F(R)$ is the left tail of the probability distribution for cash; it is the probability of demand being equal to or less than R (i.e., not running out of cash) during the period of arranging for the new funds. The probability of running out of cash is $1 - F(R)$. The rule is to hold enough cash so that the probability of not running out of cash is equal to the value of the right side of Equation (7.2).

C is a fixed cost associated with being embarrassed by the fact that we have no cash. The term $f(R)$ is the value of the density function at R. Since the values given in normal-density tables are for a standard normal-density function (mean, 0; standard deviation, 1), it is necessary to convert the values from a normal-density table by using the following relationship:

$$f(R) = \frac{f^*(R)}{\sigma} \qquad (7.3)$$

[4] See the Appendix to this section for the derivation of Equation (7.2).

where $f^*(R)$ is the value of the standard normal density function at R. Equation (7.2) may be written:

$$F(R) = \frac{Cf^*(R)}{\sigma k_c \left(\dfrac{Q}{\bar{D}}\right)} \qquad (7.4)$$

Equation (7.4) may be solved by trial and error for the value of R, for which the equality holds.[5]

EXAMPLE

Assume the demand for cash in the next week is normally distributed, with $\bar{D}$ (mean demand) being \$1,000,000, the distribution having a standard deviation of \$50,000. It is known that it will take a week to get new funds. The amount of funds to be obtained is \$20,000,000.

$C = \$4,000$ (cost of running out of funds)
$k_c = .001$ per week for each dollar held in excess of amount demanded (annual rate $= .052$, assuming simple interest)

$$F(R) = \frac{4,000\, f^*(R)}{50,000(.001)\,(20,000,000/1,000,000)}$$

$$= \frac{4,000\, f^*(R)}{1,000}$$

$$F(R) = 4f^*(R)$$

Solution by Trial and Error

Number of standard deviations to right of mean	$f^*(R)$	$F(R)$	? =	$4f^*(R)$
2	.054	.977		.216
1.5	.130	.933		.520
1.4	.150	.919		.600
1.3	.171	.903		.684
1.2	.194	.885		.776
1.1	.218	.864		.872 {Equality holds (approximately)
1.0	.242	.841		.968

The above computation indicates that at 1.1 standard deviations to the right of the mean the equality is satisfied. The computation for the optimum amount of cash, R, is as follows:

$$R = \bar{D} + 1.1\sigma$$
$$= 1,000,000 + 1.1(50,000) = \$1,055,000$$

[5] If this computation were to be made frequently, we could simplify the procedure by dividing both sides by $f^*(R)$ and then use a table of values of $F(R)/f^*(R)$.

We should arrange to obtain new funds when the amount of cash-like assets is 1,055,000. Without a positive cost of running out of cash, the optimum amount of cash-like assets to be held would be zero. Also, since we have a carrying cost of .001, or $1 per thousand per week (this is an opportunity cost connected with holding cash-like assets), it is not surprising that the computations indicate that we have a significant probability of running out of cash. In fact there is a .14 probability of running out of cash and having to borrow suddenly if we follow the decision rule indicated.

Appendix

Derivation of

$$F(R) = \frac{Cf(R)}{k_c\left(\dfrac{Q}{D}\right)}$$

The expected total cost is equal to the sum of the overage costs when $R > M$, and the underage costs when $M < R$, where M is the demand for funds and R is the amount held. The time of overlap is $(R - M)/D$. The cost of Q units for the time of overlap is Qk_c $(R - M)/D$ or $(Qk_c/D)(R - M)$. To simplify, substitute K^* for Qk_c/D.

$$E \text{ (total cost)} = \int_{-\infty}^{R} K^*(R - M)f(M)\, dM + \int_{R}^{\infty} Cf(M)\, dM$$

$$= K^*RF(R) - K^* \mathop{E}_{-\infty}^{R} (M) + CG(R)$$

where $G(R)$ is the right tail of the probability distribution. Using the relationship

$$G(R) = 1 - F(R)$$

and rearranging terms, we obtain:

$$E \text{ (total cost)} = RF(R)(K^*) + C - CF(R) - \mathop{E}_{-\infty}^{R} (M)(K^*)$$

Taking the derivative of total cost with respect to R and setting the derivative equal to zero:

$$\frac{d}{dR} = (K^*)[F(R) + Rf(R)] - Cf(R) - Rf(R)(K^*) = 0$$

$$(K^*)F(R) - Cf(R) = 0$$

$$F(R) = \frac{Cf(R)}{K^*}$$

where R is the optimum amount of cash held at the time of beginning the process of obtaining new funds. Substituting $k_c(Q/D)$ for K^*, we obtain

$$F(R) = \frac{Cf(R)}{k_c(Q/D)}$$

To obtain Q in the above equation, we can use

$$Q = \sqrt{\frac{2DK}{k_c}}$$

for an approximate solution.   For a more exact solution the following formula can be used:

$$Q = \sqrt{\frac{2D[K + CG(R)]}{k_c}}$$

Note that R which is obtained by using the equation $F(R) = Cf(R)/k_c(Q/D)$ is in the above formula, and Q is in the equation for R.   The two equations must be solved simultaneously.   This may be done by the use of an iterative procedure which starts with an estimate of Q, solves for R, then solves for a new Q, and repeats this process until a Q and R are found to satisfy both equations.

Instead of assuming C is a fixed cost associated with being short of cash, we can use k_u a cost which varies directly with the number of dollars we are short.   The equations for the optimum amount of money to be obtained and the optimum time to start the issue of new securities are:

$$Q = \sqrt{\frac{2D\left[K + k_u \int_R^{\infty} (M - R)f(M) \, dM\right]}{k_c}}$$

$$F(R) = \frac{k_u}{k_u + k_c(Q/D)}$$

These equations may also be solved by an iterative process.

chapter eight

capital budgeting

Capital budgeting is the process of deciding whether or not to commit resources to a project whose benefits will be spread over several time periods. The problem is to relate the benefits to the costs in some reasonable manner which will be consistent with a profit-maximizing objective of a firm.

There are many possible methods of relating a stream of future earnings to the cost of obtaining those earnings. We shall first define, then test the following four methods: cash payback, return on investment, rate of return, present value.

Cash Payback

Using the cash-payback method, we compute the period of time required to recover the initial investment. Thus, if an investment of $10,000 earned $5,000 cash proceeds in each of the first two years of use, it would have a cash payback of two years. The available investments are then ranked according to the length of their payback periods. An investment with a payback of two years is considered more desirable than an investment with a payback of three years. Some firms will accept or reject investments on the basis of duration of payback period; in fact this is the most common method in use at the time this book is being written.

Return on Investment

The return on investment is equal to the average income to be earned divided by the average investment. This is the same computation made in order to measure performance, but instead of being computed for one year it is based on the entire life of the investment. Instead of the average investment (i.e., a figure based on the depreciated plant assets) some companies use the initial investment (the undepreciated plant assets). Frequently the choice is not important in making investment decisions as long as all comparisons use the same procedure. The average investment will be used in this chapter since it is somewhat more logical.

Rate of Return

The rate of return is that rate of discount (interest) which equates the present value of the cash flows to zero. By trial and error, using different rates of interest, we can find that rate of interest which results in the algebraic sum of the present value of cash outlays and the present value of cash proceeds coming to zero. This is the rate of return of the investment.

It is desirable to understand the implications of the term rate of return of an investment. If an investment requires an outlay of \$173.55 and at the end of two years pays back \$210, we can find by trial and error that rate of interest which equates the present value of \$210 and an immediate outlay of \$173.55, or we can solve by some method the following equation for r:

$$210(1 + r)^{-2} - 173.55 = 0$$

We find that r is equal to .10; thus the rate of return is .10 since the algebraic sum of the present value of the cash outlays and the present value of the cash proceeds is zero.   Another interpretation of the rate of return is that it is the rate of growth of the investment.   Thus the investment may be imagined to grow as follows:

Original investment	\$173.55
.10 return	17.36
Investment plus interest	\$190.91
.10 return	19.09
Final value of investment	\$210.00

A third interpretation of rate of return is that it is the highest rate of interest that we could pay for borrowed funds to finance the investment being considered and be no worse off than if we did not undertake the investment. This interpretation assumes a conventional investment, i.e., an immediate outlay followed by periods of cash flows into the firm. It also assumes that the funds generated by the investment are used to pay the debt plus interest.

If the investment results in several unequal cash proceeds, the analysis is the same, though the computations become more complex. Let us assume that an investment costs \$281.06 and has an expected life of two years. The forecasted net cash proceeds for the first year are $100 and for the second year $200. What is the rate of return and what are the implications of the rate of return? The solution for the rate of return consists of a trial-and-error approach. (If an interest rate results in the present values being positive, a higher rate of discount is used.) After several tries we end up with the situation shown in Table 8.1. (Note the sum of the present values is zero.)

Table 8.1

Year	Proceeds (outlays)	Present value of dollar discounted at 4%	Present value of cash proceeds
0	($281.06)	$1.0000	($281.06)
1	100.00	0.9615	96.15
2	200.00	0.9246	184.91
			0

At a rate of discount of 4 per cent the present value of the cash proceeds is equated to the cost of the asset, $281.06. Thus the rate of return is 4 per cent. But what does this mean? The asset of $281.06 earns 4 per cent the first year, and then $100 is withdrawn; the remaining investment again earns 4 per cent, and then $200 is withdrawn; at this time there will be zero investment left. The asset earned a 4 per cent return during its life.

COMPUTATION

$281.06	Original investment
×4%	
$ 11.24	Earned first year
+281.06	Original investment
$292.30	Investment available
−100.00	Cash proceeds withdrawn
$192.30	Investment beginning of second year
×4%	
$ 7.69	Earned second year
+192.30	Investment beginning of second year
$199.99	Investment available
−200.00	Cash proceeds withdrawn
$ 0.01	Investment remaining ($0.01 is rounding-off error)

The rate-of-return capital-budgeting procedure implicitly assumes the above events happening, and in effect assumes the "depreciation" of the asset for year one is $100 and for year two is $200.

Table 8.2 is obtained from the computations made to illustrate what is meant by rate of return. Note that the total earnings are equal to the difference between the total cash proceeds ($300) and the cost of the asset ($281.06), except for the .01 rounding-off error.

Table 8.2

Year	Investment beginning of year	Earnings	Return on investment
1	$281.06	$11.24	4%
2	192.30	7.69	4%
		$18.93	

The rate of return of an investment is frequently used to determine the desirability of an investment. Either the investments are ranked in order of desirability according to their rates of return (the ranking may be spurious), or all independent investments with a return greater than the cost of capital are accepted and all other investments are rejected.

Present Value

Under the present-value method, cash outlays and cash proceeds are discounted back to the present period, the firm's cost of capital being taken as the discount rate. If the present value of the cash flows is positive, the investment is considered desirable. If the present value of the cash flows is negative, then the investment should not be undertaken.

What is the significance of discounting cash flows back to the present when the cost of capital is used as the rate of discount? Let us assume that a firm with a cost of capital of 10 per cent has an investment which promises to return $11,000 at the end of one year in exchange for an immediate cash outlay of $10,000. The present value of $11,000 discounted back one period at a 10 per cent rate of interest is $10,000. The present value of the outlays is also $10,000; thus the net present value of the investment is zero. This means that the firm could be just as well off not borrowing from investors and not investing in the project. The cost of borrowing the $10,000 is $1,000, which is equal to the income the investment will earn ($11,000 less $10,000). On the other hand, the firm will be no worse off investing in the project. The investment yields a return equal to the cost of capital and no more. In fact, the rate of return of the investment is 10 per cent, which is equal to the cost of capital.

Let us now change the illustration by assuming an investment which promises to earn proceeds of $20,000 at the end of period one, and costs $10,000. The present value of the proceeds is $18,182; the outlay is $10,000. The net present value of the investment is $8,182. This $8,182 is the amount that the firm could afford to pay in excess of the cost of the investment (while paying the cost of borrowing) and still be no worse off than if it had not made the investment. For example, if it paid $18,182 for the investment, the cost of borrowing would be 10 per cent of $18,182, or $1,818. Thus the total outlays would be $20,000 ($18,182 plus $1,818), an amount equal to the expected cash proceeds. The outlay of $18,182 today is equivalent to proceeds of $20,000 a year hence. We take into consideration interest of 10 per cent, either by discounting the $20,000 back to the present or by accumulating the $18,182 to the end of the year.

The net present value of the investment shows the estimated profit (unrealized, thus not to be recognized for accounting purposes) at the time of purchase. It is the amount the firm could pay in excess of the purchase price for the investment, but because of fortuitous circumstances does not have to pay.

Choosing the Best Method

Let us test the four methods which have been proposed on three investment proposals and compare the decisions suggested by the different procedures.

Investment proposed	Initial outlay (period 0)	Cash proceeds (period 1)	Cash proceeds (period 2)
A	($10,000)	$10,000	
B	(10,000)	1,000	$11,000
C	(10,000)	5,762	5,762

The cash-payback method would rank investment A as being the most desirable, since it has a payback time of one period. The absurdity of this position is obvious since investment A returns its original investment, but that is all. The cash-payback method fails as a useful device for making investment decisions, since it does not take into consideration the life of the investment after the payback period. Another weakness, not illustrated by the above example, is that the payback method fails to take into consideration the timing of proceeds during the payback period. Thus, while the payback periods of investments B and C are approximately the same, it can be seen that investment C earns its proceeds with different timing within the payback period from investment B.

The return on investment for A is zero; thus A is eliminated from consideration if we use the return-on-investment method. The return-on-investment computations of the other two investments would be as follows:

	1	*2*	*3*	*4*	*5*	*6*
Invest- ment	Outlays	Total proceeds	Net income (2 − 1)	Average income	Average investment	Return on in- vestment (4 ÷ 5)
B	$10,000	$12,000	$2,000	$1,000	$5,000	20%
C	10,000	11,524	1,524	762	5,000	15.2%

The return on investment indicates that investment B is more desirable than investment C. But the return-on-investment procedure completely fails to take into consideration the timing of the proceeds. A dollar of proceeds earned in period 2 is given the same weight as a dollar earned in period 1. This failure to take the timing of the proceeds into consideration is the weakness of return on investment, and is the reason it cannot be used as a general method of making investment decisions.

When the rates of return of the two investments B and C are computed, it will be found that both are 10 per cent. The rate of return of investment A is zero. Before accepting the equal ranking for B and C let us look at the present value of the two investments, using different interest rates (different assumed costs of capital). At a 10 per cent rate of interest the present values of both investments are zero; thus the ranking is the same as we obtained by using rate of return. With a cost of capital of less than 10 per cent, investment B will have a higher present value; but both investments will have positive present values. At a rate of interest higher than 10 per cent, investment C will have a higher present value than B, but both investments will have negative present values. Thus the rate-of-return and the present-value methods may give different rankings to investments, but they will lead to the same accept or reject decisions.

If the rate of return of a normal investment is greater than the cost of capital, the investment may be accepted; if the rate of return is less than the cost of capital, then it may be rejected. The same accept or reject decisions will be obtained, when the cost of capital is used as a rate of discount and the present values of the investments are computed, as are obtained by using the rate of return of the investments.

We have not yet decided whether the rankings obtained using the present-value or the rate-of-return method are the "correct" rankings. Unfortunately, a ranking of investments frequently appears to be correct but is actually only a function of the method used and the assumptions made. Fortunately, for most investment decisions we do not have to rank investments, but merely have to choose those investments which have a yield greater than the firm's cost of capital. If the investments are mutually exclusive, it may be necessary to choose that investment which is the best of a group.

Mutually Exclusive Investments

Mutually exclusive investments are investments which compete with each other; i.e., of the several investments being considered, only one can be undertaken. A firm may need a tanker to transport oil but may not yet have determined the size or number of tankers which is best. Tankers of all sizes and shapes are in this case mutually exclusive investments. Another illustration of mutually exclusive investments would be brick and wood as materials for building a home. The initial costs and maintenance costs through the years would be different.

Let us assume that investments B and C are mutually exclusive investments. Which is the more desirable, assuming a cost of capital of 6 per cent? The present value of the cash flows of the two investments is as follows:

	Investment B				Investment C		
Period	Cash flows	Present value factor	Present value	Period	Cash flows	Present value factor	Present value
0	($10,000)	$1.0000	($10,000)	0	($10,000)	$1.000	($10,000)
1	1,000	.9434	943	1	5,762	.9434	5,436
2	11,000	.8900	9,790	2	5,762	.8900	5,128
			$ 733				$ 564

It can be seen that the present value of the cash flows for investment B are greater than the present value of the cash flows for investment C. The rate-of-return method may not give correct rankings of mutually exclusive investments, since the method implicitly assumes that the proceeds can be reinvested at the same rate of interest as the rate of return. The present-value method assumes that the funds can be reinvested at the same rate of interest as the cost of capital.

Another objection to the rate-of-return method for making decisions involving mutually exclusive investments is that it will fail to take into consideration the size of the investment; thus it incorrectly measures the benefit to be gained by the firm. For example, let us assume two investments with the following characteristics:

Investment	Initial outlay (period 0)	Cash proceeds (period 1)	Rate of return
X	($10,000)	$12,000	20%
Y	(30,000)	35,000	16.7%

The rate-of-return criterion indicates that investment X is superior to investment Y. Let us imagine that the difference between the cash flows of investments X and Y are the cash flows of an investment Z. Thus investment Z would have outlays of $20,000 in period 0 and proceeds of $23,000 in period 1, a rate of return of 15 per cent. If we assume a cost of capital of 10 per cent, investment Z is desirable. The fact that the cash flows of investment Z are actually the difference between the cash flows of investments X and Y would indicate that investment Y is more desirable than X, since by investing an amount $20,000 greater than investment X a return of 15 per cent may be earned. If we study the incremental benefits, the rate-of-return method may be used, but it is awkward to employ it if there are many investment possibilities. Thus the present-value method is to be preferred.

A third difficulty with using the rate-of-return method is that some investments may have more than one rate of return. This occurs if, after an outlay, there are periods of positive proceeds followed by periods of negative cash flows (as when there are removal costs at the end of the investment's life). It may also occur with mutually exclusive investments. When an investment has more than one rate of return, it is easier to reach a decision if the present-value method is used.

Present Value and Mutually Exclusive Investments

The present-value method gives the correct decision in judging mutually exclusive investments if the possibility of reinvesting in the same type of equipment is taken into consideration. Let us assume a simple example where there are two mutually exclusive investments A and B with the following characteristics:

Investment	Initial outlay period	Cash proceeds Period 1	Period 2	Period 3
A	($10,000)	$12,000		
B	(10,000)	5,000	$5,000	$5,000

A and B may be different types of equipment, with A having a life of one year and B a life of three years. With a cost of capital of 10 per cent, the present values of the cash flows of A and B are as follows:

Investment	Present value of cash flows
A	$909
B	2,434

Investment B would seem to be the more desirable investment; however, this analysis is incomplete since it fails to take into consideration the fact that after one year the equipment of type A (or similar equipment) will again be purchased. Where it is likely that investment A will be repeated at the beginning of periods 2 and 3, the following cash flows would occur for investment A:

Investment	Initial outlay period 0	Period 1	Period 2	Period 3
A	($10,000)	($10,000)	($10,000)	
		12,000	12,000	$12,000

The present value of the cash flows as now presented is $2,488 for investment A; thus A is more desirable than B. Where the mutually exclusive investments have unequal lives, the possibility of reinvesting in a similar type of equipment must be taken into consideration.

In some situations the lowest common multiple of the lives of the two investments results in a length of time longer than the life of the longest-lived of the alternatives. For example, comparing the relative merits of two types of equipment, one of which has a life of three years and the other of eight years, can be awkward. In a situation of this nature the equivalent cost per year, the cost for perpetuity, or the present value of the costs for 24 years could be computed. The equipment with the lowest cost would be the most desirable alternative. The three methods of computation being discussed will all lead to the same decision.

EXAMPLE

Assume that two pieces of equipment have the following characteristics:

Equipment	Expected life (years)	Initial cost	Operating cost per year
X	3	$10,000	$2,000
Y	8	30,000	1,500

This problem can be solved by taking the lowest common multiple of 8 and 3, 24 years, and by computing the costs for a 24-year period. An alternative procedure is to compute the equivalent cost per year of an outlay of $10,000 every three years, and the equivalent cost per year of an outlay of $30,000 every eight years.

$$Ra$$
$$3\rceil 10\%$$

$10,000	R	R	R
0	1	2	3

$$Ra$$
$$3\rceil 10\% \quad = \$10,000$$
$$R \times 2.4869 = \$10,000$$
$$R = \$\ 4,021 \text{ Annual equivalent of}$$
$$\$10,000 \text{ every 3 years}$$

$$Ra$$
$$8\rceil 10\% \quad = \$30,000$$
$$R \times 5.3349 = \$30,000$$
$$R = \$\ 5,623 \text{ Annual equivalent of}$$
$$\$30,000 \text{ every 8 years}$$

The equivalent cost per year of using equipment X is $6,021 (i.e., 2,000 + 4,021), and the equivalent cost per year of using equipment Y is $7,123 (i.e., 1,500 + 5,623). On the basis of quantitative analysis X is the more desirable equipment.

To find the cost for perpetuity we multiply the equivalent cost per year by the present value of a perpetuity. The general formula for the present value of a perpetuity of $1 a period is:

$$\text{Present value of a perpetuity} = \frac{1}{r}$$

where r is the appropriate rate of interest.

Since r is equal to .10, the factor in this example is 10. The present value of using X forever is $10 \times 6,021$, or $60,210. The present value of using Y is $71,230. Since the equivalent annual costs of both alternatives are being multiplied by a constant factor of 10, the relative merits of the alternatives are not changed. X remains more desirable than Y.

Which Method?

The cash-payback method is rejected because it fails to consider the entire life of the investment. The return-on-investment method fails to consider the timing of the proceeds, and thus has severe limitations. The rate-of-return method will give acceptable reject or accept decisions except in the special situation where there are several rates of return for an investment. However, the rate-of-return procedure may incorrectly rank mutually exclusive investments, for two reasons. It implicitly assumes reinvestment of proceeds at the same rate of return, and it fails to take into consideration the size of the investment being considered. For these reasons it is suggested that the present-value method be used in making investment decisions.

Cash Flows for Investment Decisions

One of the important details of capital budgeting that is frequently neglected in discussions of the subject is the computation of the cash flows which are used in the analysis. The generally used term "cash flows" is not adequately defined. This is a serious omission since the cash flows are the basis of the computations. There are several reasonable definitions for the term "cash flow." In order to reduce the confusion in this section we shall use the term to describe a procedure which measures the change in cash in each period. Alternatively, we could base the capital-budgeting analysis on the change in working capital or funds; thus we could speak of the fund flow in reference to investment. The two methods may be equated to each other if receivables or payments of the future are recorded today at their present value. Thus there is no material difference between the two procedures.

Cash Flow

The cash-flow procedure assumes that the moment of cash disbursement or cash receipt is the moment at which we should measure the change in financial position associated with the investment. It may be argued that only when the cash is disbursed has the firm suffered any disutility, since only then are real resources, which could be engaged in other earning activities, restricted to this project. For example, the cash may be invested in government securities and interest may thus be earned; but the disbursement of cash requires that the securities be sold, thus the interest otherwise earned is lost. Or, the cash disbursement requires that new interest-bearing debt be issued, in which case the costs connected with having debt outstanding are incurred. In like manner, it is argued that until the sales result in cash, which the firm can then put to other uses, there is no real benefit from the transaction. Thus the making of the legal sale and the creation of an accounts receivable is not important for purposes of analyzing the decision; what is important is the receipt of cash.

Computation of Cash Flow

For each period of the life of the investment it is necessary to compute the change in cash resulting from the investment being considered. The following procedure accomplishes this.

Computation of Forecasted Cash Flow for 1980

Sales (as recorded by accountant) (1)		$100,000
Less: Manufacturing costs of goods sold (2)	$40,000	
Expenses of selling and administration (3)	20,000	$ 60,000
Net revenue after expense-type deductions		$ 40,000
Less: Investment-type outlays (4)	. . . .	
Decrease in revenues from other products (4)	. . . .	
Opportunity costs of factors of production (4)	5,000	
Income tax of period	10,000	$ 15,000
Less: Adjustment for changes in working capital (5)		
Decrease in current liabilities (change the sign for an increase)	4,000	
Increase in current assets (exclusive of cash)	8,000	$ 12,000
Miscellaneous uses of cash		27,000
After-tax cash flow		$ 13,000

Explanation of entries

(1) The sales on the accrual basis, were $100,000.
(2) This out-of-pocket expense is the cost of the factors of production which were utilized in generating the sales, and which required the use of working capital. Note that the manufacturing cost of goods sold expense may be different from the cost of production if we produce some units for inventory. The cost factors' contribution to the change of inventory is picked up as a change in inventory (see 5 below).
(3) The expenses for selling and administration are the expenses for which a current liability will be incurred (or cash disbursed).
(4) Investment-type outlays, decreases in revenues from other products, opportunity costs (including the use of executive time), and income taxes are deducted as cash outlays, even though there may not be a direct explicit cash disbursement. The income tax figure is after the deduction for depreciation.
(5) The adjustment for the changes in working capital is complicated by the fact that we want the change exclusive of the change in cash. The $4,000 is the result of a decrease in current liabilities (using cash). The $8,000 is an increase in current assets (for example, accounts receivable and inventories). Assume the firm produced $42,000 of goods and sold $40,000 (out-of-pocket expenses), then $2,000 would appear in this section as an increase in inventories. Also assume accounts receivable increased by $6,000; thus the total increase is $8,000.

An increase in current liabilities would be subtracted from the deductions; i.e., it would be added to the cash-flow stream. There would be some "expenses" which would not actually utilize cash since they would be financed out of current liabilities. Thus the increase in current liabilities is subtracted.

A side computation would be necessary to compute the income taxes of the period associated with this investment. There may be differences between the cash-flow computations and the computations for tax purposes. The person making these computations should be familiar with the tax code or have access to expert tax advice.

Fund Flow versus Cash Flow

The computations of cash flow are not overly difficult. The objective in each time period is to compute the change in the bank account caused by investing or not investing in the asset under consideration. This bank-account explanation is easy to understand, and with practice not difficult to apply, though the opportunity-cost concept with the possibility of no explicit cash outlay and the exclusion of interest payments weaken the bank-account analogy.

The cash-flow procedure seems to ignore the beneficial effects of other changes which may be of significance. For example, assume that in the first operating period it is expected that sales will be $10,000 (all on account, and none collected), and that the total expenses (including income taxes) are $7,000, all resulting in immediate cash disbursements. There are no other changes expected in this first time period except an increase in depreciation of $1,000 caused by the investment. The total changes are:

Increase in accounts receivable	$10,000
Decrease in cash	7,000
Increase in depreciation	1,000
Increase in retained earnings	2,000

The cash-flow procedure would indicate a negative cash flow of $7,000. The computations would be:

Sales	$10,000
Less: Out-of-pocket expenses	7,000
Excess of revenues over expenses	$ 3,000
Less: Increase in current assets (exclusive of cash)	10,000
Negative cash flow	($ 7,000)

The negative cash flow of $7,000 correctly measures the change of the cash account. But the measure seems to fail to take into consideration other events which have occurred, such as the increase of $10,000 in accounts receivable and the increase of $2,000 in retained earnings. However, in the next period the $10,000 will be collected, and the cash flows of that period will be a positive $10,000. Since there is a time delay before collection, the sales should be recorded at less than $10,000 (i.e., at the present value of $10,000); then the impression of unreasonableness disappears.

We could compute the fund flow, where fund flow is defined as the change in working capital caused by the investment being considered. In the above example the fund flow of the first year would be:

Sales	$10,000
Less: Out-of-pocket expenses	7,000
Increase in funds	$ 3,000

The fund flow is a positive $3,000, which is the same as the sum of the cash flows of the two periods. The two procedures will be different if we include the time value of money in recording the events, i.e., if we note that the cash flow of $10,000 of the second time period must be discounted back two periods. However, we can reconcile the differences by computing the fund flow on the basis of present value of the sales of $10,000 rather than indicated price.

To develop further the computation of fund flow we will use the same illustration that was used for the cash-flow exposition.

Computation of Fund Flow

Sales (as recorded by accountant)		$100,000
Less: Manufacturing cost of goods sold	$40,000	
Expenses of selling and administration	20,000	$ 60,000
Net revenue after expense-type deductions		$ 40,000
Less: Investment-type outlays	....	
Decrease in revenues from other products	....	
Opportunity costs of factors of production	5,000	
Income tax of period	10,000	$ 15,000
Fund flow		$ 25,000

The computations are exactly the same as for cash flow except that the changes in working capital are not included as a deduction. By not deducting the increase, we make the increase in working capital (such as an increase in accounts receivable) affect the computation of fund flow. Thus the fund flow in this example is $12,000 greater than the cash flow. In a situation where the current liabilities increase or the current assets (exclusive of cash) decrease, the fund flow may be less than the cash flow. Again, this difference is caused by our not taking into consideration the fact that certain events will occur in the next period which will affect the cash of that period but which are caused by the fund generation of the present period. Also, the computation assumes that a dollar of receivables not collectible for a period of time is as good to the firm as a dollar of cash. The two procedures will be reconciled if these factors are taken into consideration.

Absolute and Relative Flows

A complication arises in the computation of cash flows when a new process is being considered to replace the present process. Should the absolute revenues be used (the revenues which would be earned if there were no present process) or the relative revenues (the revenues which would be earned in excess of what could be earned under the present process)?   One possibility is to compute the present value of all possible methods (including abandonment of the project), and choose the method with the highest present value. This bypasses the question of whether the absolute or relative revenues are appropriate.

Another possible procedure is to determine if the present method would still be undertaken if there were no possibility of improved methods. If the project should be abandoned, then the relative proceeds could not be used. For example, a train may be more efficient than a bus, but it may be that a bus cannot pay its way; thus a comparison of train with bus is not valid. We want to know if a train is economically feasible. If we find that the present method is economically sound, assuming no change in method, then we can compare the old method with the new method and compute the savings. If the present value of the savings is positive compared with the present value of the outlays, then the new equipment should be adopted.

Cash Flows and Taxes

The cash flows should be on an after-income-tax basis. This means that the taxable income of each period must be determined, and that the amount of income tax arising because of the investment must be computed and included as a decrease of the cash proceeds.

Some interesting things occur when we include both interest and taxes in the analysis. For example, it may be more desirable for a company president to burn a box containing money and claim it as a tax deduction than to place the money in a safe-deposit box for a period of ten years. With a cost of capital of 10 per cent, the present value of a dollar due in ten periods is $0.3855. The present value of a tax deduction, in the presence of taxable income and with a tax rate of 52 per cent, is $0.52 per dollar of deduction.

An important complication in computing income taxes arises from the depreciation expenses allowed under the 1954 Internal Revenue Code. With new depreciable property the company will probably choose either the twice-straight-line-declining-balance method, or the sum-of-the-years'-digits method. It is difficult to generalize as to which procedure will be better, because the answer will be a function of the amount of the salvage, the life of the investment, and the firm's cost of capital.

Another complication is the fact that the firm has an option to switch from the twice-straight-line to the straight-line method of depreciation at any time. Since the twice-line procedure will generally reach a point where a switch-over is desirable, this privilege should be taken into consideration. The theoretically sound answer to the question of which depreciation method is more desirable to a firm must be solved by computing the present value of the tax deduction which will result from following the allowed procedures. The procedure which results in the highest present value is more desirable.

Note that we are speaking here of the amount of depreciation allowable for tax purposes, not the amount of depreciation to be taken for book purposes. The latter amount is not relevant to this decision at all. We are interested in cash flows; since the income tax does affect cash flows and is in turn affected by the amount of depreciation which is allowable for tax purposes, we are interested in that amount.

Cost of Capital

Determination of the cost of capital of a firm is a difficult problem; we shall do no more than survey this question. We have used the cost of capital as the rate of discount to be applied to future cash flows. This carries with it an implicit assumption that funds may be borrowed or loaned out at the cost of capital.

The term "borrowed" represents the obtaining of funds from outside markets. This money may be obtained by the issuance of debt securities or capital stock.

When we speak of the costs of debt, it should be understood that we are referring to the explicit interest costs of the debt plus the implicit costs arising from having additional debt outstanding. The implicit costs include the cost of restrictions placed on management and the cost resulting from the increased risk of bankruptcy, with the result that additional stock equity capital will be more expensive. The true cost of the stock equity capital may actually be less than the return demanded by the stockholders, since the issuance of more common stock results in decreased costs of raising more debt capital as the capital structure is strengthened.

The cost of capital is not a figure that may be determined with certainty. On the other hand, we may establish limits and determine its magnitude. For example, the cost of capital is greater than the explicit rate of interest asked by holders of debt securities, because the rate excludes the implicit costs of issuing debt. The cost of capital is probably less than the cost of common-stock money, where the common-stock cost is defined as the rate of discount required to equate the expected future cash dividends and capital gains in some future period with the price of the common stock. This is because additional common stock funds will generally enable us to issue more debt as the capital structure is strengthened. Thus the cost of capital is between the explicit cost of common stock equity and the explicit interest cost of debt.

Index of Present Value

The index-of-present-value method is a variant of the present-value method; its appeal lies in the fact that seemingly it can be used to rank investments. We shall attempt to show that the ranking is frequently spurious.

The index is computed by dividing the present value of the cash proceeds (exclusive of the initial investment) by the investment.

EXAMPLE

The X Company has a cost of capital of 10 per cent. Assume an investment has the following cash flows:

0	1	2
(1,500)	$1,000	$1,000

The present value of the $1,000-a-period cash proceeds is $1,736. The index is 1.16.

$$\text{Present value index} = \frac{1,736}{1,500} = 1.16$$

One rule to use with an independent investment is: If the index is larger than one, accept the investment.

This rule is sound. However, if the index is greater than one, the net present value is also positive, and the computation of the present value index is unnecessary.

A second rule is: Rank mutually exclusive investments by their indices, and choose the investment with the highest ranking.

This rule may lead to correct decisions; but it may just as well lead to incorrect decisions because of two factors: scale of the investment, and classification of cash flows.

EXAMPLE

Assume two mutually exclusive investments with the cash flows as indicated. Which is the more desirable?

Investment	0	1	2	Present value index
X	($1,500)	$1,000	$1,000	1.16
Y	(3,100)	2,000	2,000	1.12

The index indicates that X is preferred to Y. However, a computation of present values will show that Y is better (a net present value of $372 for Y compared to $236 for X). The present-value index is a ratio of benefits to outlay and fails to consider the scale of the investment in the same manner that other ratio measures fail, such as return on investment and rate of return. This point can be seen more clearly if we look at the incremental investment consequent on moving from X to Y. We shall label that investment $Y - X$.

Investment	0	1	2	Present value index
$Y - X$	($1,600)	$1,000	$1,000	1.08

The index is greater than one; thus the incremental investment is desirable. The problem of scale can be solved by comparing pairs of investments, but this is unnecessary since the problem can be solved more easily by using present value. Also the problem of the classification of cash flows still exists.

EXAMPLE (Classification of cash flows)

The second difficulty with the present-value index is that it requires a distinction between deductions from cash proceeds and investment-type outlays. Assume the following two mutually exclusive investments:

Investment	0	1	2	Present value index
A	($1,500)	$1,000	$1,000	1.16
B	(1,500)	2,000	2,000	1.08
		(1,000)	(1,000)	

The index ranks A over B, but close inspection of the cash flows of the investments show that the difference may be only a matter of classifying the $1,000 outlays of B as investments or as deductions from cash proceeds. Any procedure depending on arbitrary classifications is resting on a foundation of quicksand. For example, are advertising expenditures an expense or an investment?

A misconception about the present-value index is that it will rank independent investments. This ranking is not reliable. If the company does not intend to accept all independent investments with a positive present value (or an index greater than one), then the cost of capital will not be the appropriate rate of discount and the index ranking will not be reliable. It is not claimed here that the present-value method may be used to rank independent investments. It is claimed only that the present-value method will lead to correct decisions involving choices between mutually exclusive investments and will give correct accept or reject decisions when it is applied to independent investments.

Inflation and Interest Rates

We may wish to compute the effective interest for a period of time, assuming a given rate of inflation. This interest rate should not be used in discounting cash flows for capital budgeting unless the flows are expressed in constant dollars.

Let A = amount borrowed

S = amount to be repaid (A plus amount of interest)

p_0 = price index at beginning of period

p_1 = price index at end of period

r = effective interest rate

S^* = amount to be repaid terms of beginning-of-period dollars

$$S^* = S \times \frac{p_0}{p_1}$$

That is, to convert the amount to be paid at the end of the period into beginning-of-the-period purchasing power, S is multiplied by the ratio of the price indices. The formula and examples below assume the money is borrowed for a period of one year.

$$A = \frac{S^*}{1 + r}$$
$$A(1 + r) = S^*$$
$$r = \frac{S^*}{A} - 1$$

EXAMPLE 1

A = \$1000

S = \$2000

p_0 = 100

p_1 = 150

$$S^* = S \times \frac{p_0}{p_1}$$

$$S^* = \$2,000 \times \frac{100}{150} = \$1,333$$

$$r = \frac{S^*}{A} - 1 = \frac{1,333}{1,000} - 1 = 1.333 - 1 = .333$$

EXAMPLE 2

$A = \$1,000$
$S = \$1,200$
$p_0 = 100$
$p_1 = 130$

$$S^* = S \times \frac{p_0}{p_1} = 1,200 \times \frac{100}{130} = \$923$$

$$r = \frac{S^*}{A} - 1 = \frac{923}{1,000} - 1 = -.077 \text{ (a negative effective interest rate)}$$

EXAMPLE 3

$A = \$1,000$
$S = \$1,200$
$p_0 = 100$
$p_1 = 110$

$$S^* = 1,200 \times \frac{100}{110} = \$1,091$$

$$r = \frac{S^*}{A} - 1 = \frac{1,091}{1,000} - 1 = .091$$

Capital-budgeting Implications

Assume we expect the price level in a foreign country to double in the next twelve months. There is an interest rate of 100 per cent demanded by the banks in that locality (i.e., for every dollar borrowed, two must be paid one year later). Is the following investment desirable?

Period	Cash flows
0	$-1,000
1	1,400

Using the indicated interest rate of 100 per cent, we would advise rejection of the investment (which has a return of 40 per cent). With an effective interest rate of 0 per cent, the investment would seem to be desirable, however, this would be an incorrect use of the effective interest rate.

If the funds were borrowed locally, the cash flows would be as follows:

Period	Investment	Borrowings	Difference
0	$-1,000	$ 1,000	0
1	1,400	-2,000	-600

The above analysis indicates that the foreign investment is not desirable.[1] Would it be desirable if the funds were obtained from the

[1] It should not be implied that if the present value of the differences were positive

United States, where there is a cost of capital of .10? If $1,000 is borrowed, then $1,100 will have to be returned to investors. If the initial conversion rate between dollars and the foreign currency is one to one, assuming a doubling of the foreign price level and no change in the purchasing power of the dollar, then the 1,400 of foreign currency will convert back to US$700. This is less than the $1,100 required to make this a desirable investment. Thus the investment is again deemed undesirable.

A foreign investment must earn a return equal to its local cost of capital with both the interest rate and the cash flows unadjusted for the change in the price level. If the interest rate is adjusted to reflect the effective cost of the money, with due regard for inflation, and if this is used as the rate of discount, then the cash flows must be adjusted into dollars of the same purchasing power. In the example being explored, the effective rate is 0. The cash flows in terms of beginning-of-period dollars would be:

Period	Cash flows	Adjustment factor	Adjusted cash flows (beginning-of-period purchasing power)
0	$-1,000	....	$-1,000
1	1,400	$\times \frac{100}{200} =$	700

The present value of the cash flows is again negative (at a zero rate of discount, the present value is a negative $300).

If the funds are already in the foreign country and cannot be removed, then it may be necessary to invest them in absolutely undesirable investments in order to minimize a loss. That is, it may be better to undertake an undesirable investment than to have the funds eaten away by inflation.

Non-constant Cash Flows

The present value of an investment can be computed by projecting the cash flows of each period. Instead of following this detailed procedure we may wish to know the present value of the cash flows with different assumptions of rates of growth or decay of the projection of the initial period. The formulas for computing these present values are relatively easy to apply. The following formula gives the present value of the positive cash flows. To find the present value of the

---

the investment would be acceptable. Canceling debt against the investment can be used to show that the investment is not acceptable; it cannot be used to show that it is acceptable.

investment we must subtract the initial outlay. All the formulas assume a zero tax rate or the cash flows on an after tax basis.

Decreasing Cash Flows

Assumptions 1. Constant rate of decay through time
2. Cash flows continue forever

Formula
$$\text{Present value} = \frac{A}{g + r}$$

where A = cash flow of first period
g = rate of decay
r = rate of discount (continuously compounded)

Example

Assume: A = $100
g = .15
r = .10

$$\text{Present value} = \frac{\$100}{.15 + .10} = \frac{100}{.25} = \$400$$

If g = 0 (i.e., constant cash flows), then

$$\text{Present value} = \frac{\$100}{.10} = \$1,000$$

Increasing Cash Flows

Assumptions 1. Constant rate of growth through time
2. Growth continues forever
3. r (discount rate) larger than g (rate of growth)

Formula
$$\text{Present value} = \frac{A}{r - g}$$

Example

Assume: A = $100
g = .06   (g is now a rate of growth)
r = .10

$$\text{Present value} = \frac{\$100}{.10 - .06} = \frac{100}{.04} = \$2,500$$

We can prepare a table of values per dollar of initial cash flow. Change the formula to read:

$$\text{Present value} = \frac{A}{X}$$

X is equal to $r + g$ if the cash flows are decaying. X is equal to $r - g$ if the cash flows are growing. We can prepare a table of values of A divided by X for different values of X. For example, let A be $1; then we have:

Values of X	Values of $\$1/X$
1.00	1.0
.50	2.0
.25	4.0
.20	5.0
.10	10.0
.05	20.0
.04	25.0
.03	33.3
.02	50.0
.01	100.0

Increasing Cash Flows (Limited Life and Zero Terminal Value)

Instead of assuming that the growth continues for an infinite time period, let us assume that it continues for s periods. The formula becomes:[2]

$$\text{Present value} = A\left(\frac{e^{(g-r)s} - 1}{g - r}\right)$$

Example

Assume: $A = \$100$
$\quad g = .06$
$\quad r = .10$
$\quad s = 20$ years

$$\text{Present value} = 100\left(\frac{e^{(.06-.10)20} - 1}{.06 - .10}\right)$$

$$= 100\left(\frac{e^{-.8} - 1}{-.04}\right)$$

$$= 100\left(\frac{.449 - 1}{-.04}\right) = 100\left(\frac{-.551}{-.04}\right) = \$1,378$$

Previously, when we assumed that the growth continued for an infinite time period, we obtained a present value of $2,500. Thus the assumption of growth for a finite time period, even if it is of a lengthy duration, will give significantly different results from the simpler, but more inexact, assumption of infinite duration. In a situation where there is a decay rate instead of a growth rate, we can assume an infinite life since the value of the cash flows is decreasing rapidly.

Review of Capital-budgeting Decisions

After the capital-budgeting decision has been made, two control problems remain:

[2] The values of e^{-x} may be obtained from tables. For example, E. W. Cogan and R. Z. Norman, *Handbook of Calculus, Difference and Differential Equations*, Prentice-Hall, Inc., Englewood Cliffs, N.J., 1958, pp. 142–148.

1. Controlling the amount of funds spent purchasing or constructing the investment
2. Reappraisal of the investment decision once it starts operating

Controlling Investment Expenditures

Capital expenditures are difficult to control since each investment project is usually unique, and neither standards nor past experience can be used in establishing the probable expenditure of funds. When the actual costs differ from the amount originally estimated, the question remains whether the difference is caused by a bad original estimate, by changes in prices of labor and material, or by inefficiency. The action taken by top management to prevent recurrence of the variance will depend on the cause of the variance. Random uncontrollable events can also cause a difference from the estimate, further complicating the analysis. The reasons the actual expenditures exceed the budgeted expenditures will be related to all the above items, and it will frequently be impossible to isolate the causes with reasonable accuracy.

During construction, reports of percentage of completion are desirable, with the actual cost being compared to the budgeted costs. This might enable management to take action (possibly changing the construction plans) before it is too late. The report should include the probable completion date. A delay in completion of an investment may be costly since interest payments have to be made even if the operations have not yet begun. Thus there are strong incentives to meet the planned date of completion. Delay in completion should be explained just as thoroughly as differences between actual and budgeted costs.

If the actual costs are overrunning the budgeted costs significantly (say, 10 per cent), it may be necessary for the person in charge of the project to request additional funds. The decision to invest additional funds in the project is a capital-budgeting decision, and the request should be treated like any other request. The funds already expended are "sunk" costs, and thus are not relevant to the decision whether or not to invest further funds in the project.

Control of capital expenditures is an extremely inexact procedure since it is difficult to establish bench marks of performance. However, an estimate of cost is made and defended by the sponsor of a project. This estimate is the basis of the decision to invest; it should be made with care and after detailed investigations. It is not unreasonable to use the budgeted cost as the bench mark, and variances from that bench mark should be explained. Small variances can be excused, but large variances should not be ignored by saying, "Our estimate must have been off." The reason the estimate was off must be reviewed. Was the estimate off, or was there another reason for the variance?

At a minimum, review of purchase or construction costs will supply an incentive for project sponsors to make careful estimates, and those people in charge of construction will have an incentive to control costs.

Review of Operating Results

The sponsor of a capital budget request makes an estimate of revenues and expenses of the future in order to justify the proposed expenditure. If the rate-of-return or the present-value approach is used, a key item forecasted is the net cash proceeds. After the investment has been placed in operation, the actual results should be compared to the estimated information (which formed a basis of the capital-budgeting decision), and the variances should be explained.

The selection of items which can be reviewed will vary, depending to some extent on the method used to make the capital-budgeting decision. The following items are suggested as possibilities, but not all of them are to be recommended. For each item the actual results should be compared against the planned or anticipated results.

1. Cash payback or cash proceeds
2. Income
3. Return on investment

Cash Payback or Cash Proceeds

The budget request probably contained an estimate of the cash-payback period (the length of time required to recover the original investment). A comparison of the actual payback period and the expected payback period is useful for measuring the results of operations and the efficiency of the budget process, but there are several difficulties. The payback period will probably be of several years' duration; thus there will be a period with no appraisal of the decision to invest. Also, the appraisal is limited to the payback period; after that period there is no further appraisal.

These difficulties lead to a substitution for the cash-payback review, namely, a comparison of actual and predicted cash proceeds of each period. The use of cash proceeds eliminates the wait for the cash-payback period to end in order to start appraisal, and also corrects the one-shot characteristic of the cash-payback method.

The comparison of actual and predicted cash proceeds is a satisfactory method of reappraising the capital-budgeting decisions, where it can be made without difficulty. Where the projected cash flow is relative (as when equipment is being replaced), it may not be possible to determine the actual relative cash flow since we do not know what the costs of using the old equipment would have been.

Income and Return on Investment

Income (the difference between revenues and expenses) is probably the most widely accepted and used measure of performance, and the return on investment (income divided by investment) is the second. But unless they are carefully used, both these measures are inferior to the use of cash proceeds as a means of reappraising capital-budgeting decisions.

By using cash proceeds we avoid the problem of allocating the cost of an investment to specific periods of use. If income is being used to measure performance, then the depreciation cost of the investment must be computed and used as a revenue deduction since income cannot be computed without taking into consideration the cost of using the investment.

Another popular method of measuring performance is the return on investment. There are two variants of the procedure. Investment can be the gross investment (the accumulated depreciation is not subtracted) or the net investment (the accumulated depreciation is subtracted). There are many difficulties in using this measure, but we shall concentrate on one, the fact that with constant (and in some cases decreasing) proceeds the asset may have an increasing return on investment if the straight-line method of depreciation or any of the decreasing-charge methods of depreciation is used.

It is possible to develop a method of depreciation which will allow income and return on investment to be used in appraising capital-budgeting decisions without the distortion introduced by the other depreciation procedures.[3] If this method of depreciation is not used, the analyst faces the difficult task of disengaging the effect of the depreciation method from the effect of efficiency or inefficiency of the operations or the capital-budgeting process.

Capital-budgeting expenditures should be controlled during the construction period, and the decision to invest must be reappraised once operations have begun. The best measure of appraising the decision to invest and the operation of the investment after completion is a comparison of the actual and expected cash proceeds; but this is not always possible. The projected incomes and return on investment may also be used, but if they are used it is desirable that depreciation charges

[3] See Harold Bierman, Jr., "Depreciable Assets-Timing of Expense Recognition," *Accounting Review*, pp. 613–618, October, 1961.

be handled with care. In many cases reappraisal of the decision will not be possible by any of the above methods. For example, an investment which improves the product and prevents lost sales cannot be appraised, since we do not know what sales would have been without the expenditure.

Finally, it should be remembered that capital budgeting decisions are made under uncertainty. A good decision may turn out to be unsuccessful and still have been the correct decision. For example, most of us would pay $1 for an investment which had a .9 probability of an immediate return of $1,000 and a .1 probability of $0. However, if the event with .1 probability occurred, the investment on appraisal would appear to have been undesirable.

It is hoped that the reappraisal of the capital-budgeting decisions will result in two benefits: one, the presenting of better information on capital-budget requests, and two, an incentive for the operating departments to meet the income goals which they set on the request form in applying for authority to make a capital expenditure.

Appendix 1

Derivation of the formula Present value = A/(g + r) for decreasing cash flows

$$\text{Present value} = \int_0^\infty A e^{-gt} e^{-rt} \, dt$$

$$= A \int_0^\infty e^{-(g+r)t} \, dt$$

$$= \frac{A e^{-(g+r)t}}{-(g+r)} \Big|_0^\infty = 0 - \frac{A}{-(g+r)} = \frac{A}{g+r}$$

Derivation of the formula Present value = A/(r − g) for increasing cash flows
Assume *r* is larger than *g*.

$$\text{Present value} = \int_0^\infty A e^{gt} e^{-rt} \, dt$$

$$= A \int_0^\infty e^{(g-r)t} \, dt$$

$$= \frac{A e^{(g-r)t}}{g-r} \Big|_0^\infty = 0 - \frac{A}{g-r} = \frac{A}{r-g}$$

Derivation of formula when growth is assumed to continue for a finite time period s and there is zero terminal value

$$\text{Present value} = \int_0^s A e^{gt} e^{-rt} \, dt$$

$$= A \int_0^s e^{(g-r)t} \, dt$$

$$= \frac{A e^{(g-r)t}}{g-r} \Big|_0^s = A \left(\frac{e^{(g-r)s} - 1}{g-r} \right)$$

Appendix 2—The MAPI Formula

The research branch of the Machinery and Allied Products Institute has been pioneering in business investment policy for a number of years. In 1958 the research director, George Terborgh, published a new MAPI study and manual for making investment.[4] This appendix reviews the highlights of this important book and attempts to appraise the formula which it presents.

Rather than merely repeat what Terborgh states in his book, we shall review the basic components of the formula and avoid the detail. The end result of the formula is the "Urgency Rating." The higher the rating, the more desirable the project. Investments are ranked according to their urgency ratings and then classified as to whether they are acceptable or not, depending on whether or not their urgency rating is greater than the cutoff rate which the company has chosen. For example, three investments may be ranked as follows:

Investment	Urgency Rating
A	39%
B	15%
C	8%

Assuming a cut-off rate of 10 per cent, investments A and B would be accepted and investment C would be rejected.

Computing the urgency rating

The MAPI formula focuses attention and bases the investment decision on the results of the first year of operations. This is not to say that the remainder of the life of the asset is ignored. The characteristics of future operations are incorporated into the analysis via the use of graphs which project future operating characteristics. Nevertheless, the urgency rating is computed explicitly on the financial data for the first year only. In the absence of explicit information about the future, this is not an objectionable procedure, especially since the formula is capable of incorporating into the urgency rating future operating characteristics.

The urgency rating is essentially a ratio of income to investment. Income can be said to be equal to the cash proceeds earned during the period minus the capital consumption or depreciation of the period.

$$\text{Urgency rating} = \frac{\text{income}}{\text{investment}} = \frac{\text{cash proceeds} - \text{depreciation}}{\text{investment}}$$

This ratio is very similar to the return on investment, which is generally considered deficient as a tool for ranking investments since it fails to consider the time shape of the earnings and requires an assumption as to the timing of the depreciation accruals. Terborgh solves both these problems by adopting a special definition of capital consumption. In order to explain the depreciation method which Terborgh uses, it is necessary to diverge from our general explanation.

The yield of an investment

Assume an asset costs $281.06 and has an expected life of two years. The forecasted net cash proceeds of the first year are $100 and of the second year $200. The projected results of the two years are as follows:

[4] George Terborgh, *Business Investment Policy*, Machinery and Allied Products Institute, Washington, 1958.

Year	Investment, beginning of year	Earnings	Return on investment
1	$281.06	$11.25	4%
2	192.31	7.69	4%
		$18.94	

Terborgh would say that the depreciation (or capital consumption) of the investment is equal to the difference between the present value of cash proceeds at the beginning of the period and the present value of the cash flows at the end of the period.

Present value of proceeds (beginning of period)	$281.06
Present value of proceeds (end of period)	192.31
Depreciation (capital consumption)	$ 88.75

The computation is:

$$\text{Urgency rating} = \frac{\text{cash proceeds} - \text{depreciation}}{\text{investment}} = \frac{100 - 88.75}{281.06}$$

$$= \frac{11.25}{281.06} = 4\%$$

Note that the urgency rating is equal to the yield of the investment. At its best the MAPI formula will give results exactly equal to the rate-of-return method of ranking investments. Differences between the two procedures will result, since the MAPI formula derives the capital consumption not from explicit calculations similar to the above but from one of three sets of curves which make various assumptions about the pattern of future cash proceeds and incorporates a given cost of capital. If the assumptions on which the curves are drawn do not agree with the facts of the particular investment being reviewed, the formula will introduce errors.

Appraisal of the MAPI formula

Within the limitation described above, the MAPI formula will give results equivalent to the rate of return. The advantage of the procedure, if any, must be the fact that a manual has been prepared which gives explicit directions for computing the urgency rating and making the investment decision.

The prime weakness of the formula is that it inherits the weak points of the rate of return. To some extent, this is recognized and stated by Terborgh, but he fails to explain that the formula may give incorrect rankings in the case of mutually exclusive investments, just as the rate-of-return method may give incorrect rankings. Another difficulty is the problem of reinvesting cash flows. This is recognized by Terborgh, but no solution is offered.

The MAPI formula fails to accomplish two worthwhile objects. It does not determine whether the investment project should be delayed a year if technological improvements are expected. Also, the formula does not accomplish the objective of deciding whether it is better to delay the investment a year, aside from the factor of technological improvement. Terborgh in his explanatory material suggests a solution to this problem, but it is not built into the formula.

four
capital-
budgeting
decisions

income tax complications?

Lease or Buy?

An important example of a capital-budgeting decision is the lease-or-buy decision. Should land, a plant, or a piece of equipment be bought or leased? Only the quantitative aspects of the problem will be reviewed here.[1] In the discussion which follows, it is assumed that the terms of the lease require that the lease payments be made for the duration of the lease, making the lease a form of implicit debt. The procedure does not apply to a lease which is readily cancellable.

The Importance of the Rate of Interest

First we shall attempt to establish the importance of the question of the rate of interest. All other things remaining unchanged, an infinite number of solutions may be obtained, depending on the rate of interest which is chosen.

Assume that the choice is between making an immediate outlay of $50,000 or paying $18,360 a period for three periods. The tax rate is zero. With a zero rate of interest the present value or cost

[1] For other considerations see Albert H. Cohen, "Long Term Leases," *Michigan Business Studies*, vol. XI, no 5, Ann Arbor, 1954; Robert N. Anthony and Samuel Schwartz, "Office Equipment: Buy or Rent?" Management Analysis Center, Inc., Boston, 1957.

of the immediate outlay is $50,000, and the present value or cost of the rental payments is $55,080 ($18,360 times the number of payments). The immediate outlay is a better choice than the three payments of $18,360 a period.

Let us now increase the rate of interest. The present value of rental payments becomes smaller and smaller. The cost of the immediate outlay remains the same. At some rate of interest r the present value of the two cost streams will be equal, while for larger rates of interest the present value of the rental payments will be less than the $50,000 initial outlay. This is shown graphically in Figure 9.1.

If the appropriate rate of interest is less than r, the decision should be to buy the equipment since the present value of the immediate outlays resulting from purchase is less than the present value of the rental payments. If the rate of interest (cost of debt) is greater than r, the decision should be to rent the equipment. The rate of

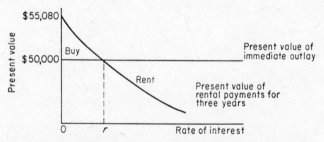

Figure 9.1   Rent versus buy with different interest rates.

interest r is equal to the rate of return or yield promised by an investment of $50,000 in equipment compared to rental of the equipment. If the cost of debt is greater than the rate of return on the outlay, the decision should be not to make the investment, that is, to rent rather than to purchase.

A possible interpretation of the above procedure is that we are finding the present outlay or debt equivalent of the three lease payments of $18,360. If the present debt equivalent is less than $50,000, the company should lease; otherwise it should buy.

Choosing the Correct Interest Rate

The above discussion and Figure 9.1 show that the relative desirability of leasing or buying is going to depend on the rate of interest chosen as the discount rate. The choice of the rate of interest to be used to discount the lease payments is even more cloudy than the computation of the cost of capital for the conventional capital-budgeting decision since a lease is a combination of an investment and a borrowing; but both these transactions are implicit, and thus not easily seen.

Assume that the investment considered for purchase (and described above) will earn proceeds of $21,000 a year for three years, and that the cost of capital is 15 per cent. First let us analyze the decision to purchase the asset.[2]

Table 9.1   Investment with No Borrowing

Period	Cash flow	Present value (15%)
0	(50,000)	(50,000)
1	21,000	18,260
2	21,000	15,880
3	21,000	13,810
		(2,050)

The present value of the cash flow is negative, and the investment would be rejected.

Next assume that a loan of $50,000 can be made, the terms being that the loan can be repaid at the rate of $18,360 a year for three years (an interest rate of 5 per cent). The cash flows from the borrowing and the investment are shown in Table 9.2.

Table 9.2   Investment with Borrowing

Period	Investment and proceeds	Proceeds from borrowing	Net cash flow	Present value (15%)
0	(50,000)	50,000	—0—	—0—
1	21,000	(18,360)	2,640	2,296
2	21,000	(18,360)	2,640	1,996
3	21,000	(18,360)	2,640	1,736
				6,028

The present value of the cash flows of Table 9.2 is positive, and the indication is that the investment and borrowing should be undertaken. But this is incorrect, since the positive present value was obtained by incorporating the borrowing of $50,000 and the repaying of the debt into

[2] The general method of analysis presented here was brought to the author's attention by William D. McEachron.

the analysis of cash flows. The source of funds should not affect the investment decision.

Let us now look at the alternative of leasing. The cash flows are shown in Table 9.3.

Table **9.3**   No Investment (Lease)

Period	Investment and proceeds	Lease payments	Cash flow	Present value (15%)
0	—0—		—0—	
1	21,000	(18,360)	2,640	2,296
2	21,000	(18,360)	2,640	1,996
3	21,000	(18,360)	2,640	1,736
				6,028

Table 9.3 leads to the same present value of cash flows as Table 9.2. This arises because of the zero tax rate and the assumption that a borrowing of an explicit amount of funds would carry the same interest rate as the implicit borrowing connected with a lease.

The lease problem highlights the general fact that any investment with a yield greater than the cost of borrowing can be made to appear acceptable by incorporating into the cash-flow analysis a sufficient amount of debt financing. Thus the investment must be analyzed without including the cash flows resulting because of borrowing. With a lease the borrowing is implicit in the contract; such implicit borrowing must be eliminated from the analysis. This can be done relatively simply by finding the immediate-payment equivalent of the lease payments. With an interest rate of 5 per cent, the immediate equivalent of a series of three payments of $18,360 each is $50,000 (the present value of the annuity, with 5 per cent as the rate of discount). Thus, instead of considering three outlays of $18,360, we can consider one outlay of $50,000. The cash flows become:

Table **9.4**   Investment with Lease Payments
Converted into an Equivalent Immediate Payment

Period	Cash flow
0	(50,000)
1	21,000
2	21,000
3	21,000

This series of cash flows is identical to the one presented in Table 9.1, and the same reject decision is reached. We have accomplished the elimination of the cash flows related to the implicit borrowing for the lease situation. We did this by computing the immediate-payment equivalent for the lease payments and by considering this payment equivalent an investment type of outlay.

In the illustration being considered the alternatives of purchasing outright and leasing were exactly equivalent. This does not have to be the case; in fact, with the introduction of income taxes and with different estimates of risk and the life of the asset, it would be rarely that the lease and buy alternatives would give exactly the same present values.

The Income Tax Complication

The income tax complication is interesting. Accelerated depreciation for tax purposes tends to make buying more attractive; but the relative merits of the alternatives must be computed, they cannot be assumed.

We want to separate the "interest" and "rent" portion of the lease payments. The first step is to separate the lease payments of $18,360 per period into implicit interest and principal. The schedule for a loan of $50,000 with a contract interest rate of 5 per cent is shown in Table 9.5.

Table **9.5**

Period	Debt balance: beginning of year	Interest (5%) on debt balance	Rent (Debt retirement)
1	50,000	2,500	15,860
2	34,140	1,707	16,653
3	17,487	873	17,487
4	–0–		

In signing a lease contract one expects services from the asset leased. The periodic payments are a return ("rent") for these services plus an amount paid to cover the interest cost on the capital tied up in the project. Table 9.5 separates these two. The amount paid for rent is the counterpart of depreciation which a firm would incur if it purchased the asset outright. Thus the "rent" to be subtracted in computing the taxable income for our analysis is equal to the return of principal computed in Table 9.5.

Table 9.6   Computation of Income Tax (Excluding Interest)

Period	Gross proceeds	Rent	Taxable income	Income tax (Income × 52%)
1	21,000	15,860	5,140	2,673
2	21,000	16,653	4,347	2,260
3	21,000	17,487	3,513	1,827

Table 9.7   Computation of Current Value of Positive Cash Flows (Lease)

Period	Gross proceeds	Income tax	After-tax cash flow	Present-value factor 15%	Present value
1	21,000	2,673	18,327	.8696	15,937
2	21,000	2,260	18,740	.7521	14,169
3	21,000	1,827	19,173	.6575	12,606
					42,712

The present value of the cash flows resulting from the lease is $42,712. It is necessary to compare this amount to the $50,000 which is the immediate outlay equivalent of the lease payments and to reach an accept or reject decision. The decision would be to reject since the present value of the lease payments is $50,000 of outlays and the present value of the positive cash flows is only $42,712.

In the above example the decision would be to reject both a lease agreement and purchase agreement. It is possible to have a situation where either purchase or rent is desirable but the other is not. If in the above example the purchase price had been $33,000 and the lease terms had remained unchanged, the decision would have been to purchase the asset since the present value of the cash flows resulting from purchase would be greater than $33,000. See Table 9.8.

Table 9.8   Computations of Present Value of Positive Cash Flows (Purchase: Cost $33,000)

Period	Gross proceeds	Income tax*	Cash flow	Present-value factor (15%)	Present value
1	21,000	5,200	15,800	.8696	13,740
2	21,000	5,200	15,800	7561	11,946
3	21,000	5,200	15,800	.6575	10,389
					36,075

* Computed with use of straight-line depreciation of $11,000 per year for tax purposes. Any method of accelerating the depreciation would increase the present value of the cash flow.

Estimating the Life of the Equipment

Figure 9.1 illustrated the relevance of the rate of interest in making a lease-or-buy decision. In order to simplify the presentation it was assumed that the life of the equipment was known to be three years. Actually, the life of the equipment may not be known with certainty. Any equipment purchased is constantly being challenged by new and more efficient models, and sooner or later will be replaced by one of these newer models. Thus the life of the equipment being considered is uncertain. It would have been possible to draw curves of present value in Figure 9.1 representing different possible lives. The present value of rental payments for less than three years would be to the left and below the curve drawn (the shorter lives reducing the possibility of buying). The present value of rental payments for lives of

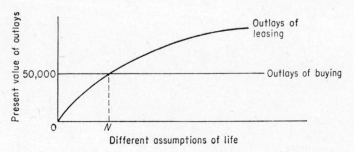

Figure 9.2   Present value of cash outlays with flexible lease.

more than three years would be to the right and above the curve drawn (the longer lives increasing the buy possibilities).

Rather than use Figure 9.1, which assumes that the appropriate discount rate has not been determined, we could use Figure 9.2, where the rate has been determined. The graph shows the different present values of rental outlays and purchase outlays for different assumptions as to the life of the investment (though the lease might be terminated at any time). With a life of zero periods the rental outlays would be zero since no payments would have to be made. The purchase outlay would be $50,000 for all possible lives. If the lease of investment is expected to be zero, or close to zero, it is more desirable to lease.

As the life of the equipment is assumed to be longer, the present value of the rental outlays increases since rent is being paid for longer and longer periods of time. Finally a point is reached where the present value of the rental cash outlays is just equal to the cash purchase out-lays, and it is a matter of indifference whether we purchase or lease if we think the life of the equipment is N years. If the life is longer than N years, the present value of the cash outlays from leasing exceeds the present value of the cash flows from purchasing, indicating that it is desirable to buy. This is consistent with the common-sense con-clusion that all things being equal, the longer the economic life of the equipment, the more desirable it is to purchase the equipment.

In the above example it was assumed that the lease would be void if the equipment was not satisfactory. Thus the zero outlay with a zero life. If the lease was not flexible and if there was a firm com-

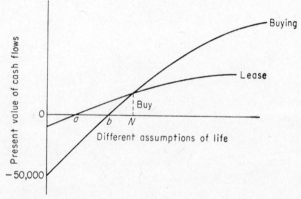

Figure 9.3   Lease versus buy with different possible lives.

mitment to make the lease payments even if the equipment turned out to be unusable, then we should show the present value of the lease payments, including the loan equivalent of the lease as an im-mediate outlay.

We have generally assumed that the equipment has been determined to be desirable and that the problem was to decide whether to buy or lease. But frequently it will be necessary to include the positive cash flows and to determine whether the equipment itself is desirable. Figure 9.3 shows the analysis where present value of cash flows is negative up to a life of b years for buying and a years for leasing.

Incorporating Uncertainty

Given the graphs shown on Figure 9.3, would it be desirable to rent or buy? It would be possible to arrive at a decision based on a general feeling that the equipment was likely to last more than N years.

A somewhat more exact procedure would be to compute the probabilities of the equipment's lasting a different number of years. Each present value could then be weighted by the probability of its occurring in order to find a weighted present value.

EXAMPLE

Assume that analysis indicates uncertain life for a piece of equipment but that management foresees the probabilities of its having different lives as follows:

Life	Probability
0	.00
1	.05
2	.50
3	.25
4	.20
5	.00
	1.00

The present values of cash flows for buying and leasing for different assumed lives are as follows:

Assumed life	Present value (buy)	Present value (lease)
1	($30,000)	–0–
2	–0–	$10,000
3	30,000	20,000
4	60,000	30,000

If management merely considered the most likely life of two years, the decision would be to lease (a present value of $10,000 versus a present value of zero). However, a more appealing procedure is to multiply the conditional present values for each possible life by the probability of the life or value's occurring.

Computations: Expected Value of Buying

(1)	(2)	(3)	(4)
		Conditional	Expected present
Assumed life	Probability	present value (buy)	value (col. 2 × col. 3)
1	.05	($30,000)	($ 1,500)
2	.50	–0–	–0–
3	.25	30,000	7,500
4	.20	60,000	12,000
		Expected value of buying	$18,000

Computations: Expected Value of Leasing

(1)	(2)	(3)	(4)
Assumed life	Probability	Conditional present value (lease)	Expected present value (col. 2 × col. 3)
1	.05	–0–	–0–
2	.50	$10,000	$ 5,000
3	.25	20,000	5,000
4	.20	30,000	6,000
		Expected value of leasing	$16,000

The expected value of buying is higher than the expected value of leasing; thus the decision should be to buy. Where there is some probability that the equipment will have a long life, even where the most likely life is short, then it will be necessary to compute the expected values of leasing and purchasing rather than rely on the decision reached by computing the present values, assuming the most likely life.

Lease or Buy—Land

A corporation which owns land cannot recover the cost of the land through tax deductions unless it sells the land. A corporation which rents land can deduct the rental payments for tax purposes. Assume a cost of debt of 5 per cent. If a firm buys land for $2,000,000, it has an immediate outlay of that amount, and there is an implicit capital cost of $100,000 per year. If a firm rents the same land for $100,000 per year, under a 50 per cent tax rate, there is a net cash outlay of $50,000 (the $100,000 reduces taxes by $50,000). The present value of outlays of $50,000 per year for perpetuity with an interest rate of 5 per cent is $1,000,000. With the facts as given, the cost of renting the land with a lease extending for perpetuity ($1,000,000) seems to be less than the cost of the land outright ($2,000,000). This assumes no speculative advantage in owning land. However, the analysis as presented is incomplete. As illustrated previously, the above analysis combines the costs of financing with the basic investment decision. The immediate payment equivalent of the rentals of $100,000 a year, using a discount rate of 5 per cent, is $2,000,000. The purchase price is also $2,000,000, thus the leasing and purchasing are equivalent in this example. The tax saving of $50,000 is properly associated with the financing and will also be present if the purchase is financed with debt.

Other Factors

The analysis has been presented as if the only factor which should be considered is the size and timing of the cash flows. There are nonquantitative factors which might be brought into the analysis. For one thing, the owning of equipment does result in additional risks (and possibly satisfactions) of ownership. The problem of servicing the equipment may exist, though this may frequently be solved by entering into a service contract with the manufacturer or an equipment servicing agency. The problem of obtaining capital or the possibility of more profitable investments is not relevant here, since both these considerations are incorporated into the analysis by means of the discounting procedures followed in making the decision.

Optimum Plant Size

The process of choosing the optimum size of plant is an interesting theoretical exercise and a question which has important practical significance. Different-sized plants will have different efficiencies for different levels of operations, will require different timing and amounts of cash outflows, and will result in different timing and amounts of cash proceeds. The incomes of future periods will be affected by the plant investment decisions made today.

The problem of optimum plant size is an example of a special type of capital-budgeting decision. The investments are mutually exclusive; i.e., if one investment plan is accepted, the others will be rejected.

In the examples which follow it is assumed that both the relative proportions and the absolute size of the factors of production affect the efficiency of the plant. Thus references to changes in size will assume that proportions will also change. All theoretically possible plants are being considered.

There are two investment decisions which have to be made. The first is whether the production of the product is desirable. The second is choosing which of several investments can do the best job in performing a particular function. For example, what size plant should be constructed? If one plant investment is undertaken, the other plants will be rejected. The fact that we are dealing to some extent with investments of this nature complicates the capital-budgeting decision in an interesting manner. The investment with the highest yield (rate of return) or present-value index (ratio of present value of cash proceeds to investment) will frequently not be the most desirable investment. The problem may be solved by using the present-value method.

Economists' Solution

The accepted procedure is to plot a series of average total-cost curves for all possible sizes of plant and all possible combinations of plants. A smooth curve, called an envelope curve, results, which just touches the cost curve of the most efficient plant for each output. (It does not touch the lowest point or minimum-cost point of the curves except for the lowest of all the average total-cost curves.)[3]

In Figure 9.4 there are three plants (or combinations of plants) which give cost curves ATC_1, ATC_2, and ATC_3 for plants 1, 2, and 3, respectively. Plant 2 is the most efficient plant, as evidenced by the fact that it shows the lowest average total cost. But if 40 units are to be produced, then plant 1 is the most efficient. At 150 units plant 3 is the most efficient. Note that 40 units is not the most efficient point

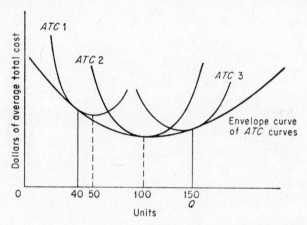

Figure 9.4   Optimum plant size for different outputs.

of operations for plant 1. It could actually produce 50 units at a lower average total cost per unit than it could 40 units. Nevertheless, plant 1 is the most efficient plant to produce 40 units. The plant which could produce 40 units at its minimum average total-cost point would not be more desirable, since at 40 units its cost would be greater than plant 1's costs.

If it is desired to build a plant to produce 100 units, then plant 2 would be the choice, for at 100 units of production plant 2, which is the most efficient of all the plants, would be operating at maximum efficiency, i.e., at the point of minimum average total cost. If the decision were based on a desired production of 150 units, plant 3

[3] See Joe S. Bain, *Price Theory*, Henry Holt and Company, New York, 1952, pp. 117–120. Also E. H. Chamberlin, *The Theory of Monopolistic Competition*, Harvard University Press, Cambridge, Mass., 1950, pp. 230–259.

would be chosen; but plant 3 would operate at a higher minimum average total cost than plant 2 producing 100 units could do.[4]

Quantitative Solutions

Let us assume that the forecast for the demand for product is such that the capacity to produce 100 units a year is required. The management must choose one of the following:

1. One or more plants which can produce 100 units per period without overtime
2. One or more plants which can produce 100 units only with overtime or multiple-shift operation

Obviously, we have an infinite number of plants from which to choose. The engineers can be called on to tell us the minimum size of plant necessary to produce this product, but the production capacity may be greater than the minimum requirement; thus the problem becomes an economic one.

Plants of different capacities are mutually exclusive investments. To choose the best of mutually exclusive investments of equal life, we can compute the present values of the cash flows of all investment possibilities; the investment with the greatest present value is the best investment. This method does not explicitly use incremental costs, but they are implicit in the solution.

EXAMPLE

There are two possible plant capacities, with the following expected cash flows if the plants operate at capacity:

Cash Flows

	0	1	2	Rate of return	Present value (.10)
100 units per day	($1,510)	$1,000	$1,000	.21	$226
500 units per day	(7,733)	5,000	5,000	.19	945

At a .10 cost of capital, the capacity of 500 units per day is the more desirable since it has the higher present value. The lower rate of return is misleading since it ignores the fact that the incremental investment is desirable. The following analysis indicates that the incremental investment is desirable.

	0	1	2	Rate of return	Present value
Incremental investment	($6,223)	$4,000	$4,000	.185	$719

The above analysis is correct as far as it goes, but it is not complete. It is necessary to incorporate into the analysis the possibility that the plants will not operate at capacity levels.

[4] The concept of optimum plant size is frequently confused with optimum size of firm. There are similarities, but the discussion here will be limited to the narrower interpretation of what is meant by "plant."

Degree of Plant Utilization

EXAMPLE

A Motor Company is considering building an assembly plant. The decision has been narrowed down to two possibilities. The company desires to choose the best plant at a level of operations of 100,000 cars a month. Both plants have an expected life of 10 years and are expected not to have any salvage value at the time of their retirement. The cost of capital is 10 per cent. Assume a zero income tax rate.

Costs for 100,000 Cars per Month

	Large plant	Small plant
Initial cost	$1,000,000	$764,500
Direct labor: First shift	500,000	260,000 per year
Second shift	....	300,000 " "
Overhead	80,000	70,000 " "

The above table assumes that the large plant will have certain economies of scale, i.e., labor efficiencies in terms of the hours of labor necessary to assemble a car. The small plant will have certain savings on service (for example, heating).

	Savings (dissaving) per year of using large plant
Direct labor: First shift	($240,000)
Second shift	300,000
Overhead	(10,000)
Saving per year of using large plant	$ 50,000

Present value of savings = $50,000 $a_{\overline{10}|.10}$ = 50,000 × 6.1446

= $307,230

Cost of large plant	$1,000,000
Cost of small plant	764,500
	$ 235,500

The present value of the savings ($307,230) resulting from use of the larger plant is $71,730 greater than the $235,500 of outlays required, indicating that the larger plant is more desirable than the smaller plant. However, there are some important elements of the problem which have not yet been considered. What is the possibility of activity being less (or more) than the expected level? Of the overhead presented in the example, how much is fixed and how much variable? How badly does the company want elbow room for the possibility that demand will be greater than expected?

Are the costs of possible idle-capacity losses arising from high fixed costs balanced by the ability of the large plant to produce more goods when needed? The small plant is designed to be worked at overtime. If demand increases, the production of the small plant may be increased somewhat by working three shifts, and Saturday and Sunday; but the basic fact still remains that the large plant has more reserve capacity. The large plant, however, is more vulnerable to decreases in production since certain costs will continue whether the plant produces or not.

We must consider the desirability of the investment not at just one level but rather at its entire range of operations. This can be accomplished by weighting the present value of cash flows for different operating rates by the probability of the flows occurring.

EXAMPLE

For different levels of operation the incremental investment of a large plant compared to a small plant is shown in the following schedule. Also shown is the probability of the different levels of demand occurring. By multiplying the probability by the present value we obtain an expected (or weighted) present value. Since the expected present value of the incremental investment is positive, the larger plant is desirable.

Level of operation cars per month	Probability of demand level	Present value of incremental investment	Expected present value
0	.10	($ 72,000)	($ 7,200)
50,000	.15	(50,000)	(7,500)
100,000	.25	(28,000)	(7,000)
150,000	.35	50,000	17,500
300,000	.15	100,000	15,000
	1.00	Expected present value	$10,800

In some industries firms may use inventories of finished goods as a means of reducing the investment in plant. By following a policy of building up finished goods inventory in anticipation of higher demand, firms may employ plants of smaller capacity than would otherwise be needed.

Make or Buy?

The make-or-buy decision may take several forms:

1. Make or buy a product (or a component) firm is not currently making
2. Continue to make or begin purchasing a product firm is currently making
3. Make more or less of a product than firm is currently making

The three variants of the make-or-buy decision could all be considered capital-budgeting decisions, or they could be considered an incremental-cost-and-revenue decision where interest is a relevant factor. Whether they are treated in one manner or the other will depend to some extent on the relative importance of the investment required to finance the operation. Where the investment is large, it would be reasonable to consider the make-or-buy decision just as the firm would other decisions involving investment of resources.

Where Significant Resources are Invested

Let us first assume a situation where new plant facilities, including a building or equipment, are required in order to make a product. Thus the initial investment is significant. In addition to the investment in plant facilities there is an investment in working capital, for example, cash outlays for rent, financing of material purchases, etc. We first determine the series of cash outlays, on the assumption that the firm makes the item. This series of cash flows should be discounted back to the present and the present value of the cash outlays determined. Against the series of cash outlays resulting from making the product would be another series of cash outlays resulting from purchase. If the present value of this second series of outlays is less than that of the first, the decision should be to purchase the product. If the present value of "make" outlays is less, then the decision should be to invest in the new facilities and make the item.

Costs not requiring cash outlays are included if there is an alternative opportunity connected with using the facilities. Thus a piece of equipment may presently be owned, but if making the new product will result in another product not being made, then there is an opportunity cost connected with making the new product, even though there may not be an out-of-pocket outlay connected with the equipment.

EXAMPLE

The cost of new equipment needed to produce the item being considered is $25,000. The equipment has an expected life of five years. Other outlays in the beginning of the first period are $1,000. Cash outlays for the next five years are expected to be $2,000 per year if the product is made. If the product is purchased, outlays of $10,000 a year will be required. The cash outlays are assumed to be made at the end of each year. The firm has a cost of capital of 10 per cent.

$$\text{Cost of purchasing} = \$10,000\ A_{\overline{5}|10\%} = \$10,000 \times 3.7908 = 37,908$$
$$\text{Cost of making} = \$25,000 + \$1,000 + \$2,000\ A_{\overline{5}|10\%} = \$26,000 + 7,582 = 33,582$$

The present value of making the product is less than the present value of purchasing the product; thus the decision should be to make.

This problem is somewhat similar to the problem of buying or leasing, though the debt-like characteristics of a long-term contract are not present. In the problem of buying or leasing we incorporated the possibility of different service lives. This procedure would also apply to the make-or-buy decision. In the above example, if the part were to be used for only four years, and if the equipment had no other use or salvage value, then the decision would be to buy the part.

No Resources Required

Let us next assume a situation where there is idle capacity in the plant and in the machinery presently owned (the opportunity cost of these facilities is zero), and that there is no significant investment in working capital required. In this case we could compute the incremental costs of producing the product and compare them with the incremental costs connected with purchasing the product. Note that we are using the incremental costs and not the accounting costs (which may include an allocation of fixed-overhead costs which would be incurred in any event). Since there may be more than one unit produced, the marginal cost of one unit is not relevant; the differential costs are relevant.

EXAMPLE

The X Company is attempting to determine whether to make or buy a component part presently being produced.   The cost of purchasing the part would be $10 per unit. There is excess capacity in the plant, and there is free machine time.   The cost of the product in the most recent time period was as follows:

Direct labor	$ 3.00
Material	4.50
Fixed overhead (allocated)	2.50
Variable overhead (identified with product)	1.00
	$11.00

If we assume that the fixed overhead would be incurred in any event, there are outlays of only $8.50 identified with the manufacture of the product.   The amount would be less if some of the variable overhead were the result of an arbitrary allocation. Since the product could not be purchased for less than $10, it would seem desirable to make the product at an incremental cost of $8.50.

If the assumption of free machine time and idle plant capacity were removed, then we might include some or all of the fixed costs.   In fact it is conceivable that the opportunity costs used for decision-making are higher than the accounting costs.

We assumed that the product was already being produced. This assumption was not necessary to our analysis, except that it lent an air of reliability to the cost information relative to making the product. Exactly the same analysis would be appropriate if the product were not currently in production. The rule to follow is to include only those costs which are incremental to the decision, that is, are incurred only if the product is made. Incomes which are lost if the product is made are also included as costs.

In the solution suggested above, interest was not considered. Generally speaking, the making of any product will require the commitment of new capital resources; thus interest should be taken into consideration. One method of incorporating interest, described earlier in this chapter, is the computing of the present values of the cash flows of the several alternatives. A second possibility is to compute the relevant costs per unit and include an interest cost per unit. This latter procedure is apt to be somewhat less sound theoretically than the present-value method, but it may be somewhat easier to present to management. The exclusion of interest in the computation of costs results in a bias toward investment in work-in-process rather than in plant and equipment. This is not desirable. All investments should be placed on a comparable basis by the recognition of interest costs incurred where there are allocations of resources.

Other Factors

We have made a quantitative analysis and ignored qualitative factors. Some of the factors we should take into consideration are the advantages and disadvantages of having several sources of supply, the quality of the product and the possibility of improvements in the product, the possibility of better uses of managers and the risks of the industry the firm is entering. The quantitative analysis may not enable us to make the final decision independently of other information, but it will supply a very important factor in making the decision, namely, the answer to the question of the direct impact of the make-or-buy decision on the profitability of the enterprise.

Outstanding Debt Refunding

A company with debt outstanding should periodically review the possibility of refunding that debt and substituting a debt contract which would reflect current interest rates. The problem of refunding has sometimes been treated as if it were a problem separate from other decisions being made in the firm, but actually it is a capital-budgeting decision under uncertainty. To simplify the analysis, the question reviewed in this chapter will be limited to whether or not to replace a debt obligation with another debt contract. The possibility of substituting stock equity securities will be passed in order to avoid complications; also, there is also a respected theory that this substitution would not affect the decision.[5] We shall first discuss bond refunding under certainty and then introduce the complications arising from our inability to predict the future interest rates with certainty.

[5] See F. Modigliani and M. H. Miller, "The Cost of Capital, Corporation Finance and the Theory of Investment," *American Economic Review*, June, 1958.

Bond Refunding under Certainty

Assume that the XYZ Company has $100,000 of debt outstanding which costs 6 per cent (i.e., $6,000) interest annually. The bond issue cost and bond discount of the old debt will be assumed to be zero to avoid explaining in this section why these complications would *not* affect the solution. The maturity date of the securities is ten years from the present. Assume that a new ten-year security could be issued which would yield 4 per cent per year. The issue costs would be $8,000, and the bond redemption penalty on the old bonds would be $4,000. Ignoring tax considerations, should the old bonds be replaced with new securities?

The conventional solution would be as follows:

1. Determine the savings per year resulting from the new contract.

Annual interest of old debt	$6,000
Annual interest of new debt	4,000
Savings per year	$2,000

2. Compute the present value of the savings per year, using the current effective yield.

   Present value of $1 per period for 10 periods at 4 per cent $8.111
   Present value of $2,000 per year for 10 years $8.111 × 2,000 = $16,222

3. Compare the present value of the savings with the present value of the outlays.

Present value of savings	$16,222
Present value of outlays	12,000
Present value of net savings	$ 4,222

Since the net savings are positive (i.e., the present value of the savings is greater than the present value of the outlays—the bond issue cost plus the redemption premium), the refunding of the old investment should be undertaken.

Possible Criticism of Procedure

A possible criticism of the above solution centers on the choice of the effective rate of interest of the new security as the appropriate rate of discount for determining the present value of the savings per year, instead of the corporation's cost of capital.

The refunding of a bond issue requires an investment of resources today just like any other capital-investment decision. If the cost of capital is used to determine the worth of capital investments, should the same criterion be used in determining whether this refunding should be undertaken? The $12,000 necessary to accomplish the refunding is an investment analogous to other investments, but there are basic differences. The benefits (savings) promised by this investment are somewhat more certain than with the average investment. Futhermore, the refunding operation will actually reduce the total debt outstanding, thus strengthening the financial position of the common stockholders and perhaps leading to a higher stock price (all things remaining unchanged except that there is less debt outstanding). Consistent with the above differences is the use of the effective rate of interest to find the present debt equivalent of the series of interest savings (the difference between the interest paid with refunding and the interest which would have to be paid if the bonds were not refunded).

Use of the Cost of Capital

Continuing the above illustration, let us assume that the cost of capital is 12 per cent and that it is appropriate to use the cost of capital to discount the cash flows connected with the refunding operation. The computations would be as follows:

1. Compute the present value of the savings per year, using the cost of capital as the appropriate rate of discount.

> Present value of $1 per period for 10 periods at 12% $5.65
> Present value of $2,000 per year for 10 years $5.65 × $2,000 = $11,300

2. Compare the present value of the savings with the present value of the outlays.

Present value of savings	$11,300
Present value of outlays	12,000
Present value of dissavings	(700)

Since the present value of the outlays is greater than the present value of the savings, it would seem that the refunding should not take place. Note that the previous solution using the effective rate of interest of the debt suggests that the refunding should take place. If the previous solution is accepted, the bond refunding will have a priority over conventional investment opportunities, and it is the author's contention that it should.

The use of the current bond yield rate will give a reasonable solution since the outlay required actually reduces the amount of debt outstanding. In decisions involving issue or retirement of debt the yield rate of the debt is appropriate for discounting the cash flows resulting from the debt. Use of the bond yield rate in refunding is predicated on the assumption that refunding is desirable if it returns more than that yield. Ordinarily a firm will have other uses for the cash required for the refunding that would yield more than the bond yield rate, but these investments have different basic characteristics from the outlays for refunding. They do not result in an improved capital structure. In the above example the present value of the debt was reduced by $16,222, the present value of the interest savings; the net savings were $4,222.

The Tax Complication

For a more complete solution of the refunding decision the income tax effect must also be included.

Whether or not particular items are deductible for tax purposes in the year of refunding depends on the exact nature of the transactions and on the tax regulations. If the retirement and issue are separate transactions (there is not an exchange), the costs of retiring the old bonds, including the redemption premiums and the book loss resulting from writing off unamortized bond discount and bond issue costs, are all deductible for tax purposes at the time of retirement. However, the costs of issuing the new bonds have to be written off over the life of the new bonds.

Continuing the example:

Assume a tax rate of 50 per cent. Should the bonds be refunded? It is necessary to include the tax saving or dissaving for each year.

1. There will be a saving equal to 50 per cent of the bond redemption costs of the old securities in the year of issue.

$$\text{Tax saving in year 1} \qquad 50\% \times \$4,000 = \$2,000$$

2. Taxes of each year will be decreased by 50 per cent of the portion of the bond issue costs (of the new issue) allocated to the period.

$$\text{Allocation of bond issue costs to each year} \qquad \frac{\$8,000}{10} = \$800$$

$$\text{Tax saving occurring each year} \qquad \$800 \times 50\% = \$400$$

3. The net savings each year will be:

After-tax savings on interest (50% × $2,000)	$1,000
Savings on taxes	400
Net saving per year	$1,400

At 4 per cent, the cost of debt and the appropriate rate of discount, discounting the tax savings of the first year for one year, the present value of the savings will be:

Present value of net savings each year	$1,400 × 8.111 = $11,355
Tax saving first year	2,000 × 0.962 = 1,924
Present value of savings, allowing for taxes	$13,279

The introduction of income taxes makes the refunding somewhat less desirable in this case. The refunding would cost $12,000, and the present value of the savings is $13,279. In the same situation, without income taxes, the present value of the savings was $16,222. But the effect of income taxes on the solution cannot be assumed, since it will depend on the size of redemption premiums, bond issue costs of the new issue, and unamortized bond issue costs and discount of the old issue.

The solution suggested here was based on the assumption that the future tax rates would be the same as the present rate of 50 per cent. If a change in rates is expected, this can be incorporated into the solution.

Extension of Maturity of Debt and Changes in Interest Rates

The new issue will probably extend the maturity of the debt, that is, push the date of repayment farther into the future. All other things being equal, this is desirable, since it reduces the pressure which accompanies a debt of early maturity.

How do we place a value expressed in dollars on the fact that the maturity date of the debt is now 1970 instead of 1965? Probably the best compromise procedure is to incorporate this as a qualitative factor to be considered in favor of refunding if the present value of the savings is not significantly greater than the costs of refunding, i.e., if refunding is not clearly advantageous.

Bond Discount

What is the relevance of unaccumulated bond discount to the refunding decision? The book value of the liability is not relevant to the refunding decision, except through its effect on income taxes. This situation is analogous to the analysis of equipment replacement, where it is agreed that the book value of the asset being replaced is not relevant to the decision. Since the bond discount account is a valuation account to the par value of the debt, it is not relevant to the refunding decision. This is true no matter how the discount has been accumulated through the years. What is relevant is the impact of the promise to pay an amount in X years and the promise to pay interest for X years. The present value of these promises represents the true liability; the liability recorded on the books does not. The computations of the preceding sections appraising refunding were made without reference to the accounting records to determine the balance in the discount account. Whether a book gain or loss will be suffered in the year of refunding as a result of the decision is not relevant to making the decision, if the appropriate computations indicate that refunding is desirable.

The presence of bond discount on the books may result in a loss on retirement of the outstanding bonds. This should be taken into consideration in computing the tax savings of the first year. Since it will increase the tax saving, the presence of bond discount, which is deductible for tax purposes, will increase the probability of refunding being desirable. (But to avoid unnecessary complications the remainder of this discussion will assume that the tax complication does not exist.)

Bond Refunding Under Uncertainty

The discussion up to this point has assumed that we are given the contractual interest rate of the debt and the present effective interest

rate, which is some rate less than the contractual rate.   A more complex problem to solve is whether to refund as soon as the rate of interest falls below a refunding break-even rate, or whether it is more desirable to wait for a further drop in the interest rate.   Thus the contractual rate may be 4 per cent, and computations may show that the firm would break even if it refunded when the interest rate fell to 3 per cent.   The question remains whether it is desirable to refund at 2.9 per cent or wait until the rate drops lower.

A Simplified Model

We shall first discuss a simplified model where changes in the interest rate are assumed to occur instantaneously.

Assume a bond is issued at a contractual rate of .04 (i.e., a \$1,000 bond paying \$40 a year).   If the market rate falls to some rate of interest r_b, the firm will just break even on refunding with another debt issue that yields r_b.   Until the interest rate falls to r_b, the firm has a relatively easy refunding decision; i.e., refunding is not desirable.   The basic formula giving the conditional saving from refunding is:

$$S_r = (r_c - r)Da_{\overline{n}|r} - R + L \qquad (9.1)$$

In the above equation the symbols have the following meaning:

r_c = contractual rate of present outstanding securities
r = current interest rate
D = debt outstanding which was issued at contractual rate of r_c
$a_{\overline{n}|r}$ = present value of annuity of \$1 a period for n periods (remaining life of the outstanding debt) discounted at r rate of interest
R = refunding cost (call premiums and bond issue costs)
L = monetary value placed on lengthening of debt accomplished by refunding

When we insert r_b, the break-even rate of interest for r, Equation (9.1) equals zero.

$$(r_c - r_b)Da_{\overline{n}|r_b} - R + L = 0 \qquad (9.2)$$

Solve for r_b by trial and error.

Since r_b is a function of the remaining life of the old issue, it will change as the time period changes.   For purposes of simplicity we are assuming that changes in interest rates will occur instantaneously.

If the rate of interest falls below r_b, the firm must decide whether to refund at that rate of interest or wait for a further fall.   Let us assume that management has definite opinions about the probability distribution of the minimum interest rate to occur shortly after the rate falls to r_b.   This distribution has a mean of r_b and a standard deviation of σ, which may be determined by past experience or by the subjective feelings of management.   We shall assume the probability distribution is normal.   (Other assumptions are reasonable.)

The expected value of the savings, $\bar{S}_r$, resulting from following a strategy of refunding when the interest rate falls to r, is the conditional saving [Equation (9.1)] times the probability of the interest rate being equal to or less than r, i.e. $F_n(r)$, or the left tail of the normal distribution.

$$\bar{S}_r = [(r_c - r)Da_{\overline{n}|r} - R + L]F_n(r) \qquad (9.3)$$

The value of r for which Equation (9.3) has the highest figure is the optimum r for which the company should wait. A reasonable method of reaching a solution is to try different trial rates of interest,

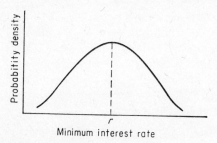

Figure 9.5   Probability distribution of minimum interest rates likely to be encountered.

bracketing the optimum r, until by trial and error a solution is reached; i.e., we find the r which gives the maximum value of $\bar{S}_r$.

Removing the Assumption of Instantaneous Interest Rate Changes

The previous model estimated the probability distribution of the minimum rate of interest to be encountered once the break-even rate of interest is reached, but it left out the waiting times till the various rates of interest are encountered. Both $\bar{S}_r$ and r_b are functions of the time till maturity and also the time till the r, chosen as the refunding rate, is likely to be encountered. We must bring time into the analysis to obtain a more exact solution than that in the previous section.

The following procedure is suggested as one method of approximating a solution.

1. For each possible rate of interest r_b (the break-even rate changes as time changes, but $r_b < r_c$) determine the waiting time till the first occurrence for every other r, where $r < r_b$. See Figure 9.6.
2. Test the desirability of refunding at each r (where $r < r_b$).
   a. Take a given r. Simulate the time of the first occurrence of r. Take a random number between .00 and .99 and enter the y

     axis of figure 9.6; then read on the x axis the time till the first occurrence.

   b. Take the simulated time and compute the saving, using Equation (9.1). Repeat the process a large number of times and compute an average saving S_r for the r.

   c. Instead of simulation, if we have a probability mass function for the times till the first occurrence, we can compute the conditional saving for each time, then multiply by the probability to find the expected saving.

3. The r which has the maximum expected saving is the optimum refunding rate.

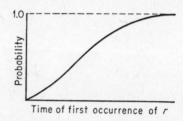

Figure 9.6   Time of first occurrence.

    Instead of using the subjective probabilities of management to compute the interest rate–waiting time probabilities, we might make a study of historical changes in interest rates. This would not change the method of analysis described above; it would change the expectation of the interest rate waiting times and base the expectation on historical evidence.

Summary

    The decision whether or not to refund an outstanding debt issue is a complex problem which is subject to different levels of analysis.

    Assuming certainty that the interest rate will not go below r, we can compute the present value of the savings from refunding; if they are positive, the refunding should be carried out.

    If there is uncertainty, we can assume interest rates change instantaneously and obtain an appropriate solution (i.e., decide to refund at r and not worry about the duration of time until r is reached). This policy is reasonable if we are making a short-range policy and are concerned only with changes in the interest rate likely to occur in a short period of time such as three or four months.

    The third procedure brings into the analysis the waiting times until interest rates are encountered. This procedure can become complex, but it is theoretically the best of the described procedures.

Appendix—Lease vs Buy?

n = period of years being analyzed
k = interest cost of debt
r = cost of capital
P_i = proceeds of year i exclusive of lease payments (outlays negative; proceeds received or disbursed at end of period)
D_i = lease payments, end of year i
V = present value of cash flows with lease
V_B = present value of cash flows with buying

Tax Rate Is Zero

$$V = \sum_{i=0}^{n} P_i(1 + r)^{-i} + \sum_{i=0}^{n} D_i(1 + k)^{-i} \tag{9.4}$$

Tax Rate Is t

t = rate of taxation per dollar of taxable income
The debt equivalent B_j at the end of year j (immediate payment equivalent) is

$$B_j = \sum_{i=j}^{n} D_i(1 + k)^{i-i} \qquad \text{where} \qquad 0 \le j \le n \tag{9.5}$$

The interest I_j of year j is

$$I_j = kB_{j-1} \tag{9.6}$$

The rent portion R_j of the lease payment of year j is

$$R_j = D_j - I_j \tag{9.7}$$

The income tax of year i is T_i

$$T_i = (P_i - R_i)t, \qquad \text{where} \qquad 1 \le i \le n \tag{9.8}$$

The present value of the cash flows of leasing, V, is

$$V = \sum_{i=0}^{n} (P_i - T_i)(1 + r)^{-i} \tag{9.9}$$

V should be compared with B_0, the immediate payment equivalent, and with the present value of the cash flows associated with buying V_B. If $V > B_0$, then leasing is acceptable. If $V > B_0$, and $V - B_0 > V_B$, then leasing is more desirable than buying.

Minimizing Costs

In many situations there are no positive cash flows; here the objective is to minimize cost. The present value of the tax saving of the "rental" payments is:

$$V_t = t \sum_{i=0}^{n} R_i(1 + r)^{-i} \tag{9.10}$$

The present value of leasing is the difference between B_0, the immediate payment equivalent of the least contract, and V_t.

$$V = B_0 - V_t \tag{9.11}$$

If V is less than the present value of the cost of buying, then leasing is desirable.

chapter ten

utility
and
capital
budgeting

Solutions to capital-budgeting decisions generally assume that the cash flows of all periods are known with certainty. If this assumption is not explicitly made, then an implicit assumption of a mean value is made, that is, the expected value, or what we might speak of inaccurately as the best guess of the cash flows. The solution generally accepted among academic authors and a growing number of businessmen is that the present-value method gives the most useful information and that the cost of capital should be used as the rate of discount. If the present value of the cash flows is positive, then the investment is acceptable if the investments are independent. If the investments are mutually exclusive, then the investment with the largest net present value is the most desirable, on the assumption that the investments are comparable, i.e., the investment periods being considered are properly adjusted.

The above solution is unsatisfactory on two counts. First, the use of the cost of capital incorporates an allowance for risk, which is inconsistent with the basic assumption that the cash flows are known with certainty. Second, it is not always appropriate to consider only the expected value of the cash flows and to ignore the other possible values, that is, the range of possible losses and gains. In this chapter we shall consider a method for separating out the adjustment for uncertainty so that it may be more clearly identified.

Investment Decisions under Uncertainty

The present-value method does not give a result suitable for ranking investments but does give information which allows management to accept or reject independent investments and to choose the best of mutually exclusive investments. Under conditions of certainty and with an appropriate discount rate available, this information is sufficient for management to make its decisions. But under conditions of uncertainty the present-value measure is not a sufficient measure of the desirability of an investment. It fails to take into consideration the reliability of the estimates or the investors' reactions to the many possible occurrences. The capital-budgeting method should take into consideration both these factors. This leads us into decision making under uncertainty.[1]

No attempt will be made to develop concepts and arguments for a cardinal measure of utility to serve as the foundation of what is to follow. We shall briefly introduce the problem and hope that the reader will investigate the subject in other sources.

Assume you are offered the choice between two lotteries (i.e., gambles) A and B.

Lottery A	Lottery B
.50 probability of $1,000	1.0 probability of X
.50 probability of $ –0–	

For you to be *indifferent* between the two lotteries A and B, what value of X should be inserted in the description of lottery B? If it is less than $500, you are somewhat averse to gambling in this situation. If X is more than $500, you are willing to pay something for the privilege of gambling. The expected monetary value of lottery A is $500. If you are indifferent between an expected value of $500 and a certain sum of $500, it is then said that your utility function is linear in this range of values. Most of us would require that X be less than $500 for us to be indifferent. That is, we would prefer a certain sum of less than $500 to the lottery A. Questions similar to the above may be

---

[1] Also see Harold Bierman, Jr., and Seymour Smidt, *The Capital Budgeting Decision*, The Macmillan Company, New York, 1960, pp. 120–132, where a rough method of solution is suggested. The concept of utility is used to analyze investments in L. E. Fouraker and R. K. Jaedicke, *Quantitative Analysis for Business Decisions*, Richard D. Irwin, Inc., Homewood, Ill., 1961.

used in determining the entire utility function. For example, we could say that the

$$U(\$X) = .5\,U(\$0) + .5\,U(\$1000)$$

where $U\,(\$X) =$ utility of $\$X$.

Arbitrarily setting the utility of $\$0$ to be 0 and the utility of $\$1,000$ to be 50, and assuming that the X chosen is $\$300$, we compute:[2]

$$U(\$300) = .5\,(0) + .5\,(.50) = 25$$

That is, the utility of $\$300$ is equal to 25. By asking a variety of similar questions we can determine the entire utility function. See Figure 10.1 for the assumed utility function of a corporation.

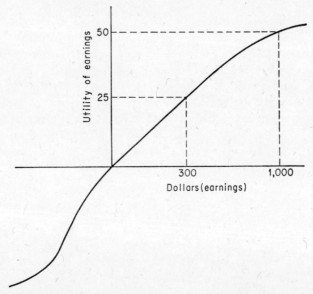

Figure 10.1   A utility function for a corporation.

The X axis measures dollars of earnings. The Y axis measures the utility of earnings. The utility function shows the utility of different earning possibilities.

Even though Figure 10.1 was created without empirical verification, there are several interesting characteristics that should be noted. It is assumed that for small amounts of money the utility function is linear;

[2] The first two utility values chosen are arbitrary; that is, the origin and interval scale are not unique. Technically, a utility function is unique up to a linear transformation.

i.e., expected monetary value is a reasonable measure of the desirability of an investment. For large amounts of gains the marginal utility is decreasing and the utility function ultimately approaches an upper bound. In like manner, as the size of a loss increases, the importance of the loss increases (the marginal disutility is increasing). Eventually a point is reached where losses of larger size result in small increases in the disutility; i.e., the utility function is bounded also from below.

Using the Utility Function

Let us return to lottery A, described as having a .5 probability of $0 and a .5 probability of $1,000. We can read the utility of the uncertain earnings from the utility function of Figure 10.1 (say the utilities are 0 and 50 respectively) and then compute the expected utility of the lottery to be 25 ($.5 \times 0 + .5 \times 50$). The next step is to determine the certainty equivalent of the lottery. Assume the certainty equivalent is $300 (the utility of $300 is 25). It can be obtained from the graph by entering the Y axis at 25 and finding the value of earnings on the X axis which has that amount of utility.

The expected monetary value of the lottery is equal to $500:

$$.5 \times \$1,000 = \$500$$
$$.5 \times 0 \quad = \quad \underline{\quad 0}$$
$$\overline{\$500}$$

The certainty equivalent is $200 less than the expected monetary value; thus the decision maker is attaching a $200 discount for risk. The information could be presented as follows:

Expected monetary value of lottery	$500
Certainty equivalent	300
Risk discount	$200

The general procedure may be summarized as follows:

1. Compute the utility of each discrete event (say, possible earnings of $0 and $1,000).
2. Compute the expected utility of the lottery by weighting the utilities of each event by the probability of occurrence.
3. Find the earnings with the same utility as the expected utility. This is the certainty equivalent.
4. Compute the expected monetary value of the investment. Compare the expected monetary value and the certainty equivalent to compute the discount for risk.

Compound Gambles

Instead of one gamble with a .5 probability of $1,000 and a .5 probability of $0, assume we have the opportunity to entering into two gambles of this nature. We must find the certainty equivalent of this opportunity. We must decide before undertaking either gamble and then we must engage in both gambles. Assume the following utility function:

Dollars	Utility measures
−800	−80
−200	−50
0	0
200	25
300	40
800	48
1,000	50
1,200	52
2,000	60

We shall first find the certainty equivalent of one gamble (which has an expected monetary value of $500).

$$.5 \ U \ (\$1,000) = .5 \times 50 = 25$$
$$.5 \ U \ (\$0) \quad\ \ = .5 \times 0 \ = 0$$
$$\text{Expected utility} \quad \overline{25}$$

We would be indifferent between $200 for certain (with a utility of 25) and undertaking one gamble. The first step was to compute the expected utility of one gamble. This was found to be 25. The amount $200 to be received for certain has a utility of 25.

An incorrect solution to the problem of finding the certainty equivalent of the two gambles would be to assume the utility measure of the second gamble to be the same as the first; thus, the total utility of the compound gamble would be 50. This would incorrectly lead to a certainty equivalent of $1,000. Also incorrect would be to assume that since we have a certainty equivalent of $200 for one gamble, we would have a certainty equivalent of twice $200, or $400, for two gambles.

The first error springs from the incorrect assumption that $U \ (A + B) = U \ (A) + U(B)$, which is not true. Both errors assume that the utility function is unchanged by the outcome of the first gamble and thus may be used for the second gamble. This assumption is not generally valid, since the utility function is affected by the state of one's resources.

If the two gambles are undertaken, there are three possible outcomes, with the following probabilities and expected utilities.

Outcomes	Probabilities of outcomes	Utilities of outcomes	Expected utilities
$0	.25	0	0
1,000	.50	50	25
2,000	.25	60	15
	Expected utility of gambles		40

We would be indifferent between a certainty equivalent of $300 (with a utility of 40) and undertaking the two gambles.

The procedure we followed was to:

1. List the possible monetary outcomes.
2. Compute the probability of each outcome.
3. Assign utility measures to each outcome.
4. Compute the expected utility of the gamble, find the sum of money with this same utility, and call this the certainty equivalent.

Instead of finding the certainty equivalent we might be interested in finding the amount we would be willing to pay for the privilege of gambling. There is no reason to assume that this amount is equal to the certainty equivalent. That is, the amount we are willing to make as an outlay may be different from the amount we would be willing to accept for certain in lieu of the gamble.

EXAMPLE

Ask yourself how much you would be willing to pay for one of the gambles described above.

Ask yourself the minimum amount you would be willing to accept for certain rather than gambling (one gamble).

Compare your two answers.

In the example being studied assume we have to pay $800 to play the compound gamble. Should we gamble?

The three possible outcomes and the expected utilities are:

Outcomes	Probabilities of outcomes	Utilities of outcomes	Expected utilities
−$ 800	.25	−80	−20
200	.50	25	12.50
1,200	.25	52	13.00
	Expected utility		5.50

The expected utility is greater than the utility of $0; thus the compound gamble is desirable.

Time Discounting

Most investments differ from the lottery described above, since the benefits do not occur instantaneously but are spread out through time. The situation involving the two gambles should be thought of as a two-period investment, the outlay occurring in period zero, the first gamble in period 1, and the second gamble in period 2. Instead of dealing with immediate amounts we have to find the present value of the outcomes of the gambles by a discounting procedure.

There remains the problem of the choice of rate of interest used in the discounting.   In computing present values previously in this book, we generally used the cost of capital, but this was for situations where there was risk associated with the cash flows.   The possibility of the cash flow not being realized and the reaction of the investor to this possibility were not effectively incorporated into the analysis.   The use of the cost of capital (which incorporates a risk allowance by including the cost of common-stock equity) was assumed to take normal risk into consideration.   We are now allowing for the possibility that the expected (or mean) cash flow will not occur; we are also taking into account the investors' reaction to this possibility via the utility function.   Thus it is now appropriate to use a risk-free measure of time discounting, say, the interest rate associated with long-term government securities.   This is a more effective way of incorporating uncertainty into the analysis than using different rates of discount for different investments or ignoring uncertainty entirely. ·

Let us assume a situation where the investment consists of the following cash flows (assume the cash flows of each period are independent):

Period	Proceeds
0	($700) outlay
1	.5 probability of $0 and .5 probability of $1,000
2	Same

Is the investment acceptable? The expected monetary value of the proceeds of each year is $500. Assume a cost of capital of .10; the present value of $500 a year for two years is $880 and the net present value is $180 (i.e., $880 minus $700). The investment is acceptable if the use of expected monetary value is appropriate.

However, we should take note of the fact that there is uncertainty connected with the cash flows. The procedure will be the same one used with the double gamble except that a discounting procedure will be incorporated. We shall compute the net present value of the investment for each possible event, determine the utility of that event, weight each utility by the probability of the event, and compute the expected utility of the investment.

EXAMPLE

There are four possible events connected with the investment being discussed. Assume the cash flows of each period are independent.

	Events			
Period	1	2	3	4
0	$-700	$-700	$-700	$-700
1	0	1,000	0	1,000
2	0	0	1,000	1,000

The probability of each of the events is .25. (Each of the events is equally likely to occur, and they form a partition of the possible outcomes.)

Assuming a discount rate of .05, we can find the net present value of each possible event and can then convert the net present value of each event to a utility measure. The final step is to multiply these conditional utilities by the probability of the event, and sum to find the expected utility of the investment.

Event	1 Net present value	2 Utilities*	3 Probability	4 Expected utility (2 × 3)	5 Expected net present value (1 × 3)
1	$-700	-80	.25	-20	$-175
2	252	20	.25	5	63
3	207	16	.25	4	52
4	1,159	56	.25	14	290
				3	$ 230

*Assume these measures are obtained from Figure 10.1.

The expected utility of the investment is positive (greater than the utility of $0), thus the investment should be undertaken.

The advantage of this procedure is that it takes into consideration both the probabilities of different events occurring and the reactions of management to the different possible events. Large negative net present values would have very large negative utilities and thus would be appropriately weighted in computing the expected utility of the investment.

The expected utility of the investment is 3. Using Figure 10.1, we can find the earnings which have a utility of 3. Assume that $U(\$40) = 3$, that is, the utility of a present value of $40 has a utility of 3. Using the expected monetary values of the investment and a discount rate of .05, we find the investment would have an expected net present value of $230. The discount for risk is $190.

Expected monetary value (present value with debt rate as rate of discount)	$230
Certainty equivalent of net present value	40
Discount for risk	$190

The $190 is the amount we are deducting from the present value of the investment because the earnings are not known with certainty.

Dependent Earnings

In the previous examples it was assumed that the earnings of the second period were independent of the results of the first period; i.e., the results of the second gamble were independent of the results of the first gamble. We shall now assume a dependency exists.

EXAMPLE

Period	Proceeds
0	($700) outlay
1	.5 probability of $0, and .5 probability of $1,000
2	Same cash flows as period 1

The possible events which may occur are as follows:

	Events	
Period	1	2
0	$-700	$-700
1	0	1,000
2	0	1,000

Assuming a discount rate of .05 and the same utility function assumed earlier, we can obtain the expected utility.

Event	Net present value	Utilities	Probability	Expected utility
1	-700	-80	.50	-40
2	1,159	56	.50	28
			Expected utility	-12

The expected utility of the investment is less than the utility of $0; thus the investment is not desirable. The assumption of independence (or dependence) is very important since it may change the investment decision. Dependency of the type illustrated tends to lead to the probability of larger profits and larger losses; i.e., the more moderate possi-

bilities are eliminated. This will reduce the desirability of the investment if the utility function is one which reflects increasing marginal
aversion to losses and decreasing marginal utility of gains.

Continuous Probability Distributions

The examples developed in this chapter assumed that only two events
were possible in each of the operating periods, zero proceeds or $1,000.
We can increase the possible events to as large a number as we wish.   In
fact the number of events may be continuous, and instead of a series
of discrete probabilities (a probability mass function), there may be
a probability density function. With a density function, earnings may
take any value within certain limits (the limits may be plus or minus
infinity), and there is some probability of the income being equal to or
less than that value.

If we are dealing with a probability density function, then the procedure is essentially the same as previously illustrated with one modi-
fication. Because the utility function is difficult to express mathematically, it may be easiest to simulate the expected utility of the
earnings of each time period.

Assume the earnings of a period are normally distributed, with a mean
of $10,000 and a standard deviation of $3,000.   The simulation procedure
would be as follows.   Take a number, say, d, from a table of standard
normal deviates (or have an electronic computer generate the number).
The d is the number of standard deviations from the mean.   It is necessary to convert the d to an earnings observation.

$$Y = \bar{M} + d\sigma$$

where Y is the earning observation, $\bar{M}$ the mean earnings, d the random
observation, and σ the standard deviation.   Say d is equal to -1.5; the
first observation is:

$$Y = 10,000 - 1.5\ (3,000)$$
$$Y = \$5,500$$

The $5,500 earnings would then be discounted back to the present,
with the debt rate as the discount rate, and the earnings of the next period
would be computed for another random selection.   The earnings of
each period should be generated and discounted back to the present, and
summed for one trial life.

We would then refer to the utility function (see Figure 10.1) to
determine the utility for the net present value of this trial.   The process
would be repeated a large number of times, and the utility observed

for each trial (each trial leading to a net present value) would be recorded. The sum of these utilities divided by the number of observations gives the mean utility of the uncertain earnings. The last step is to convert the mean utility to a certainty equivalent in the same manner in which we found the certainty equivalent $40 for the mean utility of 3. We enter the Y axis at the value of the mean utility and read the value on the X axis which has that value of utility. An investment with a positive expected utility would be an acceptable investment.

It is not necessary to assume that the earnings are normally distributed. Other continuous probability distributions could be used (though with more difficulty). A possible procedure would be to use a large number of discrete points, each with a given probability of occurrence, and compute the expected utility directly.

A Mathematical Solution

If the cash flows of each period are considered to be independent of one another, it is possible to obtain mathematically a distribution of the net present value of the investment and to use this as the basis of the expected utility computation.

Assume the appropriate rate of discount is r, the cash flow of period i is Y_i, and the standard deviation of the cash flows of the ith period is σ_i. The mean value of the cash flows of the ith period is $\bar{Y}_i$, and the mean value of the distribution of net present values is:

$$\text{Mean} = \sum_{i=0}^{n} (1 + r)^{-i} \bar{Y}_i$$

The computation of the variance of the net present value distribution is as follows:

$$\sigma^2 = \sum_{i=0}^{n} (1 + r)^{-2i} \sigma_i^2$$

It should be noted that the discount factor is raised to an exponent equal to two times the number of periods.

EXAMPLE

The expected cash flows are as follows:

Period	Mean value	Standard deviation
0	$-1,600	100
1	1,000	200
2	2,000	300

The mean value of the distribution of present value is equal to the present value of the mean values of each period.   We shall use a .05 rate of discount.

Period	Mean value	Discount factor	Present value
0	$-1,600	1.0000	$-1,600
1	1,000	0.9524	952
2	2,000	0.9070	1,814
Mean value of net present value of cash flows			$ 1,166

The computation of the standard deviation of the distribution of net present values is similar to the above except that the discount factor is raised to two times the period rather than the number of the period.

Period	1 Square of standard deviation	2 Discount factor $(1 + r)^{-2i}$	3 Product 1×2
0	10,000	1.0000	$ 10,000
1	40,000	0.9070	36,280
2	90,000	0.8227	74,043
			$120,323

The square of the standard deviation (or the variance) is equal to 120,323.   The standard deviation is equal to approximately 347.   With the standard deviation and the mean value of the probability distribution it is possible to determine the utility of this investment by the simulation method already illustrated in this chapter.

The Law of Large Numbers and Investments

An approximate statement of the law of large numbers is that if the probability of a success is p on any one trial, and if then a large number of trials are performed, the proportion of successes will differ from p by a very small amount.   If we toss a fair coin, the probability of a head is .5, but after tossing the coin once there is a .5 probability that the proportion of heads is zero (i.e., that the coin came up tails).   If the coin is tossed a million times, the proportion of heads will be very close to .5.   Even though the number of heads may differ from 500,000, the number of heads divided by the number of tosses will be close to .5.

This law of probability has application to investment analysis.   Consider the drilling for oil.   If an independent organization raises enough capital to drill one well, the probability of an economic well may be .1 and the probability of the equivalent of a dry well may be .9.   If we take into consideration the entire range of possibilities, the distribution of outcomes may appear as in Figure 10.2.

Figure 10.2 shows a high probability that the one well will be non-producing.   If instead of an independent driller one of the major oil companies is drilling 500 wells during the year, then the probability distribution of the possible events is different. There is practically no probability that all 500 wells will be dry, and there is practically no probability that all five hundred will be fabulously good. Figure 10.3 shows how the probability distribution of barrels of reserve per well has changed, with a very important change being a decrease in the variance of the distribution. The variance of the distribution of the proportion of successful wells drilled will also decrease as the number of wells drilled increases.

By drilling a large number of wells an oil company can change the over-all uncertainty connected with the outcomes of drilling. An expert can predict the proportion of producing wells to be found by drilling 500 wells and come reasonably close to his prediction (the variance is

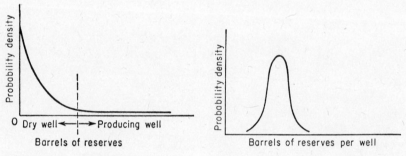

Figure 10.2   Drilling one well.   **Figure 10.3   Drilling 500 wells.**

not likely to be large). The same man making a prediction about the results of drilling any one well could be completely off; i.e., the well could be dry, or it could be the best well ever discovered. Thus, in one sense the drilling of a large number of wells does decrease the risk associated with drilling for oil.

It is possible for a person's utility function to be such that he would not be willing to invest in the situation where one well was to be drilled but be willing to participate in the drilling of the 500 wells. Thus large oil companies are considered to be reasonable investments by individuals who are essentially conservative in their investment policies.

An Appraisal of the Procedure

The procedure described in this chapter has several weaknesses. First, it assumes the same utility function for each time period and each investment. This weakness can be corrected conceptually by preparing a different utility function for each time period and changing the utility function as investments are accepted. Carrying this out operationally in a meaningful manner may be difficult.

The assumption was made in all except one example that the cash flows of each period were independent. This assumption can be changed readily without damaging the basic analysis, though the details of operation will be changed. However, the decision process becomes much more complex if the investments are no longer considered independently and if the acceptance of one investment not only changes the expected cash flows of other investments but if the utility function changes as investments are accepted. This problem is unanswered in this chapter.

The suggested procedure for solving decision problems involving several time periods offers a method of incorporating attitudes toward uncertainty which is more effective than just using the one cash flow figure as is done in the conventional present-value procedure. Making decisions on the basis of monetary expectations is reasonable if the dollar amounts involved are small. The underlying assumption is that the utility function is linear with respect to money when the dollar amounts are small. However, if the amounts are large in relation to the magnitude of operations of the entity making the decision, then expected utility is more appropriate for making decisions than is expected monetary value.

One by-product of the utility approach is that it permits a riskless discount rate to be used in computing the present value. This eliminates the necessity of computing the cost of capital. Most important, the risk of an investment is brought directly and systematically into the analysis.

Despite the fact that the determination of the utility function of a corporation is a difficult task, it is still desirable that some assumption relative to the utility function be made and that decisions be made which are consistent with that function. If this is not done, it is implicitly assumed that the utility function is linear. No corporation has a utility function which is linear for all possible earnings; thus the technique presented in this chapter has application to all corporations. The measure used to indicate the desirability (or acceptability) of the investment will be incomplete unless an attempt is made systematically to incorporate risk in the analysis.

One may ask why this procedure, which is so essential to making a rational capital-budgeting decision, is introduced in the final chapter. Several other chapters have already discussed the same general type of decision problem. The explanation is that much information can be obtained from the computations which assume certainty. Also, present corporate practice fails to use to the fullest extent possible even the present-value method. Thus it is possible to improve decision making in the area of internal investments by the wider use of the present-value method. However, the goal is to incorporate information about uncertainty and utility into the analysis, and so lead to a measure which will enable us to separate investments into acceptable and unacceptable classifications. The need for incorporating utility considerations into the analysis for major investments leads to some procedure similar to that of this chapter.

Tables

Table A*   Present Value of $1 $(1 + r)^{-n}$

n	1%	2%	3%	4%	5%	6%	7%	8%
1	0.9901	0.9804	0.9709	0.9615	0.9524	0.9434	0.9346	0.9259
2	0.9803	0.9612	0.9426	0.9246	0.9070	0.8900	0.8734	0.8573
3	0.9706	0.9423	0.9151	0.8890	0.8638	0.8396	0.8163	0.7938
4	0.9610	0.9238	0.8885	0.8548	0.8227	0.7921	0.7629	0.7350
5	0.9515	0.9057	0.8626	0.8219	0.7835	0.7473	0.7130	0.6806
6	0.9420	0.8880	0.8375	0.7903	0.7462	0.7050	0.6663	0.6302
7	0.9327	0.8706	0.8131	0.7599	0.7107	0.6651	0.6227	0.5835
8	0.9235	0.8535	0.7894	0.7307	0.6768	0.6274	0.5820	0.5403
9	0.9143	0.8368	0.7664	0.7026	0.6446	0.5919	0.5439	0.5002
10	0.9053	0.8203	0.7441	0.6756	0.6139	0.5584	0.5083	0.4632
11	0.8963	0.8043	0.7224	0.6496	0.5847	0.5268	0.4751	0.4289
12	0.8874	0.7885	0.7014	0.6246	0.5568	0.4970	0.4440	0.3971
13	0.8787	0.7730	0.6810	0.6006	0.5303	0.4688	0.4150	0.3677
14	0.8700	0.7579	0.6611	0.5775	0.5051	0.4423	0.3878	0.3405
15	0.8613	0.7430	0.6419	0.5553	0.4810	0.4173	0.3624	0.3152
16	0.8528	0.7284	0.6232	0.5339	0.4581	0.3936	0.3387	0.2919
17	0.8444	0.7142	0.6050	0.5134	0.4363	0.3714	0.3166	0.2703
18	0.8360	0.7002	0.5874	0.4936	0.4155	0.3503	0.2959	0.2502
19	0.8277	0.6864	0.5703	0.4746	0.3957	0.3305	0.2765	0.2317
20	0.8195	0.6730	0.5537	0.4564	0.3769	0.3118	0.2584	0.2145
21	0.8114	0.6598	0.5375	0.4388	0.3589	0.2942	0.2415	0.1987
22	0.8034	0.6468	0.5219	0.4220	0.3418	0.2775	0.2257	0.1839
23	0.7954	0.6342	0.5067	0.4057	0.3256	0.2618	0.2109	0.1703
24	0.7876	0.6217	0.4919	0.3901	0.3101	0.2470	0.1971	0.1577
25	0.7798	0.6095	0.4776	0.3751	0.2953	0.2330	0.1842	0.1460
26	0.7720	0.5976	0.4637	0.3607	0.2812	0.2198	0.1722	0.1352
27	0.7644	0.5859	0.4502	0.3468	0.2678	0.2074	0.1609	0.1252
28	0.7568	0.5744	0.4371	0.3335	0.2551	0.1956	0.1504	0.1159
29	0.7493	0.5631	0.4243	0.3207	0.2429	0.1846	0.1406	0.1073
30	0.7419	0.5521	0.4120	0.3083	0.2314	0.1741	0.1314	0.0994
35	0.7059	0.5000	0.3554	0.2534	0.1813	0.1301	0.0937	0.0676
40	0.6717	0.4529	0.3066	0.2083	0.1420	0.0972	0.0668	0.0460
45	0.6391	0.4102	0.2644	0.1712	0.1113	0.0727	0.0476	0.0313
50	0.6080	0.3715	0.2281	0.1407	0.0872	0.0543	0.0339	0.0213

* Reproduced by permission from Harold Bierman, Jr., and Seymour Smidt, *The Capital Budgeting Decision*, The Macmillan Company, New York. 1960.

Table A   Present Value of $1   (Continued)

n	9%	10%	11%	12%	13%	14%	15%	16%
1	0.9174	0.9091	0.9009	0.8929	0.8850	0.8772	0.8696	0.8621
2	0.8417	0.8264	0.8116	0.7972	0.7831	0.7695	0.7561	0.7432
3	0.7722	0.7513	0.7312	0.7118	0.6931	0.6750	0.6575	0.6407
4	0.7084	0.6830	0.6587	0.6355	0.6133	0.5921	0.5718	0.5523
5	0.6499	0.6209	0.5935	0.5674	0.5428	0.5194	0.4972	0.4761
6	0.5963	0.5645	0.5346	0.5066	0.4803	0.4556	0.4323	0.4104
7	0.5470	0.5132	0.4817	0.4523	0.4251	0.3996	0.3759	0.3538
8	0.5019	0.4665	0.4339	0.4039	0.3762	0.3506	0.3269	0.3050
9	0.4604	0.4241	0.3909	0.3606	0.3329	0.3075	0.2843	0.2630
10	0.4224	0.3855	0.3522	0.3220	0.2946	0.2697	0.2472	0.2267
11	0.3875	0.3505	0.3173	0.2875	0.2607	0.2366	0.2149	0.1954
12	0.3555	0.3186	0.2858	0.2567	0.2307	0.2076	0.1869	0.1685
13	0.3262	0.2897	0.2575	0.2292	0.2042	0.1821	0.1625	0.1452
14	0.2992	0.2633	0.2320	0.2046	0.1807	0.1597	0.1413	0.1252
15	0.2745	0.2394	0.2090	0.1827	0.1599	0.1401	0.1229	0.1079
16	0.2519	0.2176	0.1883	0.1631	0.1415	0.1229	0.1069	0.0930
17	0.2311	0.1978	0.1696	0.1456	0.1252	0.1078	0.0929	0.0802
18	0.2120	0.1799	0.1528	0.1300	0.1108	0.0946	0.0808	0.0691
19	0.1945	0.1635	0.1377	0.1161	0.0981	0.0829	0.0703	0.0596
20	0.1784	0.1486	0.1240	0.1037	0.0868	0.0728	0.0611	0.0514
21	0.1637	0.1351	0.1117	0.0926	0.0768	0.0638	0.0531	0.0443
22	0.1502	0.1228	0.1007	0.0826	0.0680	0.0560	0.0462	0.0382
23	0.1378	0.1117	0.0907	0.0738	0.0601	0.0491	0.0402	0.0329
24	0.1264	0.1015	0.0817	0.0659	0.0532	0.0431	0.0349	0.0284
25	0.1160	0.0923	0.0736	0.0588	0.0471	0.0378	0.0304	0.0245
26	0.1064	0.0839	0.0663	0.0525	0.0417	0.0331	0.0264	0.0211
27	0.0976	0.0763	0.0597	0.0469	0.0369	0.0291	0.0230	0.0182
28	0.0895	0.0693	0.0538	0.0419	0.0326	0.0255	0.0200	0.0157
29	0.0822	0.0630	0.0485	0.0374	0.0289	0.0224	0.0174	0.0135
30	0.0754	0.0573	0.0437	0.0334	0.0256	0.0196	0.0151	0.0116
35	0.0490	0.0356	0.0259	0.0189	0.0139	0.0102	0.0075	0.0055
40	0.0318	0.0221	0.0154	0.0107	0.0075	0.0053	0.0037	0.0026
45	0.0207	0.0137	0.0091	0.0061	0.0041	0.0027	0.0019	0.0013
50	0.0134	0.0085	0.0054	0.0035	0.0022	0.0014	0.0009	0.0006

Table **A**   Present Value of $1   (Continued)

n	17%	18%	19%	20%	21%	22%	23%	24%
1	0.8547	0.8475	0.8403	0.8333	0.8264	0.8197	0.8130	0.8065
2	0.7305	0.7182	0.7062	0.6944	0.6830	0.6719	0.6610	0.6504
3	0.6244	0.6086	0.5934	0.5787	0.5645	0.5507	0.5374	0.5245
4	0.5337	0.5158	0.4987	0.4823	0.4665	0.4514	0.4369	0.4230
5	0.4561	0.4371	0.4190	0.4019	0.3855	0.3700	0.3552	0.3411
6	0.3898	0.3704	0.3521	0.3349	0.3186	0.3033	0.2888	0.2751
7	0.3332	0.3139	0.2959	0.2791	0.2633	0.2486	0.2348	0.2218
8	0.2848	0.2660	0.2487	0.2326	0.2176	0.2038	0.1909	0.1789
9	0.2434	0.2255	0.2090	0.1938	0.1799	0.1670	0.1552	0.1443
10	0.2080	0.1911	0.1756	0.1615	0.1486	0.1369	0.1262	0.1164
11	0.1778	0.1619	0.1476	0.1346	0.1228	0.1122	0.1026	0.0938
12	0.1520	0.1372	0.1240	0.1122	0.1015	0.0920	0.0834	0.0757
13	0.1299	0.1163	0.1042	0.0935	0.0839	0.0754	0.0678	0.0610
14	0.1110	0.0985	0.0876	0.0779	0.0693	0.0618	0.0551	0.0492
15	0.0949	0.0835	0.0736	0.0649	0.0573	0.0507	0.0448	0.0397
16	0.0811	0.0708	0.0618	0.0541	0.0474	0.0415	0.0364	0.0320
17	0.0693	0.0600	0.0520	0.0451	0.0391	0.0340	0.0296	0.0258
18	0.0592	0.0508	0.0437	0.0376	0.0323	0.0279	0.0241	0.0208
19	0.0506	0.0431	0.0367	0.0313	0.0267	0.0229	0.0196	0.0168
20	0.0433	0.0365	0.0308	0.0261	0.0221	0.0187	0.0159	0.0135
21	0.0370	0.0309	0.0259	0.0217	0.0183	0.0154	0.0129	0.0109
22	0.0316	0.0262	0.0218	0.0181	0.0151	0.0126	0.0105	0.0088
23	0.0270	0.0222	0.0183	0.0151	0.0125	0.0103	0.0086	0.0071
24	0.0231	0.0188	0.0154	0.0126	0.0103	0.0085	0.0070	0.0057
25	0.0197	0.0160	0.0129	0.0105	0.0085	0.0069	0.0057	0.0046
26	0.0169	0.0135	0.0109	0.0087	0.0070	0.0057	0.0046	0.0037
27	0.0144	0.0115	0.0091	0.0073	0.0058	0.0047	0.0037	0.0030
28	0.0123	0.0097	0.0077	0.0061	0.0048	0.0038	0.0030	0.0024
29	0.0105	0.0082	0.0064	0.0051	0.0040	0.0031	0.0025	0.0020
30	0.0090	0.0070	0.0054	0.0042	0.0033	0.0026	0.0020	0.0016
35	0.0041	0.0030	0.0023	0.0017	0.0013	0.0009	0.0007	0.0005
40	0.0019	0.0013	0.0010	0.0007	0.0005	0.0004	0.0002	0.0002
45	0.0009	0.0006	0.0004	0.0003	0.0002	0.0001	0.0001	0.0001
50	0.0004	0.0003	0.0002	0.0001	0.0001	0.0000	0.0000	0.0000

Table A   Present Value of $1   (Continued)

n	25%	26%	27%	28%	29%	30%	31%	32%
1	0.8000	0.7937	0.7874	0.7813	0.7752	0.7692	0.7634	0.7576
2	0 6400	0.6299	0.6200	0.6104	0.6009	0.5917	0.5827	0.5739
3	0.5120	0.4999	0.4882	0.4768	0.4658	0.4552	0.4448	0.4348
4	0.4096	0.3968	0.3844	0.3725	0.3611	0.3501	0.3396	0.3294
5	0.3277	0.3149	0.3027	0.2910	0.2799	0.2693	0.2592	0.2495
6	0.2621	0.2499	0.2383	0.2274	0.2170	0.2072	0.1979	0.1890
7	0.2097	0.1983	0.1877	0.1776	0.1682	0.1594	0.1510	0.1432
8	0.1678	0.1574	0.1478	0.1388	0.1304	0.1226	0.1153	0.1085
9	0.1342	0.1249	0.1164	0.1084	0.1011	0.0943	0.0880	0.0822
10	0.1074	0.0992	0.0916	0.0847	0.0784	0.0725	0.0672	0.0623
11	0.0859	0.0787	0.0721	0.0662	0.0607	0.0558	0.0513	0.0472
12	0.0687	0.0625	0.0568	0.0517	0.0471	0.0429	0.0392	0.0357
13	0.0550	0.0496	0.0447	0.0404	0.0365	0.0330	0.0299	0.0271
14	0.0440	0.0393	0.0352	0.0316	0.0283	0.0253	0.0228	0.0205
15	0.0352	0.0312	0.0277	0.0247	0.0219	0.0195	0.0174	0.0155
16	0.0281	0.0248	0.0218	0.0193	0.0170	0.0150	0.0133	0.0118
17	0.0225	0.0197	0.0172	0.0150	0.0132	0.0116	0.0101	0.0089
18	0.0180	0.0156	0.0135	0.0118	0.0102	0.0089	0.0077	0.0068
19	0.0144	0.0124	0.0107	0.0092	0.0079	0.0068	0.0059	0.0051
20	0.0115	0.0098	0.0084	0.0072	0.0061	0.0053	0.0045	0.0039
21	0.0092	0.0078	0.0066	0.0056	0.0048	0.0040	0.0034	0.0029
22	0.0074	0.0062	0.0052	0.0044	0.0037	0.0031	0.0026	0.0022
23	0.0059	0.0049	0.0041	0.0034	0.0029	0.0024	0.0020	0.0017
24	0.0047	0.0039	0.0032	0.0027	0.0022	0.0018	0.0015	0.0013
25	0.0038	0.0031	0.0025	0.0021	0.0017	0.0014	0.0012	0.0010
26	0.0030	0.0025	0.0020	0.0016	0.0013	0.0011	0.0009	0.0007
27	0.0024	0.0019	0.0016	0.0013	0.0010	0.0008	0.0007	0.0006
28	0.0019	0.0015	0.0012	0.0010	0.0008	0.0006	0.0005	0.0004
29	0.0015	0.0012	0.0010	0.0008	0.0006	0.0005	0.0004	0.0003
30	0.0012	0.0010	0.0008	0.0006	0.0005	0.0004	0.0003	0.0002
35	0.0004	0.0003	0.0002	0.0002	0.0001	0.0001	0.0001	0.0001
40	0.0001	0.0001	0.0001	0.0001	0.0000	0.0000	0.0000	0.0000
45	0.0000	0.0000	0.0000	0.0000				
50								

Table A   Present Value of $1   (Continued)

n	33%	34%	35%	36%	37%	38%	39%	40%
1	0.7519	0.7463	0.7407	0.7353	0.7299	0.7246	0.7194	0.7143
2	0.5653	0.5569	0.5487	0.5407	0.5328	0.5251	0.5176	0.5102
3	0.4251	0.4156	0.4064	0.3975	0.3889	0.3805	0.3724	0.3644
4	0.3196	0.3102	0.3011	0.2923	0.2839	0.2757	0.2679	0.2603
5	0.2403	0.2315	0.2230	0.2149	0.2072	0.1998	0.1927	0.1859
6	0.1807	0.1727	0.1652	0.1580	0.1512	0.1448	0.1386	0.1328
7	0.1358	0.1289	0.1224	0.1162	0.1104	0.1049	0.0997	0.0949
8	0.1021	0.0962	0.0906	0.0854	0.0806	0.0760	0.0718	0.0678
9	0.0768	0.0718	0.0671	0.0628	0.0588	0.0551	0.0516	0.0484
10	0.0577	0.0536	0.0497	0.0462	0.0429	0.0399	0.0371	0.0346
11	0.0434	0.0400	0.0368	0.0340	0.0313	0.0289	0.0267	0.0247
12	0.0326	0.0298	0.0273	0.0250	0.0229	0.0210	0.0192	0.0176
13	0.0245	0.0223	0.0202	0.0184	0.0167	0.0152	0.0138	0.0126
14	0.0185	0.0166	0.0150	0.0135	0.0122	0.0110	0.0099	0.0090
15	0.0139	0.0124	0.0111	0.0099	0.0089	0.0080	0.0072	0.0064
16	0.0104	0.0093	0.0082	0.0073	0.0065	0.0058	0.0051	0.0046
17	0.0078	0.0069	0.0061	0.0054	0.0047	0.0042	0.0037	0.0033
18	0.0059	0.0052	0.0045	0.0039	0.0035	0.0030	0.0027	0.0023
19	0.0044	0.0038	0.0033	0.0029	0.0025	0.0022	0.0019	0.0017
20	0.0033	0.0029	0.0025	0.0021	0.0018	0.0016	0.0014	0.0012
21	0.0025	0.0021	0.0018	0.0016	0.0013	0.0012	0.0010	0.0009
22	0.0019	0.0016	0.0014	0.0012	0.0010	0.0008	0.0007	0.0006
23	0.0014	0.0012	0.0010	0.0008	0.0007	0.0006	0.0005	0.0004
24	0.0011	0.0009	0.0007	0.0006	0.0005	0.0004	0.0004	0.0003
25	0.0008	0.0007	0.0006	0.0005	0.0004	0.0003	0.0003	0.0002
26	0.0006	0.0005	0.0004	0.0003	0.0003	0.0002	0.0002	0.0002
27	0.0005	0.0004	0.0003	0.0002	0.0002	0.0002	0.0001	0.0001
28	0.0003	0.0003	0.0002	0.0002	0.0001	0.0001	0.0001	0.0001
29	0.0003	0.0002	0.0002	0.0001	0.0001	0.0001	0.0001	0.0001
30	0.0002	0.0002	0.0001	0.0001	0.0001	0.0001	0.0001	0.0000
35	0.0000	0.0000	0.0000	0.0000	0.0000	0.0000	0.0000	
40								
45								
50								

Table A Present Value of $1 (Continued)

n	41%	42%	43%	44%	45%	46%	47%	48%
1	0.7092	0.7042	0.6993	0.6944	0.6897	0.6849	0.6803	0.6757
2	0.5030	0.4959	0.4890	0.4823	0.4756	0.4691	0.4628	0.4565
3	0.3567	0.3492	0.3420	0.3349	0.3280	0.3213	0.3148	0.3085
4	0.2530	0.2459	0.2391	0.2326	0.2262	0.2201	0.2142	0.2u84
5	0.1794	0.1732	0.1672	0.1615	0.1560	0.1507	0.1457	0.1408
6	0.1273	0.1220	0.1169	0.1122	0.1076	0.1032	0.0991	0.0952
7	0.0903	0.0859	0.0818	0.0779	0.0742	0.0707	0.0674	0.0643
8	0.0640	0.0605	0.0572	0.0541	0.0512	0.0484	0.0459	0.0434
9	0.0454	0.0426	0.0400	0.0376	0.0353	0.0332	0.0312	0.0294
10	0.0322	0.0300	0.0280	0.0261	0.0243	0.0227	0.0212	0.0198
11	0.0228	0.0211	0.0196	0.0181	0.0168	0.0156	0.0144	0.0134
12	0.0162	0.0149	0.0137	0.0126	0.0116	0.0107	0.0098	0.0091
13	0.0115	0.0105	0.0096	0.0087	0.0080	0.0073	0.0067	0.0061
14	0.0081	0.0074	0.0067	0.0061	0.0055	0.0050	0.0045	0.0041
15	0.0058	0.0052	0.0047	0.0042	0.0038	0.0034	0.0031	0.0028
16	0.0041	0.0037	0.0033	0.0029	0.0026	0.0023	0.0021	0.0019
17	0.0029	0.0026	0.0023	0.0020	0.0018	0.0016	0.0014	0.0013
18	0.0021	0.0018	0.0016	0.0014	0.0012	0.0011	0.0010	0.0009
19	0.0015	0.0013	0.0011	0.0010	0.0009	0.0008	0.0007	0.0006
20	0.0010	0.0009	0.0008	0.0007	0.0006	0.0005	0.0005	0.0004
21	0.0007	0.0006	0.0005	0.0005	0.0004	0.0004	0.0003	0.0003
22	0.0005	0.0004	0.0004	0.0003	0.0003	0.0002	0.0002	0.0002
23	0.0004	0.0003	0.0003	0.0002	0.0002	0.0002	0.0001	0.0001
24	0.0003	0.0002	0.0002	0.0002	0.0001	0.0001	0.0001	0.0001
25	0.0002	0.0002	0.0001	0.0001	0.0001	0.0001	0.0001	0.0001
26	0.0001	0.0001	0.0001	0.0001	0.0001	0.0001	0.0000	0.0000
27	0.0001	0.0001	0.0001	0.0001	0.0000	0.0000		
28	0.0001	0.0001	0.0000	0.0000				
29	0.0000	0.0000						
30								
35								
40								
45								
50								

Table B*   Present Value of \$1 Received per Period $\dfrac{1-(1+r)^{-n}}{r}$

n	1%	2%	3%	4%	5%	6%	7%
1	0.9901	0.9804	0.9709	0.9615	0.9524	0.9434	0.9346
2	1.9704	1.9416	1.9135	1.8861	1.8594	1.8334	1.8080
3	2.9410	2.8839	2.8286	2.7751	2.7232	2.6730	2.6243
4	3.9020	3.8077	3.7171	3.6299	3.5460	3.4651	3.3872
5	4.8534	4.7135	4.5797	4.4518	4.3295	4.2124	4.1002
6	5.7955	5.6014	5.4172	5.2421	5.0757	4.9173	4.7665
7	6.7282	6.4720	6.2303	6.0021	5.7864	5.5824	5.3893
8	7.6517	7.3255	7.0197	6.7327	6.4632	6.2098	5.9713
9	8.5660	8.1622	7.7861	7.4353	7.1078	6.8017	6.5152
10	9.4713	8.9826	8.5302	8.1109	7.7217	7.3601	7.0236
11	10.3676	9.7868	9.2526	8.7605	8.3064	7.8869	7.4987
12	11.2551	10.5753	9.9540	9.3851	8.8633	8.3838	7.9427
13	12.1337	11.3484	10.6350	9.9856	9.3936	8.8527	8.3577
14	13.0037	12.1062	11.2961	10.5631	9.8986	9.2950	8.7455
15	13.8651	12.8493	11.9379	11.1184	10.3797	9.7122	9.1079
16	14.7179	13.5777	12.5611	11.6523	10.8378	10.1059	9.4466
17	15.5623	14.2919	13.1661	12.1657	11.2741	10.4773	9.7632
18	16.3983	14.9920	13.7535	12.6593	11.6896	10.8276	10.0591
19	17.2260	15.6785	14.3238	13.1339	12.0853	11.1581	10.3356
20	18.0456	16.3514	14.8775	13.5903	12.4622	11.4699	10.5940
21	18.8570	17.0112	15.4150	14.0292	12.8212	11.7641	10.8355
22	19.6604	17.6580	15.9369	14.4511	13.1630	12.0416	11.0612
23	20.4558	18.2922	16.4436	14.8568	13.4886	12.3034	11.2722
24	21.2434	18.9139	16.9355	15.2470	13.7986	12.5504	11.4693
25	22.0232	19.5235	17.4131	15.6221	14.0939	12.7834	11.6536
26	22.7952	20.1210	17.8768	15.9828	14.3752	13.0032	11.8258
27	23.5596	20.7069	18.3270	16.3296	14.6430	13.2105	11.9867
28	24.3164	21.2813	18.7641	16.6631	14.8981	13.4062	12.1371
29	25.0658	21.8444	19.1885	16.9837	15.1411	13.5907	12.2777
30	25.8077	22.3965	19.6004	17.2920	15.3725	13.7648	12.4090
31	26.5423	22.9377	20.0004	17.5885	15.5928	13.9291	12.5318
32	27.2696	23.4683	20.3888	17.8736	15.8027	14.0840	12.6466
33	27.9897	23.9886	20.7658	18.1476	16.0025	14.2302	12.7538
34	28.7027	24.4986	21.1318	18.4112	16.1929	14.3681	12.8540
35	29.4086	24.9986	21.4872	18.6646	16.3742	14.4982	12.9477
40	32.8347	27.3555	23.1148	19.7928	17.1591	15.0463	13.3317
45	36.0945	29.4902	24.5187	20.7200	17.7741	15.4558	13.6055
50	39.1961	31.4236	25.7298	21.4822	18.2559	15.7619	13.8007

* Reproduced by permission from Harold Bierman, Jr., and Seymour Smidt, *The Capital Budgeting Decision*, The Macmillian Company, New York, 1960.

Table B   Present Value of $1 Received per Period   (Continued)

n	8%	9%	10%	11%	12%	13%	14%
1	0.9259	0.9174	0.9091	0.9009	0.8929	0.8850	0.8772
2	1.7833	1.7591	1.7355	1.7125	1.6901	1.6681	1.6467
3	2.5771	2.5313	2.4869	2.4437	2.4018	2.3612	2.3216
4	3.3121	3.2397	3.1699	3.1024	3.0373	2.9745	2.9137
5	3.9927	3.8897	3.7908	3.6959	3.6048	3.5172	3.4331
6	4.6229	4.4859	4.3553	4.2305	4.1114	3.9975	3.8887
7	5.2064	5.0330	4.8684	4.7122	4.5638	4.4226	4.2883
8	5.7466	5.5348	5.3349	5.1461	4.9676	4.7988	4.6389
9	6.2469	5.9952	5.7590	5.5370	5.3282	5.1317	4.9464
10	6.7101	6.4177	6.1446	5.8892	5.6502	5.4262	5.2161
11	7.1390	6.8051	6.4951	6.2065	5.9377	5.6869	5.4527
12	7.5361	7.1607	6.8137	6.4924	6.1944	5.9176	5.6603
13	7.9038	7.4869	7.1034	6.7499	6.4235	6.1218	5.8424
14	8.2442	7.7862	7.3667	6.9819	6.6282	6.3025	6.0021
15	8.5595	8.0607	7.6061	7.1909	6.8109	6.4624	6.1422
16	8.8514	8.3126	7.8237	7.3792	6.9740	6.6039	6.2651
17	9.1216	8.5436	8.0216	7.5488	7.1196	6.7291	6.3729
18	9.3719	8.7556	8.2014	7.7016	7.2497	6.8399	6.4674
19	9.6036	8.9501	8.3649	7.8393	7.3658	6.9380	6.5504
20	9.8181	9.1285	8.5136	7.9633	7.4694	7.0248	6.6231
21	10.0168	9.2922	8.6487	8.0751	7.5620	7.1015	6.6870
22	10.2007	9.4424	8.7715	8.1757	7.6446	7.1695	6.7429
23	10.3711	9.5802	8.8832	8.2664	7.7184	7.2297	6.7921
24	10.5288	9.7066	8.9847	8.3481	7.7843	7.2829	6.8351
25	10.6748	9.8226	9.0770	8.4217	7.8431	7.3300	6.8729
26	10.8100	9.9290	9.1609	8.4881	7.8957	7.3717	6.9061
27	10.9352	10.0266	9.2372	8.5478	7.9426	7.4086	6.9352
28	11.0511	10.1161	9.3066	8.6016	7.9844	7.4412	6.9607
29	11.1584	10.1983	9.3696	8.6501	8.0218	7.4701	6.9830
30	11.2578	10.2737	9.4269	8.6938	8.0552	7.4957	7.0027
31	11.3498	10.3428	9.4790	8.7331	8.0850	7.5183	7.0199
32	11.4350	10.4062	9.5264	8.7686	8.1116	7.5383	7 0350
33	11.5139	10.4644	9.5694	8.8005	8.1354	7.5560	7.0482
34	11.5869	10.5178	9.6086	8.8293	8.1566	7.5717	7.0599
35	11.6546	10.5668	9.6442	8.8552	8.1755	7.5856	7.0700
40	11.9246	10.7574	9.7791	8.9511	8.2438	7.6344	7.1050
45	12.1084	10.8812	9.8628	9.0079	8.2825	7.6609	7.1232
50	12.2335	10.9617	9.9148	9.0417	8.3045	7.6752	7.1327

Table B   Present Value of $1 Received per Period   (Continued)

n	15%	16%	17%	18%	19%	20%	21%
1	0.8696	0.8621	0.8547	0.8475	0.8403	0.8333	0.8264
2	1.6257	1.6052	1.5852	1.5656	1.5465	1.5278	1.5095
3	2.2832	2.2459	2.2096	2.1743	2.1399	2.1065	2.0739
4	2.8550	2.7982	2.7432	2.6901	2.6386	2.5887	2.5404
5	3.3522	3.2743	3.1993	3.1272	3.0576	2.9906	2.9260
6	3.7845	3.6847	3.5892	3.4976	3.4098	3.3255	3.2446
7	4.1604	4.0386	3.9224	3.8115	3.7057	3.6046	3.5079
8	4.4873	4.3436	4.2072	4.0776	3.9544	3.8372	3.7256
9	4.7716	4.6065	4.4506	4.3030	4.1633	4.0310	3.9054
10	5.0188	4.8332	4.6586	4.4941	4.3389	4.1925	4.0541
11	5.2337	5.0286	4.8364	4.6560	4.4865	4.3271	4.1769
12	5.4206	5.1971	4.9884	4.7932	4.6105	4.4392	4.2784
13	5.5831	5.3423	5.1183	4.9095	4.7147	4.5327	4.3624
14	5.7245	5.4675	5.2293	5.0081	4.8023	4.6106	4.4317
15	5.8474	5.5755	5.3242	5.0916	4.8759	4.6755	4.4890
16	5.9542	5.6685	5.4053	5.1624	4.9377	4.7296	4.5364
17	6.0472	5.7487	5.4746	5.2223	4.9897	4.7746	4.5755
18	6.1280	5.8178	5.5339	5.2732	5.0333	4.8122	4.6079
19	6.1982	5.8775	5.5845	5.3162	5.0700	4.8435	4.6346
20	6.2593	5.9288	5.6278	5.3527	5.1009	4.8696	4.6567
21	6.3125	5.9731	5.6648	5.3837	5.1268	4.8913	4.6750
22	6.3587	6.0113	5.6964	5.4099	5.1486	4.9094	4.6900
23	6.3988	6.0442	5.7234	5.4321	5.1668	4.9245	4.7025
24	6.4338	6.0726	5.7465	5.4509	5.1822	4.9371	4.7128
25	6.4641	6.0971	5.7662	5.4669	5.1951	4.9476	4.7213
26	6.4906	6.1182	5.7831	5.4804	5.2060	4.9563	4.7284
27	6.5135	6.1364	5.7975	5.4919	5.2151	4.9636	4.7342
28	6.5335	6.1520	5.8099	5.5016	5.2228	4.9697	4.7390
29	6.5509	6.1656	5.8204	5.5098	5.2292	4.9747	4.7430
30	6.5660	6.1772	5.8294	5.5168	5.2347	4.9789	4.7463
31	6.5791	6.1872	5.8371	5.5227	5.2392	4.9824	4.7490
32	6.5905	6.1959	5.8437	5.5277	5.2430	4.9854	4.7512
33	6.6005	6.2034	5.8493	5.5320	5.2462	4.9878	4.7531
34	6.6091	6.2098	5.8541	5.5356	5.2489	4.9898	4.7546
35	6.6166	6.2153	5.8582	5.5386	5.2512	4.9915	4.7559
40	6.6418	6.2335	5.8714	5.5482	5.2582	4.9966	4.7596
45	6.6543	6.2421	5.8773	5.5523	5.2611	4.9986	4.7610
50	6.6605	6.2463	5.8801	5.5541	5.2623	4.9995	4.7616

Table B   Present Value of $1 Received per Period   (Continued)

n	22%	23%	24%	25%	26%	27%	28%
1	0.8197	0.8130	0.8065	0.8000	0.7937	0.7874	0.7813
2	1.4915	1.4740	1.4568	1.4400	1.4235	1.4074	1.3916
3	2.0422	2.0114	1.9813	1.9520	1.9234	1.8956	1.8684
4	2.4936	2.4438	2.4043	2.3616	2.3202	2.2800	2.2410
5	2.8636	2.8035	2.7454	2.6893	2.6351	2.5827	2.5320
6	3.1669	3.0923	3.0205	2.9514	2.8850	2.8210	2.7594
7	3.4155	3.3270	3.2423	3.1611	3.0833	3.0087	2.9370
8	3.6193	3.5179	3.4212	3.3289	3.2407	3.1564	3.0758
9	3.7863	3.6731	3.5655	3.4631	3.3657	3.2728	3.1842
10	3.9232	3.7993	3.6819	3.5705	3.4648	3.3644	3.2689
11	4.0354	3.9018	3.7757	3.6564	3.5435	3.4365	3.3351
12	4.1274	3.9852	3.8514	3.7251	3.6059	3.4933	3.3868
13	4.2028	4.0530	3.9124	3.7801	3.6555	3.5381	3.4272
14	4.2646	4.1082	3.9616	3.8241	3.6949	3.5733	3.4587
15	4.3152	4.1530	4.0013	3.8593	3.7261	3.6010	3.4834
16	4.3567	4.1894	4.0333	3.8874	3.7509	3.6228	3.5026
17	4.3908	4.2190	4.0591	3.9099	3.7705	3.6400	3.5177
18	4.4187	4.2431	4.0799	3.9279	3.7861	3.6536	3.5294
19	4.4415	4.2627	4.0967	3.9424	3.7985	3.6642	3.5386
20	4.4603	4.2786	4.1103	3.9539	3.8083	3.6726	3.5458
21	4.4756	4.2916	4.1212	3.9631	3.8161	3.6792	3.5514
22	4.4882	4.3021	4.1300	3.9705	3.8223	3.6844	3.5558
23	4.4985	4.3106	4.1371	3.9764	3.8273	3.6885	3.5592
24	4.5070	4.3176	4.1428	3.9811	3.8312	3.6918	3.5619
25	4.5139	4.3232	4.1474	3.9849	3.8342	3.6943	3.5640
26	4.5196	4.3278	4.1511	3.9879	3.8367	3.6963	3.5656
27	4.5243	4.3316	4.1542	3.9903	3.8387	3.6979	3.5669
28	4.5281	4.3346	4.1566	3.9923	3.8402	3.6991	3.5679
29	4.5312	4.3371	4.1585	3.9938	3.8414	3.7001	3.5687
30	4.5338	4.3391	4.1601	3.9950	3.8424	3.7009	3.5693
31	4.5359	4.3407	4.1614	3.9960	3.8432	3.7015	3.5697
32	4.5376	4.3421	4.1624	3.9968	3.8438	3.7019	3.5701
33	4.5390	4.3431	4.1632	3.9975	3.8443	3.7023	3.5704
34	4.5402	4.3440	4.1639	3.9980	3.8447	3.7026	3.5706
35	4.5411	4.3447	4.1644	3.9984	3.8450	3.7028	3.5708
40	4.5439	4.3467	4.1659	3.9995	3.8458	3.7034	3.5712
45	4.5449	4.3474	4.1664	3.9998	3.8460	3.7036	3.5714
50	4.5452	4.3477	4.1666	3.9999	3.8461	3.7037	3.5714

Table B Present Value of $1 Received per Period (Continued)

n	29%	30%	31%	32%	33%	34%	35%
1	0.7752	0.7692	0.7634	0.7576	0.7519	0.7463	0.7407
2	1.3761	1.3609	1.3461	1.3315	1.3172	1.3032	1.2894
3	1.8420	1.8161	1.7909	1.7663	1.7423	1.7188	1.6959
4	2.2031	2.1662	2.1305	2.0957	2.0618	2.0290	1.9969
5	2.4830	2.4356	2.3897	2.3452	2.3021	2.2604	2.2200
6	2.7000	2.6427	2.5875	2.5342	2.4828	2.4331	2.3852
7	2.8682	2.8021	2.7368	2.6775	2.6187	2.5620	2.5075
8	2.9986	2.9247	2.8539	2.7860	2.7208	2.6582	2.5982
9	3.0997	3.0190	2.9419	2.8681	2.7976	2.7300	2.6653
10	3.1781	3.0915	3.0091	2.9304	2.8553	2.7836	2.7150
11	3.2388	3.1473	3.0604	2.9776	2.8987	2.8236	2.7519
12	3.2859	3.1903	3.0995	3.0133	2.9314	2.8534	2.7792
13	3.3224	3.2233	3.1294	3.0404	2.9559	2.8757	2.7994
14	3.3507	3.2487	3.1522	3.0609	2.9744	2.8923	2.8144
15	3.3726	3.2682	3.1696	3.0764	2.9883	2.9047	2.8255
16	3.3896	3.2832	3.1829	3.0882	2.9987	2.9140	2.8337
17	3.4028	3.2948	3.1931	3.0971	3.0065	2.9209	2.8398
18	3.4130	3.3037	3.2008	3.1039	3.0124	2.9260	2.8443
19	3.4210	3.3105	3.2067	3.1090	3.0169	2.9299	2.8476
20	3.4271	3.3158	3.2112	3.1129	3.0202	2.9327	2.8501
21	3.4319	3.3198	3.2147	3.1158	3.0227	2.9349	2.8520
22	3.4356	3.3230	3.2173	3.1180	3.0246	2.9365	2.8533
23	3.4384	3.3253	3.2193	3.1197	3.0260	2.9377	2.8543
24	3.4406	3.3272	3.2209	3.1210	3.0271	2.9386	2.8550
25	3.4423	3.3286	3.2220	3.1220	3.0279	2.9392	2.8556
26	3.4437	3.3297	3.2229	3.1227	3.0285	2.9397	2.8560
27	3.4447	3.3305	3.2236	3.1233	3.0289	2.9401	2.8563
28	3.4455	3.3312	3.2241	3.1237	3.0293	2.9404	2.8565
29	3.4461	3.3316	3.2245	3.1240	3.0295	2.9406	2.8567
30	3.4466	3.3321	3.2248	3.1242	3.0297	2.9407	2.8568
31	3.4470	3.3324	3.2251	3.1244	3.0299	2.9408	2.8569
32	3.4473	3.3326	3.2252	3.1246	3.0300	2.9409	2.8569
33	3.4475	3.3328	3.2254	3.1247	3.0301	2.9410	2.8570
34	3.4477	3.3329	3.2255	3.1248	3.0301	2.9410	2.8570
35	3.4478	3.3330	3.2256	3.1248	3.0302	2.9411	2.8571
40	3.4481	3.3332	3.2257	3.1250	3.0303	2.9412	2.8571
45	3.4482	3.3333	3.2258	3.1250	3.0303	2.9412	2.8571
50	3.4483	3.3333	3.2258	3.1250	3.0303	2.9412	2.8571

Table B Present Value of $1 Received per Period (Continued)

n	36%	37%	38%	39%	40%	41%	42%
1	0.7353	0.7299	0.7246	0.7194	0.7143	0.7092	0.7042
2	1.2760	1.2627	1.2497	1.2370	1.2245	1.2122	1.2002
3	1.6735	1.6516	1.6302	1.6093	1.5889	1.5689	1.5494
4	1.9658	1.9355	1.9060	1.8772	1.8492	1.8219	1.7954
5	2.1807	2.1427	2.1058	2.0699	2.0352	2.0014	1.9686
6	2.3388	2.2939	2.2506	2.2086	2.1680	2.1286	2.0905
7	2.4550	2.4043	2.3555	2.3083	2.2628	2.2189	2.1764
8	2.5404	2.4849	2.4315	2.3801	2.3306	2.2829	2.2369
9	2.6033	2.5437	2.4866	2.4317	2.3790	2.3283	2.2795
10	2.6495	2.5867	2.5265	2.4689	2.4136	2.3605	2.3095
11	2.6834	2.6180	2.5555	2.4956	2.4383	2.3833	2.3307
12	2.7084	2.6409	2.5764	2.5148	2.4559	2.3995	2.3455
13	2.7268	2.6576	2.5916	2.5286	2.4685	2.4110	2.3560
14	2.7403	2.6698	2.6026	2.5386	2.4775	2.4192	2.3634
15	2.7502	2.6787	2.6106	2.5457	2.4839	2.4249	2.3686
16	2.7575	2.6852	2.6164	2.5509	2.4885	2.4290	2.3722
17	2.7629	2.6899	2.6206	2.5546	2.4918	2.4319	2.3748
18	2.7668	2.6934	2.6236	2.5573	2.4941	2.4340	2.3766
19	2.7697	2.6959	2.6258	2.5592	2.4958	2.4355	2.3779
20	2.7718	2.6977	2.6274	2.5606	2.4970	2.4365	2 3788
21	2.7734	2.6991	2.6285	2.5616	2.4979	2.4372	2.3794
22	2.7746	2.7000	2.6294	2.5623	2.4985	2.4378	2.3799
23	2.7754	2.7008	2.6300	2.5628	2.4989	2.4381	2.3802
24	2.7760	2.7013	2.6304	2.5632	2.4992	2.4384	2.3804
25	2.7765	2.7017	2.6307	2.5634	2.4994	2.4386	2.3806
26	2.7768	2.7019	2.6310	2.5636	2.4996	2.4387	2.3807
27	2.7771	2.7022	2.6311	2.5637	2.4997	2.4388	2.3808
28	2.7773	2.7023	2.6313	2.5638	2.4998	2.4389	2.3808
29	2.7774	2.7024	2.6313	2.5639	2.4999	2.4389	2.3809
30	2.7775	2.7025	2.6314	2.5640	2.4999	2.4389	2.3809
31	2.7776	2.7025	2.6315	2.5640	2.4999	2.4390	2.3809
32	2.7776	2.7026	2.6315	2.5640	2.4999	2.4390	2.3809
33	2.7777	2.7026	2.6315	2.5641	2.5000	2.4390	2.3809
34	2.7777	2.7026	2.6315	2.5641	2.5000	2.4390	2.3809
35	2.7777	2.7027	2.6315	2.5641	2.5000	2.4390	2.3809
40	2.7778	2.7027	2.6316	2.5641	2.5000	2.4390	2.3810
45	2.7778	2.7027	2.6316	2.5641	2.5000	2.4390	2.3810
50	2.7778	2.7027	2.6316	2.5641	2.5000	2.4390	2.3810

Table **B**   Present Value of $1 Received per Period   (Continued)

n	43%	44%	45%	46%	47%	48%	49%
1	0.6993	0.6944	0.6897	0.6849	0.6803	0.6757	0.6711
2	1.1883	1.1767	1.1653	1.1541	1.1430	1.1322	1.1216
3	1.5303	1.5116	1.4933	1.4754	1.4579	1.4407	1.4239
4	1.7694	1.7442	1.7195	1.6955	1.6720	1.6491	1.6268
5	1.9367	1.9057	1.8755	1.8462	1.8177	1.7899	1.7629
6	2.0536	2.0178	1.9831	1.9495	1.9168	1.8851	1.8543
7	2.1354	2.0957	2.0573	2.0202	1.9842	1.9494	1.9156
8	2.1926	2.1498	2.1085	2.0686	2.0301	1.9928	1.9568
9	2.2326	2.1874	2.1438	2.1018	2.0613	2.0222	1.9844
10	2.2605	2.2134	2.1681	2.1245	2.0825	2.0420	2.0030
11	2.2801	2.2316	2.1849	2.1401	2.0969	2.0554	2.0154
12	2.2938	2.2441	2.1965	2.1507	2.1068	2.0645	2.0238
13	2.3033	2.2529	2.2045	2.1580	2.1134	2.0706	2.0294
14	2.3100	2.2589	2.2100	2.1630	2.1180	2.0747	2.0331
15	2.3147	2.2632	2.2138	2.1665	2.1211	2.0775	2.0357
16	2.3180	2.2661	2.2164	2.1688	2.1232	2.0794	2.0374
17	2.3203	2.2681	2.2182	2.1704	2.1246	2.0807	2.0385
18	2.3219	2.2695	2.2195	2.1715	2.1256	2.0815	2.0393
19	2.3230	2.2705	2.2203	2.1723	2.1263	2.0821	2.0398
20	2.3238	2.2712	2.2209	2.1728	2.1267	2.0825	2.0401
21	2.3243	2.2717	2.2213	2.1731	2.1270	2.0828	2.0403
22	2.3247	2.2720	2.2216	2.1734	2.1272	2.0830	2.0405
23	2.3250	2.2722	2.2218	2.1736	2.1274	2.0831	2.0406
24	2.3251	2.2724	2.2219	2.1737	2.1275	2.0832	2.0407
25	2.3253	2.2725	2.2220	2.1737	2.1275	2.0832	2.0407
26	2.3254	2.2726	2.2221	2.1738	2.1276	2.0833	2.0408
27	2.3254	2.2726	2.2221	2.1738	2.1276	2.0833	2.0408
28	2.3255	2.2726	2.2222	2.1739	2.1276	2.0833	2.0408
29	2.3255	2.2727	2.2222	2.1739	2.1276	2.0833	2.0408
30	2.3255	2.2727	2.2222	2.1739	2.1276	2.0833	2.0408
31	2.3255	2.2727	2.2222	2.1739	2.1276	2.0833	2.0408
32	2.3256	2.2727	2.2222	2.1739	2.1277	2.0833	2.0408
33	2.3256	2.2727	2.2222	2.1739	2.1277	2.0833	2.0408
34	2.3256	2.2727	2.2222	2.1739	2.1277	2.0833	2.0408
35	2.3256	2.2727	2.2222	2.1739	2.1277	2.0833	2.0408
40	2.3256	2.2727	2.2222	2.1739	2.1277	2.0833	2.0408
45	2.3256	2.2727	2.2222	2.1739	2.1277	2.0833	2.0408
50	2.3256	2.2727	2.2222	2.1739	2.1277	2.0833	2.0408

Table C Standardized Normal Density Function, f(s)*

$$f(s) = f(-s)$$

s	0.00	0.01	0.02	0.03	0.04	0.05	0.06	0.07	0.08	0.09
0.0	0.3989	0.3989	0.3989	0.3988	0.3986	0.3984	0.3982	0.3980	0.3977	0.3973
0.1	0.3970	0.3965	0.3961	0.3956	0.3951	0.3945	0.3939	0.3932	0.3925	0.3918
0.2	0.3910	0.3902	0.3894	0.3885	0.3876	0.3867	0.3857	0.3847	0.3836	0.3825
0.3	0.3814	0.3802	0.3790	0.3778	0.3765	0.3752	0.3739	0.3725	0.3712	0.3697
0.4	0.3683	0.3668	0.3653	0.3637	0.3621	0.3605	0.3589	0.3572	0.3555	0.3538
0.5	0.3521	0.3503	0.3485	0.3467	0.3448	0.3429	0.3410	0.3391	0.3372	0.3352
0.6	0.3332	0.3312	0.3292	0.3271	0.3251	0.3230	0.3209	0.3187	0.3166	0.3144
0.7	0.3123	0.3101	0.3079	0.3056	0.3034	0.3011	0.2989	0.2966	0.2943	0.2920
0.8	0.2897	0.2874	0.2850	0.2827	0.2803	0.2780	0.2756	0.2732	0.2709	0.2685
0.9	0.2661	0.2637	0.2613	0.2589	0.2565	0.2541	0.2516	0.2492	0.2468	0.2444
1.0	0.2420	0.2396	0.2371	0.2347	0.2323	0.2299	0.2275	0.2251	0.2227	0.2203
1.1	0.2179	0.2155	0.2131	0.2107	0.2083	0.2059	0.2036	0.2012	0.1989	0.1965
1.2	0.1942	0.1919	0.1895	0.1872	0.1849	0.1826	0.1804	0.1781	0.1758	0.1736
1.3	0.1714	0.1691	0.1669	0.1647	0.1626	0.1604	0.1582	0.1561	0.1539	0.1518
1.4	0.1497	0.1476	0.1456	0.1435	0.1415	0.1394	0.1374	0.1354	0.1334	0.1315
1.5	0.1295	0.1276	0.1257	0.1238	0.1219	0.1200	0.1182	0.1163	0.1145	0.1127
1.6	0.1109	0.1092	0.1074	0.1057	0.1040	0.1023	0.1006	0.09893	0.09728	0.09566
1.7	0.09405	0.09246	0.09089	0.08933	0.08780	0.08628	0.08478	0.08329	0.08183	0.08038
1.8	0.07895	0.07754	0.07614	0.07477	0.07341	0.07206	0.07074	0.06943	0.06814	0.06687
1.9	0.06562	0.06438	0.06316	0.06195	0.06077	0.05959	0.05844	0.05730	0.05618	0.05508

s	0.00	0.01	0.02	0.03	0.04	0.05	0.06	0.07	0.08	0.09
2.0	0.05399	0.05292	0.05186	0.05082	0.04980	0.04879	0.04780	0.04682	0.04586	0.04491
2.1	0.04398	0.04307	0.04217	0.04128	0.04041	0.03955	0.03871	0.03788	0.03706	0.03626
2.2	0.03547	0.03470	0.03394	0.03319	0.03246	0.03174	0.03103	0.03034	0.02965	0.02898
2.3	0.02833	0.02768	0.02705	0.02643	0.02582	0.02522	0.02463	0.02406	0.02349	0.02294
2.4	0.02239	0.02186	0.02134	0.02083	0.02033	0.01984	0.01936	0.01888	0.01842	0.01797
2.5	0.01753	0.01709	0.01667	0.01625	0.01585	0.01545	0.01506	0.01468	0.01431	0.01394
2.6	0.01358	0.01323	0.01289	0.01256	0.01223	0.01191	0.01160	0.01130	0.01100	0.01071
2.7	0.01042	0.01014	$0.0^{2}9871$	$0.0^{2}9606$	$0.0^{2}9347$	$0.0^{2}9094$	$0.0^{2}8846$	$0.0^{2}8605$	$0.0^{2}8370$	$0.0^{2}8140$
2.8	$0.0^{2}7915$	$0.0^{2}7697$	$0.0^{2}7483$	$0.0^{2}7274$	$0.0^{2}7071$	$0.0^{2}6873$	$0.0^{2}6679$	$0.0^{2}6491$	$0.0^{2}6307$	$0.0^{2}6127$
2.9	$0.0^{2}5953$	$0.0^{2}5782$	$0.0^{2}5616$	$0.0^{2}5454$	$0.0^{2}5296$	$0.0^{2}5143$	$0.0^{2}4993$	$0.0^{2}4847$	$0.0^{2}4705$	$0.0^{2}4567$
3.0	$0.0^{2}4432$	$0.0^{2}4301$	$0.0^{2}4173$	$0.0^{2}4049$	$0.0^{2}3928$	$0.0^{2}3810$	$0.0^{2}3695$	$0.0^{2}3584$	$0.0^{2}3475$	$0.0^{2}3370$
3.1	$0.0^{2}3267$	$0.0^{2}3167$	$0.0^{2}3070$	$0.0^{2}2975$	$0.0^{2}2884$	$0.0^{2}2794$	$0.0^{2}2707$	$0.0^{2}2623$	$0.0^{2}2541$	$0.0^{2}2461$
3.2	$0.0^{2}2384$	$0.0^{2}2309$	$0.0^{2}2236$	$0.0^{2}2165$	$0.0^{2}2096$	$0.0^{2}2029$	$0.0^{2}1964$	$0.0^{2}1901$	$0.0^{2}1840$	$0.0^{2}1780$
3.3	$0.0^{2}1723$	$0.0^{2}1667$	$0.0^{2}1612$	$0.0^{2}1560$	$0.0^{2}1508$	$0.0^{2}1459$	$0.0^{2}1411$	$0.0^{2}1364$	$0.0^{2}1319$	$0.0^{2}1275$
3.4	$0.0^{2}1232$	$0.0^{2}1191$	$0.0^{2}1151$	$0.0^{2}1112$	$0.0^{2}1075$	$0.0^{2}1038$	$0.0^{2}1003$	$0.0^{3}9689$	$0.0^{3}9358$	$0.0^{3}9037$
3.5	$0.0^{3}8727$	$0.0^{3}8426$	$0.0^{3}8135$	$0.0^{3}7853$	$0.0^{3}7581$	$0.0^{3}7317$	$0.0^{3}7061$	$0.0^{3}6814$	$0.0^{3}6575$	$0.0^{3}6343$
3.6	$0.0^{3}6119$	$0.0^{3}5902$	$0.0^{3}5693$	$0.0^{3}5490$	$0.0^{3}5294$	$0.0^{3}5105$	$0.0^{3}4921$	$0.0^{3}4744$	$0.0^{3}4573$	$0.0^{3}4408$
3.7	$0.0^{3}4248$	$0.0^{3}4093$	$0.0^{3}3944$	$0.0^{3}3800$	$0.0^{3}3661$	$0.0^{3}3526$	$0.0^{3}3396$	$0.0^{3}3271$	$0.0^{3}3149$	$0.0^{3}3032$
3.8	$0.0^{3}2919$	$0.0^{3}2810$	$0.0^{3}2705$	$0.0^{3}2604$	$0.0^{3}2506$	$0.0^{3}2411$	$0.0^{3}2320$	$0.0^{3}2232$	$0.0^{3}2147$	$0.0^{3}2065$
3.9	$0.0^{3}1987$	$0.0^{3}1910$	$0.0^{3}1837$	$0.0^{3}1766$	$0.0^{3}1698$	$0.0^{3}1633$	$0.0^{3}1569$	$0.0^{3}1508$	$0.0^{3}1449$	$0.0^{3}1393$
4.0	$0.0^{3}1338$	$0.0^{3}1286$	$0.0^{3}1235$	$0.0^{3}1186$	$0.0^{3}1140$	$0.0^{3}1094$	$0.0^{3}1051$	$0.0^{3}1009$	$0.0^{4}9687$	$0.0^{4}9299$

* From A. Hald, *Statistical Tables and Formulas*, John Wiley & Sons, Inc., New York, 1952; reproduced by permission of Professor A. Hald and the publishers.

Table D The Standardized Normal Distribution Function, F(s)

s	0.00	0.01	0.02	0.03	0.04	0.05	0.06	0.07	0.08	0.09
0.0	0.5000	0.5040	0.5080	0.5120	0.5160	0.5199	0.5239	0.5279	0.5319	0.5359
0.1	0.5398	0.5438	0.5478	0.5517	0.5557	0.5596	0.5636	0.5675	0.5714	0.5753
0.2	0.5793	0.5832	0.5871	0.5910	0.5948	0.5987	0.6026	0.6064	0.6103	0.6141
0.3	0.6179	0.6217	0.6255	0.6293	0.6331	0.6368	0.6406	0.6443	0.6480	0.6517
0.4	0.6554	0.6591	0.6628	0.6664	0.6700	0.6736	0.6772	0.6808	0.6844	0.6879
0.5	0.6915	0.6950	0.6985	0.7019	0.7054	0.7088	0.7123	0.7157	0.7190	0.7224
0.6	0.7257	0.7291	0.7324	0.7357	0.7389	0.7422	0.7454	0.7486	0.7517	0.7549
0.7	0.7580	0.7611	0.7642	0.7673	0.7703	0.7734	0.7764	0.7794	0.7823	0.7852
0.8	0.7881	0.7910	0.7939	0.7967	0.7995	0.8023	0.8051	0.8078	0.8106	0.8133
0.9	0.8159	0.8186	0.8212	0.8238	0.8264	0.8289	0.8315	0.8340	0.8365	0.8389
1.0	0.8413	0.8438	0.8461	0.8485	0.8508	0.8531	0.8554	0.8577	0.8599	0.8621
1.1	0.8643	0.8665	0.8686	0.8708	0.8729	0.8749	0.8770	0.8790	0.8810	0.8830
1.2	0.8849	0.8869	0.8888	0.8907	0.8925	0.8944	0.8962	0.8980	0.8997	0.90147
1.3	0.90320	0.90490	0.90658	0.90824	0.90988	0.91149	0.91309	0.91466	0.91621	0.91774
1.4	0.91924	0.92073	0.92220	0.92364	0.92507	0.92647	0.92785	0.92922	0.93056	0.93189
1.5	0.93319	0.93448	0.93574	0.93699	0.93822	0.93943	0.94062	0.94179	0.94295	0.94408
1.6	0.94520	0.94630	0.94738	0.94845	0.94950	0.95053	0.95154	0.95254	0.95352	0.95449
1.7	0.95543	0.95637	0.95728	0.95818	0.95907	0.95994	0.96080	0.96164	0.96246	0.96327
1.8	0.96407	0.96485	0.96562	0.96638	0.96712	0.96784	0.96856	0.96926	0.96995	0.97062
1.9	0.97128	0.97193	0.97257	0.97320	0.97381	0.97441	0.97500	0.97558	0.97615	0.97670
2.0	0.97725	0.97778	0.97831	0.97882	0.97932	0.97982	0.98030	0.98077	0.98124	0.98169
2.1	0.98214	0.98257	0.98300	0.98341	0.98382	0.98422	0.98461	0.98500	0.98537	0.98574
2.2	0.98610	0.98645	0.98679	0.98713	0.98745	0.98778	0.98809	0.98840	0.98870	0.98899
2.3	0.98928	0.98956	0.98983	$0.9^{2}0097$	$0.9^{2}0358$	$0.9^{2}0613$	$0.9^{2}0863$	$0.9^{2}1106$	$0.9^{2}1344$	$0.9^{2}1576$
2.4	$0.9^{2}1802$	$0.9^{2}2024$	$0.9^{2}2240$	$0.9^{2}2451$	$0.9^{2}2656$	$0.9^{2}2857$	$0.9^{2}3053$	$0.9^{2}3244$	$0.9^{2}3431$	$0.9^{2}3613$
2.5	$0.9^{2}3790$	$0.9^{2}3963$	$0.9^{2}4132$	$0.9^{2}4297$	$0.9^{2}4457$	$0.9^{2}4614$	$0.9^{2}4766$	$0.9^{2}4915$	$0.9^{2}5060$	$0.9^{2}5201$
3.0	$0.9^{2}8650$	$0.9^{2}8694$	$0.9^{2}8736$	$0.9^{2}8777$	$0.9^{2}8817$	$0.9^{2}8856$	$0.9^{2}8893$	$0.9^{2}8930$	$0.9^{2}8965$	$0.9^{2}8999$
3.5	$0.9^{3}7674$	$0.9^{3}7759$	$0.9^{3}7842$	$0.9^{3}7922$	$0.9^{3}7999$	$0.9^{3}8074$	$0.9^{3}8146$	$0.9^{3}8215$	$0.9^{3}8282$	$0.9^{3}8347$
4.0	$0.9^{4}6833$	$0.9^{4}6964$	$0.9^{4}7090$	$0.9^{4}7211$	$0.9^{4}7327$	$0.9^{4}7439$	$0.9^{4}7546$	$0.9^{4}7649$	$0.9^{4}7748$	$0.9^{4}7843$

For example: $F(2.41) = .9^{2}024 = .99024$.

* From A. Hald, Statistical Tables and Formulas, John Wiley & Sons, Inc., New York, 1952; reproduced by permission of Professor A. Hald and the publishers.

Table E N(D)—Loss Function*

Loss line

$\overline{X}$ $-D$ $\overline{X}$ D

D	.00	.01	.02	.03	.04	.05	.06	.07	.08	.09
.0	.3989	.3940	.3890	.3841	.3793	.3744	.3697	.3649	.3602	.3556
.1	.3509	.3464	.3418	.3373	.3328	.3284	.3240	.3197	.3154	.3111
.2	.3069	.3027	.2986	.2944	.2904	.2863	.2824	.2784	.2745	.2706
.3	.2668	.2630	.2592	.2555	.2518	.2481	.2445	.2409	.2374	.2339
.4	.2304	.2270	.2236	.2203	.2169	.2137	.2104	.2072	.2040	.2009
.5	.1978	.1947	.1917	.1887	.1857	.1828	.1799	.1771	.1742	.1714
.6	.1687	.1659	.1633	.1606	.1580	.1554	.1528	.1503	.1478	.1453
.7	.1429	.1405	.1381	.1358	.1334	.1312	.1289	.1267	.1245	.1223
.8	.1202	.1181	.1160	.1140	.1120	.1100	.1080	.1061	.1042	.1023
.9	.1004	.09860	.09680	.09503	.09328	.09156	.08986	.08819	.08654	.08491
1.0	.08332	.08174	.08019	.07866	.07716	.07568	.07422	.07279	.07138	.06999
1.1	.06862	.06727	.06595	.06465	.06336	.06210	.06086	.05964	.05844	.05726
1.2	.05610	.05496	.05384	.05274	.05165	.05059	.04954	.04851	.04750	.04650
1.3	.04553	.04457	.04363	.04270	.04179	.04090	.04002	.03916	.03831	.03748
1.4	.03667	.03587	.03508	.03431	.03356	.03281	.03208	.03137	.03067	.02998
1.5	.02931	.02865	.02800	.02736	.02674	.02612	.02552	.02494	.02436	.02380
1.6	.02324	.02270	.02217	.02165	.02114	.02064	.02015	.01967	.01920	.01874
1.7	.01829	.01785	.01742	.01699	.01658	.01617	.01578	.01539	.01501	.01464
1.8	.01428	.01392	.01357	.01323	.01290	.01257	.01226	.01195	.01164	.01134
1.9	.01105	.01077	.01049	.01022	$.0^29957$	$.0^29698$	$.0^29445$	$.0^29198$	$.0^28957$	$.0^28721$
2.0	$.0^28491$	$.0^28266$	$.0^28046$	$.0^27832$	$.0^27623$	$.0^27418$	$.0^27219$	$.0^27024$	$.0^26835$	$.0^26649$
2.1	$.0^26468$	$.0^26292$	$.0^26120$	$.0^25952$	$.0^25788$	$.0^25628$	$.0^25472$	$.0^25320$	$.0^25172$	$.0^25028$
2.2	$.0^24887$	$.0^24750$	$.0^24616$	$.0^24486$	$.0^24358$	$.0^24235$	$.0^24114$	$.0^23996$	$.0^23882$	$.0^23770$
2.3	$.0^23662$	$.0^23556$	$.0^23453$	$.0^23352$	$.0^23255$	$.0^23159$	$.0^23067$	$.0^22977$	$.0^22889$	$.0^22804$
2.4	$.0^22720$	$.0^22640$	$.0^22561$	$.0^22484$	$.0^22410$	$.0^22337$	$.0^22267$	$.0^22199$	$.0^22132$	$.0^22067$
2.5	$.0^22005$	$.0^21943$	$.0^21883$	$.0^21826$	$.0^21769$	$.0^21715$	$.0^21662$	$.0^21610$	$.0^21560$	$.0^21511$
3.0	$.0^33822$	$.0^33689$	$.0^33560$	$.0^33436$	$.0^33316$	$.0^33199$	$.0^33087$	$.0^32978$	$.0^32873$	$.0^32771$
3.5	$.0^45848$	$.0^45620$	$.0^45400$	$.0^45188$	$.0^44984$	$.0^44788$	$.0^44599$	$.0^44417$	$.0^44242$	$.0^44073$
4.0	$.0^57145$	$.0^56835$	$.0^56538$	$.0^56253$	$.0^55980$	$.0^55718$	$.0^55468$	$.0^55227$	$.0^54997$	$.0^54777$

* By permission from R. Schlaifer, *Probability and Statistics for Business Decisions*, McGraw-Hill Book Company, Inc., New York, 1959.

$N(-D) = D + N(D)$.

Example:

$N(2) = .008491$

$N(-2) = 2 + .008491 = 2.008491$.

Index